With ex_____
course to_____ or career opportunities while gaining valuable insight into yourself and others. Offering a daily outlook for 18 full months, this fascinating guide shows you:

- The important dates in your life
- What to expect from an astrological reading
- How the stars can help you stay healthy and fit
And more!

Let this sound advice guide you through a year of heavenly possibilities—for today and for every day of 2007!

SYDNEY OMARR'S® DAY-BY-DAY ASTROLOGICAL GUIDE FOR

ARIES—March 21–April 19
TAURUS—April 20–May 20
GEMINI—May 21–June 20
CANCER—June 21–July 22
LEO—July 23–August 22
VIRGO—August 23–September 22
LIBRA—September 23–October 22
SCORPIO—October 23–November 21
SAGITTARIUS—November 22–December 21
CAPRICORN—December 22–January 19
AQUARIUS—January 20–February 18
PISCES—February 19–March 20

IN 2007

SYDNEY OMARR'S®

DAY-BY-DAY ASTROLOGICAL GUIDE FOR

VIRGO

AUGUST 23–SEPTEMBER 22

2007

By Trish MacGregor
with Carol Tonsing

A SIGNET BOOK

SIGNET
Published by New American Library, a division of
Penguin Group (USA) Inc., 375 Hudson Street,
New York, New York 10014, USA
Penguin Group (Canada), 90 Eglinton Avenue East, Suite 700, Toronto,
Ontario M4P 2Y3, Canada (a division of Pearson Penguin Canada Inc.)
Penguin Books Ltd., 80 Strand, London WC2R 0RL, England
Penguin Ireland, 25 St. Stephen's Green, Dublin 2,
Ireland (a division of Penguin Books Ltd.)
Penguin Group (Australia), 250 Camberwell Road, Camberwell, Victoria 3124,
Australia (a division of Pearson Australia Group Pty. Ltd.)
Penguin Books India Pvt. Ltd., 11 Community Centre, Panchsheel Park,
New Delhi - 110 017, India
Penguin Group (NZ), cnr Airborne and Rosedale Roads, Albany,
Auckland 1310, New Zealand (a division of Pearson New Zealand Ltd.)
Penguin Books (South Africa) (Pty.) Ltd., 24 Sturdee Avenue,
Rosebank, Johannesburg 2196, South Africa

Penguin Books Ltd., Registered Offices:
80 Strand, London WC2R 0RL, England

First published by Signet, an imprint of New American Library,
a division of Penguin Group (USA) Inc.

First Printing, June 2006
10 9 8 7 6 5 4 3 2 1

Copyright © The Estate of Sydney Omarr, 2006
All rights reserved

Sydney Omarr's is a registered trademark of Writers House, LLC.

Sydney Omarr® is syndicated worldwide by
Los Angeles Times Syndicate.

REGISTERED TRADEMARK—MARCA REGISTRADA

Printed in the United States of America

Without limiting the rights under copyright reserved above, no part of this publication may be reproduced, stored in or introduced into a retrieval system, or transmitted, in any form, or by any means (electronic, mechanical, photocopying, recording, or otherwise), without the prior written permission of both the copyright owner and the above publisher of this book.

PUBLISHER'S NOTE
While the author has made every effort to provide accurate telephone numbers and Internet addresses at the time of publication, neither the publisher nor the author assumes any responsibility for errors, or for changes that occur after publication. Further, publisher does not have any control over and does not assume any responsibility for author or third-party Web sites or their content.

If you purchased this book without a cover you should be aware that this book is stolen property. It was reported as "unsold and destroyed" to the publisher and neither the author nor the publisher has received any payment for this "stripped book."

The scanning, uploading and distribution of this book via the Internet or via any other means without the permission of the publisher is illegal and punishable by law. Please purchase only authorized electronic editions, and do not participate in or encourage electronic piracy of copyrighted materials. Your support of the author's rights is appreciated.

CONTENTS

Introduction: Astrology to Use Every Day ... 1
1. The Big Trends of 2007 ... 3
2. Your Best Times This Year ... 10
3. What Planets Could Rock Your World This Year ... 22
4. The Moon and Your Emotions ... 28
5. Basic Astrology: Your Owner's Manual ... 33
6. Your Planetary Recipe ... 44
7. Your Rising Sign Tells Where the Action Is ... 99
8. Learn the Glyphs and Read Your Own Chart! ... 108
9. Astrology on Your Computer: Where to Find Software That Suits Your Budget and Ability ... 120
10. How to Connect with Astrology Fans Around the Globe ... 126
11. Got a Big Question? A Personal Reading Might Give You the Answer ... 132
12. Your Pet-scope for 2007: How to Choose Your Best Friend for Life ... 138
13. Your Baby-scope: Children Born in 2007 ... 145
14. Is This the Right Time to Fall in Love? ... 155
15. Is There Prosperity in Your Future? ... 171
16. Health and Diet Makeovers from the Stars ... 177

17. Discover Your Virgo Personality	191
18. Virgo Stellar Style: The Fashion Trends, Home Decor, Colors, and Getaways That Suit Virgo Best	198
19. Your Virgo Career Finder	203
20. Let Virgo Celebrities Teach You About Your Sun Sign	206
21. The Virgo Power of Attraction: Your Chemistry with Every Other Sign	212
22. Astrological Overview for Virgo in 2007	221
23. Eighteen Months of Day-by-Day Predictions—July 2006 to December 2007	224

INTRODUCTION

Astrology to Use Every Day

Are you living your life to the fullest? Whether you want a more rewarding career, financial freedom, better relationships, or a romantic love life, astrology can help you make it happen. No matter what your goal, astrology's age-old techniques work just as well today as they did thousands of years ago. You can apply them to so many areas of your life to make the best decisions concerning your career, love, money, health, and even clothing and vacations.

In relationships, astrology can help you understand every sun-sign combination, which is very handy when you meet someone special. You'll be amazed at how knowing only the person's sun sign can help resolve a conflict or improve communication. What's more, astrology gives you a way to troubleshoot potential problems in advance and, if they crop up, find a way to turn them around.

On a deeper level, astrology can be a tool for personal growth and insight into your own special place in the cosmos. Like your genetic imprint, your astrology chart is unique. It is a map of your moment in time, which has its own code, based on the sun, moon, and planets at the time and place you were born. What is especially intriguing is that this system can offer specific, practical guidance, even when using only one of the elements of the code, your sun sign.

For those who would like to know more about astrology, this book provides user-friendly information to start you on your astrological journey. Then you can put your whole astrological portrait together by looking up the other planets in your horoscope. If you want to delve deeper, we'll show you the best astrology Web sites, where you can find sophisticated software and free education. If you're interested in connecting with other astrologers, we provide an extensive resource list of contacts and organizations, as well as computer program recommendations for fun or serious study.

As the saying goes, "Timing is everything." We'll deal in many ways with the question of timing: the difficult times (which also present positive challenges), times with potential for delays and misunderstandings, and the best times to take risks and to kick back and relax. You will learn when to use the downtime when Mercury is retrograde to reconnect with old friends, troubleshoot, and reevaluate where you're going and with whom.

This guide provides the tools you need to plan the best year ever, to enhance every aspect of your life, plus astonishingly accurate day-by-day forecasts to follow along in your own activities. Let it empower you to make 2007 a year of growth and prosperity!

CHAPTER 1

The Big Trends of 2007

Prepare for Changes Ahead

Astrologers judge the trends of a year by following the slow-moving planets, from Jupiter through Pluto. A change in sign indicates a new cycle, with new emphasis. The farthest planets (Uranus, Neptune, and Pluto), which stay in a sign for at least seven years, cause a very significant change in the atmosphere when they change signs. Shifts in Jupiter, which changes every year, and Saturn, every two years, are more obvious in current events and daily lives. Jupiter generally brings a fortunate, expansive emphasis to its new sign, while Saturn's two-year cycle is a reality check, bringing tests of maturity, discipline, and responsibility.

Sagittarius Is the Sign to Watch

In the final year of Pluto's transit of Sagittarius, it will be accompanied and intensified by Jupiter, the planet of expansion. This duo is superpowerful because Sagittarius is the sign Jupiter rules, making 2007 the grand finale for many of the key trends that began in 1995, when Pluto first entered Sagittarius.

Until January 2008, slow-moving Pluto will be emphasizing everything associated with Sagittarius to prepare us philosophically and spiritually for things to come. Perhaps the most pervasive sign of Pluto in Sagittarius over the past few years has been globalization in all its forms. We are re-forming boundaries, creating new forms of travel, interacting with exotic cultures and religions as never before.

In truth-telling Sagittarius, Pluto has shifted our emphasis away from acquiring wealth to a quest for the meaning of it all, as upward strivers discover that money and power are not enough and religious extremists assert themselves. We search the cosmos for something to believe in when many lies and scandals are brought to public view, exposing leaders in the corporate, political and religious domains. When ideals and idols are shattered, we reevaluate our goals and ask ourselves what is really important.

Sagittarius is the sign of linking everything together; therefore, the trend has been to find ways to connect on spiritual, philosophical, and intellectual levels. The spiritual emphasis of Pluto in Sagittarius has filtered down to our home lives, as religion and religious controversy have entered local communities. Vast church complexes that combine religious activities with sports centers, health clubs, malls, and theme parks are being built. Religious education and book publishing have expanded as well.

Sagittarius is known for love of animals, especially horses. It's no surprise that horse racing has become popular again and that America has never been more pet happy. Look for extremes related to animal welfare, such as vegetarianism as a lifestyle. As habitats are destroyed, the care, feeding, and control of wild animals will become a larger issue, especially when deer, bears, and coyotes invade our backyards.

The Sagittarius love of the outdoors combined with Pluto's power has already promoted extreme sports, especially those that require strong legs, like rock climbing, trekking, or snowboarding. Expect the trend toward more adventurous travel to continue, as well as fitness- or sports-oriented vacations. Exotic hiking trips to unexplored territories, mountain-climbing expeditions, spa vacations, and sports-associated resorts are part of this trend.

Publishing, which is associated with Sagittarius, has been transformed by global conglomerates and the Internet. Look for more inspirational books aimed at those who are interested in spirituality outside of traditional religions.

What's Next? Capricorn Brings Us Down to Earth

Next year, Pluto will join Jupiter in Capricorn, which marks a major shift in emphasis to Capricorn-related themes. Capricorn is a practical, building, healing earth sign. It is an active, cardinal sign that symbolizes rising from the waters of the emotions to the top of the mountain, surmounting obstacles all the way, demanding maturity and down-to-earth common sense. Capricorn relates to structures, institutions, order, mountains and mountain countries, mineral rights, issues involving the elderly and growing older—all of which will be emphasized in the coming years.

This shift begins in December 2007, which starts activating all the cardinal signs (Aries, Cancer, Libra, Capricorn). At the end of 2007, you should feel the rumblings of change in the Capricorn area of your horoscope and in the world at large. The last time Pluto was in Capricorn was the period of the Revolutionary War. Therefore this may be an important time in U.S. politics, as well as a reflection of the aging and maturing of American society in general.

Saturn Moves from Leo to Virgo: The Maturing of the Baby Boomers, Reforms in Care and Maintenance

Saturn, the planet of limitation, testing, and restriction, has been transiting Leo since mid-July 2005, forcing us to grow up and get serious in the Leo areas of our lives. Many of the fun things in life fall under the banner of Leo: entertainment, show business, children, play, recreation, love affairs, hobbies, performing, talent, the creative arts, and recognition by others. Since Saturn tends to put a damper on Leo's fun, expect some restrictions on the entertainment business, shows with more serious themes and actors. Leo is associated with children, and with Saturn come the burdens and responsibilities of bringing them up.

The subject of aging in general belongs to Saturn, and

the Leo archetype in this area is the aging film star determined to hold on to youth. Love affairs and flirtations, part of Leo's sunny side, may this year involve older people. Maturing baby boomers will demand more awareness from the media. Therefore we will see more older people on television and in films, more entertainment tailored to an aging population, a harbinger of the even stronger Saturnian trends coming up in 2008. Since Leo is also associated with speculation and gambling, in fact all games, expect more stringent regulation and controversy around big-time casinos and sports.

Saturn in Leo demands hard work in creative ventures, responsibility when interacting with others. Leo types can't get away with casual love affairs, or with being high-handed, arrogant, or divalike in any way. Leo divas will have to earn their applause. This could tone down the blatant celebrity-worshipping culture that has arisen over the past few years. No longer will it be enough to be famous for being famous. The emphasis will be on true values rather than the trappings of success. Flashy lifestyles, bling bling jewelry, and showing off will be out.

Saturn moves into Virgo on September 2, 2007, which is followed soon after by a solar eclipse in Virgo on September 11. This is a time when Virgo issues—health care and maintenance and moral standards and controls—will come to the fore. We will adjust the structures of our lives, making changes so that we can function at an efficient level. We'll be challenged with a reality check in areas where we have been too optimistic or expansive.

Jupiter in Sagittarius

During the year that Jupiter remains in a sign, the fields associated with that sign—comedy, fun, travel, laughter—will be the ones that arouse excitement and enthusiasm, usually providing excellent opportunities for expansion, fame, and fortune. Jupiter remains in fun-loving Sagittarius, the sign it rules, until December 18.

One place we will notice the Jupiter influence is in fashion, which should have a cheerful, colorful look. Sagittarius has great fashion flair, which should show up in ethnic influences and exciting new sportswear.

Those born under Sagittarius should have many opportunities during the year. However, keep your feet on the ground. The flip side of Jupiter is that there are no limits. You can expand off the planet under a Jupiter transit, which is why the planet is often called the Gateway to Heaven. If something is going to burst (such as an artery) or overextend or go over the top in some way, it could happen under a supposedly lucky Jupiter transit. So be aware.

Those born under Gemini may find their best opportunities working with partners this year, as Jupiter will be transiting their seventh house of relationships.

Continuing Trends

Uranus and Neptune continue to do a kind of astrological dance called a mutual reception. This is a supportive relationship where Uranus is in Pisces, the sign ruled by Neptune, while Neptune is in Aquarius, the sign ruled by Uranus. When this dance is over in 2011, it is likely that we will be living under very different political and social circumstances.

Uranus in Pisces

Uranus, known as the Great Awakener, tends to cause both upheaval and innovation in the sign it transits. During previous episodes of Uranus in Pisces, great religions and spiritual movements have come into being, most recently Mormonism and Christian Fundamentalism. In its most positive mode, Pisces promotes imagination and creativity, the art of illusion in theater and film, the inspiration of great artists. A water sign, Pisces is naturally associated with all things liquid—oceans, oil, alcohol—and with those creatures that live in the water—fish, the fishing industry, fish habitats, and fish farming. Currently there is a great debate going on about overfishing, contamination of fish, and fish farming. The underdog, the enslaved, and the disenfranchised should also benefit from Uranus in Pisces.

Since Uranus is a disruptive influence that aims to challenge the status quo, the forces of nature that manifest will most likely be in the Pisces area: oceans, seas, and rivers. We have seen unprecedented rainy seasons, floods, mud slides, and disastrous hurricanes. Note that 2005's devastating Hurricane Katrina hit an area known for both the oil and fishing industries.

Pisces is associated with the prenatal phase of life, which is related to regenerative medicine. The controversy over embryonic stem cell research should continue to be debated. Petroleum issues, both in the oil-producing countries and offshore oil drilling, will come to a head. Uranus in Pisces suggests that development of new hydroelectric sources may provide the power we need to continue our current power-thirsty lifestyle.

As in previous eras, there should continue to be a flourishing of the arts. We are seeing many new artistic forms developing now, such as computer-created actors and special effects. The sky's the limit on this influence.

Those who have problems with Uranus are those who resist change, so the key is to embrace the future.

Neptune in Aquarius

Neptune is a planet of imagination and creativity, but also of deception and illusion. Neptune is associated with hospitals, which have been the subject of much controversy. On the positive side, hospitals are acquiring cutting-edge technology. The atmosphere of many hospitals is already changing from the intimidating and sterile environment of the past to that of a health-promoting spa. Alternative therapies, such as massage, diet counseling, and aromatherapy, are becoming commonplace, which expresses this Neptune trend. New procedures in plastic surgery, also a Neptune glamour field, and anti-aging therapies are restoring the illusion of youth.

However, issues involving the expense and quality of

health care and the evolving relationship between doctors, drug companies, and HMOs reflect a darker side of this trend.

What About the New Planets?

Our solar system is becoming more complex; astronomers continue to discover new objects circling the sun. In addition to the familiar planets, there are comets, cometoids, asteroids, and strange icy bodies in the Kuiper Belt beyond Neptune. The newest object at this writing is a planetlike orb that has a tiny moon. It is tentatively nicknamed Xena, after the TV heroine. Once Xena's orbit is established, astrologers will observe what effect this planet has on our horoscopes. Astrologers have long hypothesized about distant planets on the outer reaches of the solar system, but most astrologers stop with Pluto, which itself is quite controversial. Some scientists insist that tiny Pluto, only one-fifth the size of Earth, is not a full-fledged planet. However, anyone experiencing a zap to the horoscope from this little object knows that it is a force to be reckoned with! Time will tell about Xena and her yet to be discovered siblings!

CHAPTER 2

Your Best Times This Year

Have you ever felt that success is a matter of timing, that you could set your schedule on a successful course if you coordinated your activities with times when the planets give you the green light? On the other hand, it's useful to know when not to act, when it would be better to kick back and review where you're going.

For instance, when mischievous Mercury creates havoc with communications and you can't seem to make progress with projects, you'll use the time to best advantage by backing up your vital computer files, clearing out your files and closets and reading between the lines of contracts. That's the time to be extra patient with coworkers and double-check all messages. Mark your social calendar when Venus passes through your sign—that's when you're the flavor of the month. You've got extra sex appeal, so it's time to get a knockout new outfit or hairstyle. Then ask someone you'd like to know better to dinner. Venus timing can also help you charm clients with a stunning sales pitch or make an offer they won't refuse.

In this chapter, you will learn how to find your best times as well as which times to avoid. You will also learn how to read the moods of the moon and make them work for you. Use the information and tables in this chapter and the planet tables in this book, and also use the moon sign listings in your daily forecasts.

Here are the happenings to note on your agenda:

- Dates of your sun sign (high-energy period)
- The month previous to your sun sign (low-energy period)
- Dates of planets in your sign this year

- Full and new moons (pay special attention when these fall in your sun sign!)
- Eclipses
- Moon in your sun sign every month, as well as moon in the opposite sign (listed in daily forecast)
- Mercury retrogrades
- Other retrograde periods

Your High-Power Time

Every birthday starts off a new cycle of solar energy for you. You should feel a new surge of vitality as the powerful sun enters your sign. This is the time when predominant energies are most favorable to you. So go for it! Start new projects, make your big moves (especially when the new moon is in your sign, doubling your charisma). You'll get the recognition you deserve now, when everyone is attuned to your sun sign. Look in the tables in this book to see if other planets will also be passing through your sun sign at this time. Venus (love, beauty), Mars (energy, drive), and Mercury (communication, mental sharpness) reinforce the sun and give an extra boost to your life in the areas they affect. Venus will rev up your social and love life, making you seem especially attractive. Mars amplifies your energy and drive. Mercury fuels your brainpower and helps you communicate. Jupiter signals an especially lucky period of expansion.

There are two downtimes related to the sun. During the month before your birthday period, when you are winding up your annual cycle, you could be feeling especially vulnerable and depleted. So at that time get extra rest, watch your diet, and take it easy. Don't overstress yourself. Use this time to gear up for a big "push" when the sun enters your sign.

Another downtime is when the sun is in a sign opposite your sun sign (six months from your birthday). That's when the prevailing energies are very different from yours. You may feel at odds with the world. You'll have to work harder for recognition because people are not on your wavelength.

However, this could be a good time to work on a team, in cooperation with others, or behind the scenes.

Plan Your Day with the Moon

The moon is a powerful tool to divine the mood of the moment. You can work with the moon in two ways. Plan by the *sign* the moon is in; plan by the *phase* of the moon. The sign will tell you the kind of activities that suit the moon's mood. The phase will tell you the best time to start or finish a certain activity.

Working with the phases of the moon is as easy as looking up at the night sky. During the new moon, when both the sun and moon are in the same sign, begin new ventures—especially activities that are favored by that sign. Then you'll utilize the powerful energies pulling you in the same direction. You'll be focused outward, toward action, and in a doing mode. Postpone breaking off, terminating, deliberating, or reflecting—activities that require introspection and passive work. These are better suited to a later moon phase.

Get your project under way during the first quarter. Then go public at the full moon, a time of high intensity, when feelings come out into the open. This is your time to shine—to express yourself. Be aware, however, that because pressures are being released, other people will also be letting off steam. Since confrontations are possible, take advantage of this time either to air grievances or to avoid arguments. Traditionally, astrologers often advise against surgery at this time, which could produce heavier bleeding.

About three days after the full moon comes the disseminating phase, a time when the energy of the cycle begins to wind down. From the last quarter of the moon to the next new moon, it's a time to cut off unproductive relationships, do serious thinking, and focus on inward-directed activities.

You'll feel some new and full moons more strongly than others, especially those new moons that fall in your sun sign and full moons in your opposite sign. Because that full moon happens at your low-energy time of year, it is likely to be an especially stressful time in a relationship, when any hidden problems or unexpressed emotions could surface.

Full and New Moons in 2007

All dates are calculated for eastern standard time and eastern daylight time.

Full Moon—January 3 in Cancer
New Moon—January 18 in Capricorn

Full Moon—February 2 in Leo
New Moon—February 17 in Aquarius

Full Moon—March 3 in Virgo (lunar eclipse)
New Moon—March 18 in Pisces (total solar eclipse)

Full Moon—April 2 in Libra
New Moon—April 17 in Aries

Full Moon—May 2 in Scorpio
New Moon—May 16 in Taurus

Full Moon—May 31 in Sagittarius
New Moon—June 14 in Gemini

Full Moon—June 30 in Capricorn
New Moon—July 14 in Cancer

Full Moon—July 29 in Aquarius
New Moon—August 12 in Leo

Full Moon—August 28 in Pisces (lunar eclipse)
New Moon—September 11 in Virgo (solar eclipse)

Full Moon—September 26 in Aries
New Moon—October 11 in Libra

Full Moon—October 26 in Taurus
New Moon—November 9 in Scorpio

Full Moon—November 24 in Gemini
New Moon—December 9 in Sagittarius
Full Moon—December 23 in Cancer

How to Time by the Moon Sign

To forecast the daily emotional "weather," to determine your monthly high and low days, or to synchronize your activities with the cycles of the moon, take note of the moon sign under your daily forecast at the end of the book. Here are some of the activities favored and the moods you are likely to encounter under each moon sign.

Moon in Aries: Get Moving!

The new moon in Aries is an ideal time to start new projects. Everyone is pushy, raring to go, rather impatient, and short-tempered. Leave details and follow-up for later. Competitive sports or martial arts are great ways to let off steam. Quiet types could use some assertiveness, but it's a great day for dynamos. Be careful not to step on too many toes.

Moon in Taurus: Lay the Foundations for Success

Do solid, methodical tasks like follow-through or backup work. Make investments, buy real estate, do appraisals, do some hard bargaining. Attend to your property. Get out in the country or spend some time in your garden. Enjoy creature comforts, music, a good dinner, sensual lovemaking. Forget starting a diet—this is a day when you'll feel self-indulgent.

Moon in Gemini: Communicate

Talk means action today. Telephone, write letters, fax! Make new contacts, stay in touch with steady customers.

You can juggle lots of tasks today. It's a great time for mental activity of any kind. Don't try to pin people down—they, too, are feeling restless. Keep it light. Flirtations and socializing are good. Watch gossip—and don't give away secrets.

Moon in Cancer: Pay Attention to Loved Ones

This is a moody, sensitive, emotional time. People respond to personal attention, to mothering. Stay at home, have a family dinner, call your mother. Nostalgia, memories, and psychic powers are heightened. You'll want to hang on to people and things (don't clean out your closets now). You could have shrewd insights into what others really need and want. Pay attention to dreams, intuition, and gut reactions.

Moon in Leo: Be Confident

Everybody is in a much more confident, warm, generous mood. It's a good day to ask for a raise, show what you can do, dress like a star. People will respond to flattery, enjoy a bit of drama and theater. You may be extravagant, treat yourself royally, and show off a bit—but don't break the bank! Be careful you don't promise more than you can deliver.

Moon in Virgo: Be Practical

Do practical down-to-earth chores. Review your budget, make repairs, be an efficiency expert. Not a day to ask for a raise. Tend to personal care and maintenance. Have a health checkup, go on a diet, buy vitamins or health food. Make your home spotless. Take care of details and piled-up chores. Reorganize your work and life so they run more smoothly and efficiently. Save money. Be prepared for others to be in a critical, faultfinding mood.

Moon in Libra: Be Diplomatic

Attend to legal matters. Negotiate contracts. Arbitrate. Do things with your favorite partner. Socialize. Be romantic. Buy a special gift, a beautiful object. Decorate yourself or your surroundings. Buy new clothes. Throw a party. Have an elegant, romantic evening. Smooth over any ruffled feathers. Avoid confrontations. Stick to civilized discussions.

Moon in Scorpio: Solve Problems

This is a day to do things with passion. You'll have excellent concentration and focus. Try not to get too intense emotionally. Avoid sharp exchanges with loved ones. Others may tend to go to extremes, get jealous, overreact. Great for troubleshooting, problem solving, research, scientific work—and making love. Pay attention to those psychic vibes.

Moon in Sagittarius: Sell and Motivate

A great time for travel, philosophical discussions, setting long-range career goals. Work out, do sports, buy athletic equipment. Others will be feeling upbeat, exuberant, and adventurous. Risk taking is favored. You may feel like taking a gamble, betting on the horses, visiting a local casino, buying a lottery ticket. Teaching, writing, and spiritual activities also get the green light. Relax outdoors. Take care of animals.

Moon in Capricorn: Get Organized

You can accomplish a lot now, so get on the ball! Attend to business. Issues concerning your basic responsibilities, duties, family, and elderly parents could crop up. You'll be expected to deliver on promises. Weed out the deadwood from your life. Get a dental checkup. Not a good day for gambling or taking risks.

Moon in Aquarius: Join the Group

A great day for doing things with groups—clubs, meetings, outings, politics, parties. Campaign for your candidate. Work for a worthy cause. Deal with larger issues that affect humanity—the environment and metaphysical questions. Buy a computer or electronic gadget. Watch TV. Wear something outrageous. Try something you've never done before. Present an original idea. Don't stick to a rigid schedule—go with the flow. Take a class in meditation, mind control. yoga.

Moon in Pisces: Be Creative

This can be a very creative day, so let your imagination work overtime. Film, theater, music, ballet could inspire you. Spend some time alone, resting and reflecting, reading or writing poetry. Daydreams can also be profitable. Help those less fortunate. Lend a listening ear to someone who may be feeling blue. Don't overindulge in self-pity or escapism, however. People are especially vulnerable to substance abuse now. Turn your thoughts to romance and someone special.

Retrogrades: When the Planets Seem to Backstep

All the planets, except for the sun and moon, have times when they appear to move backward—or retrograde—as it seems from our point of view on earth. At these times, planets do not work as they normally do. So it's best to "take a break" from that planet's energies in our life and to do some work on an inner level.

Mercury Retrograde: The Key Is in "Re"

Mercury goes retrograde most often, and its effects can be especially irritating. When it reaches a short distance ahead of the sun several times a year, it seems to move backward from our point of view. Astrologers often compare retrograde motion to the optical illusion that occurs when we ride on a train that passes another train traveling at a different speed—the second train appears to be moving in reverse.

What this means to you is that the Mercury-ruled areas of your life—analytical thought processes, communications, scheduling—are subject to all kinds of confusion. Be prepared. Communications equipment can break down. Schedules may be changed on short notice. People are late for appointments or don't show up at all. Traffic is terrible. Major purchases malfunction, don't work out, or get delivered in the wrong color. Letters don't arrive or are delivered to the wrong address. Employees will make errors that have to be corrected later. Contracts don't work out or must be renegotiated.

Since most of us can't put our lives on "hold" during Mercury retrogrades, we should learn to tame the trickster and make it work for us. The key is in the prefix *re-*. This is the time to go back over things in your life, *re*flect on what you've done during the previous months. Now you can get deeper insights, spot errors you've missed. So take time to *re*view and *re*evaluate what has happened. *Re*st and *re*ward yourself—it's a good time to take a vacation, especially if you *re*visit a favorite place. *Re*organize your work and finish up projects that are backed up. Clean out your desk and closets. Throw away what you can't *re*cycle. If you must sign contracts or agreements, do so with a contingency clause that lets you *re*evaluate the terms later.

Postpone major purchases or commitments for the time being. Don't get married (unless you're *re*marrying the same person). Try not to *re*ly on other people keeping appointments, contracts, or agreements to the letter; have several alternatives. Double-check and *re*ad between the lines. Don't buy anything connected with communications or transportation (if you must, be sure to cover yourself).

Mercury retrograding through your sun sign will intensify its effect on your life.

If Mercury was retrograde when you were born, you may be one of the lucky people who don't suffer the frustrations of this period. If so, your mind probably works in a very intuitive, insightful way.

The sign in which Mercury is retrograding can give you an idea of what's in store—as well as the sun signs that will be especially challenged.

Mercury Retrogrades in 2007

Mercury has three retrograde periods this year.
February 14 to March 8 from Pisces back to Aquarius
June 15 to July 9 in Cancer
October 11 to November 1 from Scorpio back to Libra

Venus Retrograde: Relationships Move Backward

Retrograding Venus can cause your relationships to take a backward step, or it can make you extravagant and impractical. Shopping till you drop and buying what you cannot afford are problems at this time. It's *not* a good time to redecorate—you'll hate the color of the walls later. Postpone getting a new hairstyle. Try not to fall in love either. But if you wish to make amends in an already troubled relationship, make peaceful overtures at this time.

Venus Retrogrades in 2007

Venus turns retrograde in Virgo from July 27 until September 8, when it turns direct in Leo.

Use the Go Power of Mars

Mars shows how and when to get where you want to go. Timing your moves with Mars on your side can give you a big push. On the other hand, pushing Mars the wrong way can guarantee that you'll run into frustrations in every corner. Your best times to forge ahead are during the weeks when Mars is traveling through your sun sign or your Mars sign (look these up in the tables in this book). Also consider times when Mars is in a compatible sign (fire with air signs, or earth with water signs). You'll be sure to have planetary power on your side.

Mars Retrogrades in 2007

Mars turns retrograde on November 15 until January 30, 2008, from Cancer to Gemini.

When Other Planets Retrograde

The slower-moving planets stay retrograde for months at a time (Jupiter, Saturn, Neptune, Uranus, and Pluto).

When Saturn is retrograde, it's an uphill battle with self-discipline. You may not be in the mood for work. You may feel more like hanging out at the beach than getting things done.

Neptune retrograde promotes a dreamy escapism from reality, when you may feel you're in a fog (Pisces will feel this, especially).

Uranus retrograde may mean setbacks in areas where there have been sudden changes, when you may be forced to regroup or reevaluate the situation.

Pluto retrograde is a time to work on establishing proportion and balance in areas where there have been recent dramatic transformations.

When the planets move forward again, there's a shift in the atmosphere. Activities connected with each planet start moving ahead, plans that were stalled get rolling. Make a special note of those days on your calendar and proceed accordingly.

Other Retrogrades in 2007

The five slower-moving planets all go retrograde in 2007.

Jupiter retrogrades four months from April 5 to August 6 in Sagittarius.

Saturn turned retrograde on December 5, 2006, until

April 19, 2007. It turns retrograde again on December 19 for the duration of the year.

Uranus retrogrades from June 23 to November 24 in Pisces.

Neptune retrogrades from May 24 to October 31 in Aquarius.

Pluto retrogrades from March 31 to September 7 in Sagittarius.

CHAPTER 3

What Planets Could Rock Your World This Year

It's been said that knowledge is power, so why not use astrology's wisdom to ride with the tide this year and make the planets work for you?

Eclipses Clear the Air

Eclipses can bring on milestones in your life, if they aspect a key point in your horoscope. In general, they shake up the status quo, bringing hidden areas out into the open. During this time, problems you've been avoiding or have brushed aside can surface to demand your attention. A good coping strategy is to accept whatever comes up as a challenge that could make a positive difference in your life. And don't forget the power of your sense of humor. If you can laugh at something, you'll never be afraid of it.

What Is the Best Thing to Do During an Eclipse?

When the natural rhythms of the sun and moon are disturbed, it's best to postpone important activities. Be sure to mark eclipse days on your calendar, especially if the eclipse falls in your birth sign. This year, those born under Aries, Pisces, and Virgo should take special note of the feelings that arise. With lunar eclipses, some possibilities could be a break from attachments or the healing of an illness or substance abuse, which had been triggered by the subconscious. The temporary event could be a healing time, when you gain perspective. During solar eclipses, when you might be in a highly subjective state, pay attention to the hidden subconscious patterns that surface, the emotional truth that is revealed at this time.

The effect of the eclipse can reverberate for some time, often months after the event. But it is especially important to stay cool and make no major moves during the period known as the shadow of the eclipse, which begins about a week before and lasts until at least three days after the eclipse. After three days, the daily rhythms should return to normal, and you can proceed with business as usual.

This Year's Eclipse Dates

March 3: Lunar eclipse in Virgo
March 18: Solar eclipse in Pisces
August 28: Lunar eclipse in Pisces
September 11: Solar eclipse in Virgo

Saturn Gives You a Reality Check

When Saturn hits a critical point in your horoscope, you can count on an experience that will make you slow up, pull back, and reexamine your life. It is a call to eliminate what is not working, to shape up, to set priorities, to examine the boundaries and structures in your life (or lack of them) and set new ones. During this process, you may feel restricted, frustrated, or inhibited—not a fun time, but one that will serve you well in the long run. You may need to take on more responsibilities that will test your limits.

By the end of its twenty-eight-year trip around the zodiac, Saturn will have tested you in all areas of your life. The major tests happen in seven-year cycles, when Saturn passes over the angles of your chart, which means your rising sign, the top of your chart or midheaven, your descendant, and the nadir or bottom of your chart. This is when the real life-changing experiences happen. But you are also in for a testing period whenever Saturn passes a planet in your chart or stresses that planet from a distance. It is useful to check your planetary positions with the timetable of Saturn or prepare in advance, or at least to brace yourself.

When Saturn returns to its location at the time of your birth, at approximately age twenty-eight, you'll have your first Saturn return. At this time, a person usually takes stock or settles down to find his mission in life and assume full adult duties and responsibilities.

Another way Saturn helps us is to reveal the karmic lessons from previous lives and give us the chance to overcome them. So look at Saturn's challenges as much-needed opportunities for self-improvement.

Outwitting the Planets

Second-guessing Saturn and the eclipses this year is easy if you have a copy of your horoscope calculated by a computer. This enables you to pinpoint the area of your life that will be affected. However, you can make an educated guess, by setting up a rough diagram on your own. If you'd like to find out which area of your life this year's Saturn change is most likely to affect, follow these easy steps.

First, you must know the time of day you were born and look up your rising sign listed on the tables in this book (see chapter 7). Set up an estimated horoscope by drawing a circle, then dividing it into four parts by making a cross directly through the center. Continue to divide each of the parts into thirds, as if you were dividing a cake, until you have twelve slices. Write your rising sign on the middle left-hand slice, which would be the nine o'clock point, if you were looking at your watch. Then write the following signs on the dividing line of each slice, working counterclockwise, until you have listed all twelve signs of the zodiac.

You should now have a basic diagram of your horoscope chart (minus the planets, of course). Starting with your rising-sign slice, number each portion consecutively, again working counterclockwise.

Since this year's eclipses will fall in Pisces and Virgo, find the number of these slices, or houses, on the chart and read the following descriptions for the kinds of issues that are likely to be emphasized. On September 2, Saturn will move from Leo to Virgo, so check those houses in your chart for Saturn-related events.

If an eclipse or Saturn falls in your FIRST HOUSE:
Events cause you to examine the ways you are acting independently and push you to become more visible, to assert yourself. This is a time when you feel compelled to make your own decisions. You may want to change your physical appearance, body image, or style of dress in some way. Under affliction, there might be illness or physical harm.

If an eclipse or Saturn falls in your SECOND HOUSE:
This is the place where you consider all matters of security. You consolidate your resources, earn money, acquire property, and decide what you value and what you want to own. On a deeper level, this house reveals your sense of self-worth.

If an eclipse or Saturn falls in your THIRD HOUSE:
Here you reach out to others, express your ideas, and explore different courses of action. You may feel especially restless or have confrontations with neighbors or siblings. In your search for more knowledge, you may decide to improve your skills, get more education, or sign up for a course that interests you. Local transportation, especially your car, might be affected by an eclipse here.

If an eclipse or Saturn falls in your FOURTH HOUSE:
Here is where you put down roots and establish a base. You'll consider what home really means to you. Issues involving parents, the physical setup or location of your home, and your immediate family demand your attention. You may be especially concerned with parenting or relationships with your own mother. You may consider moving your home to a new location or leaving home.

If an eclipse or Saturn falls in your FIFTH HOUSE:
Here is where you express yourself, either through your personal talents or through procreating children. You are interested in making your special talents visible. This is also the house of love affairs and the romantic aspect of life, where you flirt, have fun, and enjoy the excitement of love. Hobbies and crafts fall in this area.

If an eclipse or Saturn falls in your SIXTH HOUSE:
How well are you doing your job? This is your maintenance department, where you take care of your health, organize your life, and set up a daily routine. It is also the place where you perfect your skills and add polish to your life. The chores you do every day, the skills you learn, and the techniques you use fall here. If something doesn't work in your life, an eclipse is sure to bring this to light. If you've been neglecting your health, diet, and fitness, you'll probably pay the consequences during an eclipse. Or you may be faced with work that requires much routine organization and steady effort, rather than creative ability. Or you may be required to perform services for others.

If an eclipse or Saturn falls in your SEVENTH HOUSE:
This is the area of committed relationships, of those which involve legal agreements, of working in a close relationship with another. Here you'll be dealing with how you relate, what you'll be willing to give up for the sake of a marriage or partnership. Eclipses here can put extra pressure on a relationship and, if it's not working, precipitate a breakup. Lawsuits and open enemies also reside here.

If an eclipse or Saturn falls in your EIGHTH HOUSE:
This area is concerned with power and control. Consider what you are willing to give up in order that something might happen. Power struggles, intense relationships, and desires to penetrate deeper mysteries belong here. Debts, loans, financial matters that involve another party, and wheeling and dealing also come into focus. So does sex, where you surrender your individual power to create a new life together. Matters involving birth and death are also involved here.

If an eclipse or Saturn falls in your NINTH HOUSE:

Here is where you look at the big picture. You'll seek information that helps you find meaning in life: higher education, religion, travel, global issues. Eclipses here can push you to get out of your rut, to explore something you've never done before, and to expand your horizons.

If an eclipse or Saturn falls in your TENTH HOUSE:

This is the high-profile point in your chart. Here is where you consider how society looks at you and your position in the outside world. You'll be concerned about whether you receive proper credit for your work and if you're recognized by higher-ups. Promotions, raises, and other forms of recognition can be given or denied. If you have worked hard, Saturn can give you well-deserved rewards here. Either your standing in your career or in your community can be challenged, or you'll be publicly acknowledged for achieving a goal. An eclipse here can make you famous or burst your balloon if you've been too ambitious or neglecting other areas of your life.

If an eclipse or Saturn falls in your ELEVENTH HOUSE:

Your relationship with groups of people comes under scrutiny during an eclipse: whom you are identified with, whom you socialize with, and how well you are accepted by other members of your team. Activities of clubs and political parties, networking, and other social interactions become important. You'll be concerned about what other people think.

If an eclipse or Saturn falls in your TWELFTH HOUSE:

This is the time when the focus turns to your inner life. An especially favorable eclipse here might bring you great insight and inspiration. On the other hand, events may happen that cause you to retreat from public life. Here is where we go to be alone or to work in retreats, hospitals, or religious institutions, or to explore psychotherapy. Here is where you deliver selfless service, through charitable acts. Good aspects from an eclipse could promote an ability to go with the flow or to rise above the competition to find an inner, almost mystical strength that enables you to connect with the deepest needs of others.

CHAPTER 4

The Moon and Your Emotions

How do you react to life's problems? What do you care about? What makes you feel comfortable, secure, or romantic? The answers are a few secrets revealed by the moon sign in your horoscope, where the moon represents your receptive, reflective, female, nurturing self. It also reflects who you were nurtured by—the mother or mother figure in your chart. In a man's chart, the moon position describes his receptive, emotional, yin side, as well as the woman in his life who will have the deepest effect, usually his mother. (Venus reveals the kind of woman who will attract him physically.)

It's well worth having an accurate chart cast to determine your moon sign or that of someone you'd like to know better, since this reveals much about your inner life. You can learn what appeals to a person subconsciously by knowing the person's moon sign, which reflects the instinctive emotional nature.

The moon is more at home in some signs than others. It rules maternal Cancer and is exalted in Taurus—both comforting, home-loving signs where the natural emotional energies of the moon are easily and productively expressed. But when the moon is in the opposite signs—Capricorn and Scorpio—it leaves the comfortable nest and deals with emotional issues of power and achievement in the outside world. Those of you with the moon in these signs are likely to find your emotional role more challenging in life.

Since detailed moon tables are too extensive for this book, check through the following listing to find the moon sign that feels most familiar.

Moon in Aries

This placement makes you both independent and ardent. An idealist, you tend to fall in and out of love easily. You love a challenge but could cool once your quarry is captured. Your emotional reactions are fast and fiery, quickly expressed and quickly forgotten. You may not think before expressing your feelings. It's not easy to hide how you feel. Channeling all your emotional energy could be one of your big challenges.

Moon in Taurus

A sentimental soul, you are very fond of the good life, and you gravitate toward solid, secure relationships. You like displays of affection and creature comforts—all the tangible trappings of a cozy, safe, calm atmosphere. You are sensual and steady emotionally, but very stubborn, possessive, and determined. You can't be pushed, and you tend to dislike changes. You should make an effort to broaden your horizons and to take a risk sometimes. You may become very attached to your home turf. You may also be a collector of objects that are meaningful to you.

Moon in Gemini

You crave mental stimulation and variety in life, which you usually get through either an ever-varied social life, the excitement of flirtation and/or multiple professional involvements. You may marry more than once and have a rather chaotic emotional life due to your difficulty with commitment and settling down, as well as your need to be constantly on the go. (Be sure to find a partner who is as outgoing as you are.) You will have to learn at some point to focus your energies because you tend to be somewhat fragmented—to do two things at once, to have two homes or even two lovers. If you can find a creative way to express your many-faceted nature, you'll be ahead of the game.

Moon in Cancer

This is the most powerful lunar position, which is sure to make a deep imprint on your character. Your needs are very much associated with your reaction to the needs of others. You are very sensitive, caring, and self-protective, though some of you may mask this with a hard shell, like the moon-sensitive crab. This placement also gives an excellent memory, keen intuition, and an uncanny ability to perceive the needs of others. All of the lunar phases will affect you, especially full moons and eclipses, so you would do well to mark them on your calendar. Because you're happiest at home, you may work at home or turn your office into a second home, where you can nurture and comfort people. (You may tend to mother the world.) With natural psychic, intuitive ability, you might be drawn to occult work in some way. Or you may get professionally involved with providing food and shelter to others.

Moon in Leo

This warm, passionate moon takes everything to heart. You are attracted to all that is noble, generous, and aristocratic in life (and may be a bit of a snob). You have an innate ability to take command emotionally, but you do need strong support, loyalty, and loud applause from those you love. You are possessive of your loved ones and your turf and will roar if anyone threatens to take over your territory.

Moon in Virgo

You are rather cool until you decide if others measure up. But once someone or something meets your ideal standards, you hold up your end of the arrangement perfectly. You may, in fact, drive yourself too hard to attain some notion of perfection. Try to be a bit easier on yourself and others. Don't always act the censor! You love to be the teacher and are drawn to situations where you can change others for the better, but sometimes you must learn to accept others for what they are—enjoy what you have!

Moon in Libra

Like other air-sign moons, you think before you feel. Therefore, you may not immediately recognize the emotional needs of others. However, you are relationship oriented and may find it difficult to be alone or to do things alone. After you have learned emotional balance by leaning on yourself first, you can have excellent partnerships. It is best for you to avoid extremes, which set your scales swinging and can make your love life precarious. You thrive in a rather conservative, traditional, romantic relationship, where you receive attention and flattery—but not possessiveness—from your partner. You'll be your most charming in an elegant, harmonious atmosphere.

Moon in Scorpio

This is a moon that enjoys and responds to intense, passionate feelings. You may go to extremes and have a very dramatic emotional life, full of ardor, suspicion, jealousy, and obsession. It would be much healthier to channel your need for power and control into meaningful work. This is a good position for anyone in the fields of medicine, police work, research, the occult, psychoanalysis, or intuitive work, because life-and-death situations don't faze you. However, you do take personal disappointments very hard.

Moon in Sagittarius

You take life's ups and downs with good humor and the proverbial grain of salt. You'll love 'em and leave 'em— take off on a great adventure at a moment's notice. Born free could be your slogan. Attracted by the exotic, you have wanderlust mentally and physically. You may be too much in search of new mental and spiritual stimulation to ever settle down.

Moon in Capricorn

Are you ever accused of being too cool and calculating? You have an earthy side, but you take prestige and position very seriously. Your strong drive to succeed extends to your romantic life, where you will be devoted to improving your lifestyle, rising to the top. A structured situation where you can advance methodically makes you feel wonderfully secure. You may be attracted to someone older or very much younger or from a different social world. It may be difficult to look at the lighter side of emotional relationships. Though this moon is placed in the sign of its detriment, the good news is that you tend to be very dutiful and responsible to those you care for.

Moon in Aquarius

You are a people collector with many friends of all backgrounds. You are happiest surrounded by people and may feel uneasy when left alone. Though you usually stay friends with lovers, intense emotions and demanding one-on-one relationships turn you off. You don't like anything to be too rigid or scheduled. Though tolerant and understanding, you can be emotionally unpredictable and may opt for an unconventional love life. With plenty of space, you will be able to sustain relationships with liberal, freedom-loving types.

Moon in Pisces

You are very responsive and empathetic to others, especially if they have problems or are the underdog. (Be on guard against attracting too many people with sob stories.) You'll be happiest if you can express your creative imagination in the arts or in the spiritual or healing professions. Because you may tend to escape in fantasies or overreact to the moods of others, you need an emotional anchor to help you keep a firm foothold in reality. Steer clear of too much escapism (especially in alcohol) or reclusiveness. Places near water soothe your moods. Working in a field that gives you emotional variety will also help you be productive.

CHAPTER 5

Basic Astrology: Your Owner's Manual

You probably know your zodiac sign and those of your friends. But do you know the difference between a sign and a constellation? And what is a house? Is yours an earth sign or a water sign? If you'd like to venture around the zodiac into the deeper areas of astrology, this chapter can get you up and running. It's a quick owner's manual, your fast track to understanding the basic principles of this fascinating but often confusing subject.

Signs and Constellations: What's the Difference?

First, let's get our sign language straight, because for most readers, that's the starting point of astrology.

Signs are actually a type of celestial real estate, located on the zodiac, an imaginary 360-degree belt circling the earth. This belt is divided into twelve equal thirty-degree portions, which are the signs. There's a lot of confusion about the difference between the signs and the constellations of the zodiac. The latter are patterns of stars that originally marked the twelve divisions, like signposts. Though a sign is named after the constellation that once marked the same area, the constellations are no longer in the same place relative to the earth that they were many centuries ago. Over hundreds of years, the earth's orbit has shifted, so that from our point of view here on earth, the constellations seem to have moved. However, the signs remain in place. (Most Western astrology uses the twelve-equal-part division of the zodiac, though there are some other methods of astrology that still use the constellations instead of the signs.)

Most people think of themselves in terms of their sun sign. A sun sign refers to the sign the sun is orbiting through at a given moment (from our point of view here on earth). For instance, "I'm an Aries" means that the sun was passing through Aries when that person was born. However, there are nine other planets (plus asteroids, fixed stars, and sensitive points) that also form our total astrological personality, and some or many of these will be located in other signs. No one is completely Aries, with all astrological components in one sign! (Please note that, in astrology, the sun and moon are usually referred to as planets, though of course they're not.)

As we mentioned before, the sun signs are places on the zodiac. They do not do anything (the planets are the doers). However, they are associated with many things, depending on their location.

How We Define the Signs

The definitions of the signs evolved systematically from four components that interrelate. These four different criteria are a sign's element: its quality, its polarity or sex, and its order in the progression of the zodiac. All these factors work together to tell us what the sign is like.

The system is magically mathematical. The number 12—as in the twelve signs of the zodiac—is divisible by 4, by 3, and by 2. There are four elements, three qualities, and two polarities, which follow each other in sequence around the zodiac.

The four elements (earth, air, fire, and water) are the building blocks of astrology. The use of an element to describe a sign probably dates from man's first attempts to categorize what he saw. Ancient sages believed that all things were composed of combinations of these basic elements—earth, air, fire, and water. This included the human character, which was fiery/choleric, earthy/melancholy, airy/sanguine, or watery/phlegmatic. The elements also correspond to our emotional (water), physical (earth), mental (air) and spiritual (fire) natures. The energies of each of the elements were then observed to be related to the time of year when the sun was passing through a certain segment of the zodiac.

Those born with the sun in fire signs—Aries, Leo, Sagittarius—embody the characteristic of that element. Optimism, warmth, hot tempers, enthusiasm, and spirit are typical of these signs. Taurus, Virgo, and Capricorn are earthy—more grounded, physical, materialistic, organized and deliberate than fire-sign people. Air-sign people—Gemini, Libra, and Aquarius—are mentally oriented communicators. Water signs—Cancer, Scorpio, and Pisces—are emotional, sensitive, and creative.

Think of what each element does to the others. Water puts out fire or evaporates under heat. Air fans the flames or blows them out. Earth smothers fire, drifts and erodes with too much wind, becomes mud or fertile soil with water. Those are often perfect analogies for the relationships between people of different sun-sign elements. This astrochemistry was one of the first ways man described his relationships. Fortunately, no one is entirely air or fire. We all have a bit, or a lot, of each element in our horoscopes. It is this unique mix that defines each astrological personality.

Within each element, there are three qualities that describe types of behavior associated with the sign. Those of cardinal signs are activists, go-getters. These four signs—Aries, Cancer, Libra, and Capricorn—begin each season. Fixed signs, which happen in the middle of the season, are associated with builders, stabilizers. You'll find that sun signs Taurus, Leo, Scorpio, and Aquarius are usually gifted with concentration, stamina, and focus. Mutable signs—Gemini, Virgo, Sagittarius, and Pisces—fall at the end of each season and thus are considered catalysts for change. People born under mutable signs are flexible, adaptable.

The polarity of a sign is either its positive or negative charge. It can be masculine, active, positive, and yang like air or fire signs. Or feminine, reactive, negative, and yin like the water and earth signs.

Finally, we consider the sign's place in the order of the

zodiac. This is vital to the balance of all the forces and the transmission of energy moving through the signs. You may have noticed that your sign is quite different from your neighboring sign on either side. Yet each seems to grow out of its predecessor like links in a chain and transmits a synthesis of energy gathered along the chain to the following sign, beginning with the fire-powered, active, positive charge of Aries.

How the Signs Add Up

SIGN	ELEMENT	QUALITY	POLARITY	PLACE
Aries	fire	cardinal	masculine	first
Taurus	earth	fixed	feminine	second
Gemini	air	mutable	masculine	third
Cancer	water	cardinal	feminine	fourth
Leo	fire	fixed	masculine	fifth
Virgo	earth	mutable	feminine	sixth
Libra	air	cardinal	masculine	seventh
Scorpio	water	fixed	feminine	eighth
Sagittarius	fire	mutable	masculine	ninth
Capricorn	earth	cardinal	feminine	tenth
Aquarius	air	fixed	masculine	eleventh
Pisces	water	mutable	feminine	twelfth

Your Sign's Special Planet

Each sign has a ruling planet that is most compatible with its energies. Mars adds its fiery assertive characteristics to

Aries. The sensual beauty and comfort-loving side of Venus rules Taurus, whereas the idealistic side of Venus rules Libra. Quick-moving Mercury rules two mutable signs, Gemini and Virgo. Its mental agility belongs to Gemini while its analytical, critical side is best expressed in Virgo. The changeable emotional moon is associated with Cancer, while the outgoing Leo personality is ruled by the sun. Scorpio originally shared Mars, but when Pluto was discovered in this century, its powerful magnetic energies were deemed more suitable to the intense vibrations of the fixed water sign Scorpio. Disciplined Capricorn is ruled by Saturn, and expansive Sagittarius by Jupiter. Unpredictable Aquarius is ruled by Uranus and creative, imaginative Pisces by Neptune. In a horoscope, if a planet is placed in the sign it rules, it is sure to be especially powerful.

The Layout of a Horoscope Chart

A horoscope chart is a map of the heavens at a given moment in time. It looks like a wheel divided with twelve spokes. In between each of the spokes is a section called a house.

Each house deals with a different area of life and is influenced by a special sign and a planet. Astrologers look at the house to tell in what area of life an event is happening or about to happen.

The house is governed by the sign passing over the spoke (or cusp of the house) at that particular moment. Though the first house is naturally associated with Aries and Mars, it would also have an additional Capricorn influence if that sign was passing over the house cusp at the time the chart was cast. The sequence of the houses starts with the first house located at the left center spoke (or the number 9 position, if you were reading a clock). The houses are then read counterclockwise around the chart, with the fourth house at the bottom of the chart, the tenth house at the top or twelve o'clock position.

Where do the planets belong? Around the horoscope, planets are placed within the houses according to their location at the time of the chart. That is why it is so important to have an accurate time; with no specific time, the planets have no specific location in the houses and one cannot determine which area of life they will apply to. Since the signs move across the houses as the earth turns, planets in a house will naturally intensify the importance of that house. The house that contains the sun is naturally one of the most prominent.

The First House: Home of Aries and Mars

The sign passing over the first house at the time of your birth is known as your *ascendant,* or *rising sign.* The first house is the house of "firsts"—the first impression you make, how you initiate matters, the image you choose to project. This is where you advertise yourself, where you project your personality. Planets that fall here will intensify the way you come across to others.

The Second House: Home of Taurus and Venus

This house is where you experience the material world—what you value. Here are your attitudes about money, possessions, finances, whatever belongs to you, and what you own, as well as your earning and spending capacity. On a deeper level, this house reveals your sense of self-worth, the inner values that draw wealth in various forms.

The Third House: Home of Gemini and Mercury

This house describes how you communicate with others, how you reach out to others nearby, and how you interact with the immediate environment. It shows how your thinking process works and the way you express your thoughts. Are you articulate or tongue-tied? Can you think on your feet? This house also shows your first relationships, your experiences with brothers and sisters, and how you deal with people close to you such as your neighbors or pals. It's where you take short trips, write letters, or use the telephone. It shows how your mind works in terms of left-brain logical and analytical functions.

The Fourth House: Home of Cancer and the Moon

The fourth house shows the foundation of life, the psychological underpinnings. At the bottom of the chart, this house shows how you are nurtured and made to feel secure—your roots! It shows your early home environment and the circumstances at the end of your life (your final "home") as well as the place you call home now. Astrologers look here for information about the parental nurturers in your life.

The Fifth House: Home of Leo and the Sun

The fifth house is where the creative potential develops. Here you express yourself and procreate in the sense that children are outgrowths of your creative ability. But this house most represents your inner childlike self who delights in play. If your inner security has been established by the time you reach this house, you are now free to have fun, romance, and love affairs and to give of yourself. This is also the place astrologers look for playful love affairs, flirtations, and brief romantic encounters (rather than long-term commitments).

The Sixth House: Home of Virgo and Mercury

The sixth house has been called the "care and maintenance" department. This house shows how you take care of your body and organize yourself to perform efficiently in the world. Here is where you get things done, where you look after others, and fulfill service duties such as taking care of pets. Here is what you do to survive on a day-to-day basis. The sixth house demands order in your life; otherwise there would be chaos. This house is your "job" (as opposed to your career, which is the domain of the tenth house), your diet, and your health and fitness regimens.

The Seventh House: Home of Libra and Venus

This house shows your attitude toward partners and those with whom you enter into commitments, contracts, or agreements. Here is the way you relate to others, as well as your close, intimate, one-on-one relationships (including open enemies—those you "face off" with). Open hostilities, lawsuits, divorces, and marriages happen here. If the first house represents the "I," the seventh or opposite house is the "not-I"—the complementary partner you attract by the way you come across. If you are having trouble with partnerships, consider what you are attracting by the energies of your first and seventh houses.

The Eighth House: Home of Scorpio and Pluto (also Mars)

The eighth house refers to how you merge with something or someone, and how you handle power and control. This is one of the most mysterious and powerful houses, where your energy transforms itself from "I" to "we." As you give up power and control by uniting with something or someone, two kinds of energies merge and become something greater, leading to a regeneration of the self on a higher level. Here are your attitudes toward sex, shared resources, taxes (what you share with the government). Because this house involves what belongs to others, you face issues of control and power struggles, or undergo a deep psychological transformation as you bond with another. Here you transcend yourself with dreams, drugs, and occult or psychic experiences that reflect the collective unconscious.

The Ninth House: Home of Sagittarius and Jupiter

The ninth house shows your search for wisdom and higher knowledge—your belief system. As the third house represents the "lower mind," its opposite on the wheel, the ninth house, is the "higher mind"—the abstract, intuitive, spiritual mind that asks "big" questions like "Why are we here?" After the third house has explored what was close at hand, the ninth stretches out to broaden you mentally with higher education and travel. Here you stretch spiritually with religious activity. Since you are concerned with how everything is related, you tend to push boundaries, take risks. Here is where you express your ideas in a book or thesis, where you pontificate, philosophize, or preach.

The Tenth House: Home of Capricorn and Saturn

The tenth house is associated with your public life and high-profile activities. Located directly overhead at the "high noon" position on the horoscope wheel, this is the most "visible" house in the chart, the one where the world sees you. It deals with your career (but not your routine "job") and your reputation. Here is where you go public, take on responsibilities, (as opposed to the fourth house, where you stay home). This will affect the career you choose and your "public relations." This house is also associated with your father figure or the main authority figure in your life.

The Eleventh House: Home of Aquarius and Uranus

The eleventh house is where you extend yourself to a group, a goal, or a belief system. This house is where you define what you really want, the kinds of friends you have, your political affiliations, and the kind of groups you identify with as an equal. Here is where you become concerned with "what other people think" or where you rebel against social conventions. Here is where you could become a socially conscious humanitarian or a partygoing social butterfly. It's where you look to others to stimulate you and discover your kinship to the rest of humanity. The sign on this house can help you understand what you gain and lose from friendships.

The Twelfth House: Home of Pisces and Neptune

Old-fashioned astrologers used to put a rather negative spin on this house, calling it the house of self-undoing. When we undo ourselves, we surrender control, boundaries, limits, and rules. The twelfth house is where the boundaries between yourself and others become blurred and you become selfless. But instead of being self-undoing, the twelfth house can be a place of great creativity and talent. It is the place where you can tap into the collective unconscious, where your imagination is limitless.

In your trip around the zodiac, you've gone from the I of self-assertion in the first house to the final house, which symbolizes the dissolution that happens before rebirth. The twelfth house is where accumulated experiences are processed in the unconscious. Spiritually oriented astrologers look to this house for evidence of past lives and karma. Places where we go for solitude or to do spiritual or reparatory work belong here, such as retreats, religious institutions, or hospitals. Here is also where we withdraw from society voluntarily or involuntarily or are put in prison because of antisocial activity. Selfless giving through charitable acts is part of this house, as is dependence on charity.

In your daily life, the twelfth house reveals your deepest intimacies, your best-kept secrets, especially those you hide from yourself and keep repressed deep in the unconscious. It is where we surrender a sense of a separate self to a deep feeling of wholeness, such as selfless service in religion or any activity that involves merging with the greater whole. Many sports stars have important planets in the twelfth house that enable them to play in the zone, finding an inner, almost mystical, strength that transcends their limits.

Who's Home in Your Houses?

Houses are stronger or weaker depending on how many planets are inhabiting them. If there are many planets in a given house, it follows that the activities of that house will be especially important in your life. If the planet that rules the house is also located there, this too adds power to the house.

CHAPTER 6

Your Planetary Recipe

Besides the sun and moon, there are eight planets in your horoscope. Each is an ingredient representing a basic force in life that interacts with the other planets to make up a recipe that is uniquely yours. The location of a planet in your horoscope can determine how strongly that planet will affect you. A planet that's close to your rising sign will be emphasized in your chart. If two or more planets are grouped together in one sign, they usually operate together, playing off each other, rather than expressing their energy singularly. A lone planet that stands far away from the others is usually outstanding and often calls the shots in a horoscope.

The sign of each planet also has a powerful influence. In some signs, the planetary energies are very much at home and can easily express themselves. In others, the planet has to work harder and is slightly out of sorts. The sign that most corresponds to the energies of a planet is said to be ruled by that planet and obviously is the best place for it to be. The next best place is in a sign where it is exalted, or especially harmonious. On the other hand, there are places in the horoscope where a planet has to work harder to play its role, such as the sign opposite a planet's rulership, which embodies the opposite area of life, and the sign opposite its exaltation. However, a planet that must work harder can actually be more complete, because it must stretch itself to meet the challenges of living in a more difficult sign. Like world leaders who've had to struggle for greatness, this planet may actually develop great strength and character.

Here's a list of the best places for each planet to be. Note that, as new planets were discovered, they replaced the traditional rulers of signs which best complemented their energies.

ARIES—Mars
TAURUS—Venus, in its most sensual form
GEMINI—Mercury, in its communicative role
CANCER—the moon
LEO—the sun
VIRGO—also Mercury, this time in its more critical capacity
LIBRA—also Venus, in its more aesthetic, judgmental form
SCORPIO—Pluto, replacing Mars, the sign's original ruler
SAGITTARIUS—Jupiter
CAPRICORN—Saturn
AQUARIUS—Uranus, replacing Saturn, its original ruler
PISCES—Neptune, replacing Jupiter, its original ruler

A person who has many planets in exalted signs is lucky indeed, for here is where the planet can accomplish the most and be its most influential and creative.

SUN—exalted in Aries, where its energy creates action
MOON—exalted in Taurus, where instincts and reactions operate on a highly creative level
MERCURY—exalted in Aquarius, where it can reach analytical heights
VENUS—exalted in Pisces, a sign whose sensitivity encourages love and creativity
MARS—exalted in Capricorn, a sign that puts energy to work productively
JUPITER—exalted in Cancer, where it encourages nurturing and growth
SATURN—at home in Libra, where it steadies the scales of justice and promotes balanced, responsible judgment
URANUS—powerful in Scorpio, where it promotes transformation
NEPTUNE—especially favored in Cancer, where it gains the security to transcend to a higher state
PLUTO—exalted in Pisces, where it dissolves the old cycle to make way for transition to the new

The Personal Planets: Mercury, Venus, and Mars

These planets work in your immediate personal life.

Mercury affects how you communicate and how your mental processes work. Are you a quick study who grasps information rapidly? Or do you learn more slowly and thoroughly? How is your concentration? Can you express yourself easily? Are you a good writer? All these questions can be answered by your Mercury placement.

Venus shows what you react to. What turns you on? What appeals to you aesthetically? Are you charming to others? Are you attractive to look at? Your taste, your refinement, your sense of balance and proportion are all Venus-ruled.

Mars is your outgoing energy, your drive and ambition. Do you reach out for new adventures? Are you assertive? Are you motivated? Self-confident? Hot-tempered? How you channel your energy and drive is revealed by your Mars placement.

Mercury Shows How Your Mind Works

In our cookbook analogy, Mercury would be the recipe instructions. Mercury shows how you think and speak, how logical you are. Since it stays close to the sun, read the description for Mercury in your sun sign, then the sign preceding and following it. Then decide which reflects the way you think.

Mercury in Aries

Your mind is very active and assertive. It approaches a plan aggressively. You never hesitate to say what you think, never shy away from a battle. In fact, you may relish a verbal confrontation. Tact is not your strong point, so you may have to learn not to trip over your tongue.

Mercury in Taurus

This is a cautious Mercury. Though you may be a slow learner, you have good concentration and mental stamina. You want to make your ideas really happen. You'll attack a problem methodically and consider every angle thoroughly, never jumping to conclusions. You'll stick with a subject until you master it.

Mercury in Gemini

You are a wonderful communicator with great facility for expressing yourself both verbally and in writing. You love gathering all kinds of information. You probably finish other people's sentences, and express yourself with eloquent hand gestures. You can talk to anybody anytime . . . and probably have phone and e-mail bills to prove it. You read anything from sci-fi to Shakespeare, and might need an extra room just for your book collection. Though you learn fast, you may lack focus and discipline. Watch a tendency to jump from subject to subject.

Mercury in Cancer

You rely on intuition more than logic. Your mental processes are usually colored by your emotions, so you may seem shy or hesitant to voice your opinions. However, this placement gives you the advantage of great imagination and empathy in the way you communicate with others.

Mercury in Leo

You are enthusiastic and very dramatic in the way you express yourself. You like to hold the attention of groups, and could be a great public speaker. Your mind thinks big, so you prefer to deal with the overall picture rather than with the details.

Mercury in Virgo

This is one of the best places for Mercury. It should give you critical ability, attention to details, and thorough analysis. Your mind focuses on the practical side of things. This type of thinking is very well suited to being a teacher or editor.

Mercury in Libra

You're either a born diplomat who smoothes over ruffled feathers or a talented debater. Many lawyers have this placement. However, since you're forever weighing the pros and cons of a situation, you may vacillate when making decisions.

Mercury in Scorpio

This is an investigative mind that stops at nothing to get the answers. You may have a sarcastic, stinging wit or a gift for the cutting remark. There's always a grain of truth to your verbal sallies, thanks to your penetrating insight.

Mercury in Sagittarius

You are a supersalesman with a tendency to expound. Though you are very broad-minded, you can be dogmatic when it comes to telling others what's good for them. You won't hesitate to tell the truth as you see it, so watch a tendency toward tactlessness. On the plus side, you have a great sense of humor. This position of Mercury is often considered by astrologers to be at a disadvantage because Sagittarius opposes Gemini, the sign Mercury rules, and squares off with Virgo, another Mercury-ruled sign. What often happens is that Mercury in Sagittarius oversteps its bounds and loses sight of the facts in a situation. Do a reality check before making promises you may not be able to deliver.

Mercury in Capricorn

This placement endows good mental discipline. You have a love of learning and a very orderly approach to your subjects. You will patiently plod through the facts and figures until you have mastered the tasks. You grasp structured situations easily, but may be short on creativity.

Mercury in Aquarius

An independent, original thinker, you'll have more cutting-edge ideas than the average person. You will be quick to check out any unusual opportunities. Your opinions are so well-researched and grounded that once your mind is made up, it is difficult to change.

Mercury in Pisces

You have the psychic and intuitive mind of a natural poet. Learn to make use of your creative imagination. You may think in terms of helping others, but check a tendency to be vague and forgetful of details.

Venus: The Sweet Things

In our recipe analogy, Venus would be dessert. Venus shows where you receive pleasure, what you love to do. Find your Venus placement from the charts at the end of this chapter by looking for the year of your birth in the left-hand column. Then follow the line of that year across the page until you reach the time period of your birthday. The sign heading that column will be your Venus. If you were born on a day when Venus was changing signs, check the signs preceding or following that day to determine if that sign feels more like your Venus nature.

Venus in Aries

You can't stand to be bored, confined, or ordered around. But a good challenge, maybe even a rousing row, turns you on. Confess—don't you pick a fight now and then just to get someone stirred up? You're attracted by the chase, not the catch, which could cause some problems in your love life if the object of your affection becomes too attainable. You like to wear red, and you can spot a trend before anyone else.

Venus in Taurus

All your senses work in high gear. You love to be surrounded by glorious tastes, smells, textures, sounds, and visuals. Austerity is not for you! Neither is being rushed. You like time to enjoy your pleasures. Soothing surroundings with plenty of creature comforts are your cup of tea. You like to feel secure in your nest, with no sudden jolts or surprises. You like familiar objects—in fact, you may hate to let anything or anyone go.

Venus in Gemini

You are a lively, sparkling personality who thrives in a situation that affords a constant variety and a frequent change of scenery. A varied social life is important to you, with plenty of stimulation and a chance to engage in some light flirtation. Commitment may be difficult, because playing the field is so much fun.

Venus in Cancer

An atmosphere where you feel protected, coddled, and mothered is best for you. You love to be surrounded by children in a cozy, homelike situation. You are attracted to those who are tender and nurturing, who make you feel secure and well provided for. You may be quite secretive about your emotional life, or attracted to clandestine relationships.

Venus in Leo

First-class attention in large doses turns you on, and so does the glitter of real gold and the flash of mirrors. You like to feel like a star at all times, surrounded by your admiring audience. The side effect is that you may be attracted to flatterers and tinsel, while the real gold requires some digging.

Venus in Virgo

Everything neatly in its place? On the surface, you are attracted to an atmosphere where everything is in perfect order, but underneath are some basic, earthy urges. You are attracted to those who appeal to your need to teach, to be of service, or to play out a Pygmalion fantasy. You are at your best when you are busy doing something useful.

Venus in Libra

Elegance and harmony are your key words. You can't abide an atmosphere of contention. Your taste tends toward the classic, with light harmonies of color—nothing clashing, trendy, or outrageous. You love doing things with a partner, and should be careful to pick one who is decisive but patient enough to let you weigh the pros and cons. And steer clear of argumentative types!

Venus in Scorpio

Hidden mysteries intrigue you. In fact, anything that is too open and aboveboard is a bit of a bore. You surely have a stack of whodunits by the bed, along with an erotic magazine or two. You like to solve puzzles, and may also be fascinated with the occult, crime, or scientific research. Intense, all-or-nothing situations add spice to your life, and you love to ferret out the secrets of others. But you could get burned by your flair for living dangerously. The color black, spicy food, dark wood furniture, and heady perfume all get you in the right mood.

Venus in Sagittarius

If you are not actually a world traveler, your surroundings are sure to reflect your love of faraway places. You like a casual outdoor atmosphere and a dog or two to pet. There should be plenty of room for athletic equipment and suitcases. You're attracted to kindred souls who love to travel and who share your freedom-loving philosophy of life. Athletics and spiritual or New Age pursuits could be other interests.

Venus in Capricorn

No fly-by-night relationships for you! You want substance in life, and you are attracted to whatever will help you get where you are going. Status objects turn you on. And so do those who have a serious, responsible, businesslike approach as well as those who remind you of a beloved parent. It is characteristic of this placement to be attracted to someone of a different generation. Antiques, traditional clothing, and dignified behavior are becoming to you.

Venus in Aquarius

This Venus wants to make friends, to be "cool." You like to be in a group, particularly one pushing a worthy cause. You feel quite at home surrounded by people, and could even court fame. Yet all the while you remain detached from any intense commitment. Original ideas and unpredictable people fascinate you. You don't like everything to be planned out in advance, preferring spontaneity and delightful surprises.

Venus in Pisces

This Venus loves to give of yourself, and you find plenty of takers. Stray animals and people appeal to your heart and your pocketbook, but be careful to look at their motives realistically once in a while. You are extremely vulnerable to sob stories of all kinds. Fantasy, the arts (especially film, dance, and theater), and psychic or spiritual activities also speak to you.

Mars: Hot and Spicy

In your cosmic recipe, Mars provides the heat and spice. It is the mover and shaker in your life. It shows how you pursue your goals, whether you have energy to burn or proceed at a slow, steady pace. It will also show how you get angry. Do you explode or do a slow burn or hold everything inside, then get revenge later?

To find your Mars, turn to the charts on pages 86–94. Then find your birth year in the left-hand column and trace the line across horizontally until you come to the column headed by the month of your birth. There you will find an abbreviation of your Mars sign. If the description of your Mars sign doesn't ring true, read the description of the sign preceding and following it. You may have been born on a day when Mars was changing signs, in which case your Mars might be in the adjacent sign.

Mars in Aries

In the sign it rules, Mars shows its brilliant fiery nature. You have an explosive temper and can be quite impatient. On the other hand, you have tremendous courage, energy, and drive. You'll let nothing stand in your way as you race to be first! Obstacles are met head-on and broken through by force. However, those that require patience and persistence can have you exploding in rage. You're a great starter, but not necessarily around for the finish.

Mars in Taurus

Slow, steady, concentrated energy gives you staying power to last until the finish line. You have great stamina, and you never give up. Your tactic is to wear away obstacles with your persistence. Often you come out a winner because you've had the patience to hang in there. When angered, you do a slow burn.

Mars in Gemini

You can't sit still for long. This Mars craves variety. You often have two or more things going on at once—it's all an amusing game to you. Your life can get very complicated, but that only adds spice and stimulation. What drives you into a nervous, hyper state? Boredom, sameness, routine, and confinement. You can do wonderful things with your hands, and you have a way with words.

Mars in Cancer

You rarely attack head-on. Instead, you'll keep things to yourself, make plans in secret, and always cover your actions. This might be interpreted by some as manipulative, but you are only being self-protective. You get furious when anyone knows too much about you. But you do like to know all about others. Your mothering and feeding instincts can be put to good use if you work in the food, hotel, or child-care business. You may have to overcome your fragile sense of security, which prompts you not to take risks and to get physically upset when criticized. Don't take things so personally!

Mars in Leo

You have a very dominant personality that takes center stage. Modesty is not one of your traits, nor is taking a backseat. You prefer giving the orders, and have been known to make a dramatic scene if they are not obeyed. Properly used, this Mars confers leadership ability, endurance, and courage.

Mars in Virgo

You are the faultfinder of the zodiac. You notice every detail. Mistakes of any kind make you very nervous. You may worry, even if everything is going smoothly. You may not express your anger directly, but you sure can nag. You have definite likes and dislikes, and you are sure you can do the job better than anyone else. You are certainly more industrious and detail-oriented than other signs. Your Mars energy is often most positively expressed in some kind of teaching role.

Mars in Libra

This Mars will have a passion for beauty, justice, and art. Generally, you will avoid confrontations at all costs. You prefer to spend your energy finding diplomatic solutions or weighing pros and cons. Your other techniques are passive aggression or exercising your well-known charm to get people to do what you want.

Mars in Scorpio

This is a powerful placement, so intense that it demands careful channeling into worthwhile activities. Otherwise, you could become obsessed with your sexuality or might use your need for power and control to manipulate others. You are strong-willed, shrewd, and very private about your affairs, and you'll usually have a secret agenda behind your actions. Your great stamina, focus, and discipline would be excellent assets for careers in the military or medical fields, especially research or surgery. When angry, you don't get mad—you get even!

Mars in Sagittarius

This expansive Mars often propels people into sales, travel, athletics, or philosophy. Your energies function well when you are on the move. You have a hot temper, and are inclined to say what you think before you consider the consequences. You shoot for high goals—and talk endlessly about them—but you may be weak on groundwork. This Mars needs a solid foundation. Watch a tendency to take unnecessary risks.

Mars in Capricorn

This is an ambitious Mars with an excellent sense of timing. You have an eye for those who can be of use to you, and you may dismiss people ruthlessly when you're angry, but you drive yourself hard and deliver full value. This is a good placement for an executive. You'll aim for status and a high material position in life, and you'll keep climbing despite the odds. A great Mars to have!

Mars in Aquarius

This is the most rebellious Mars. You seem to have a drive to assert yourself against the status quo. You may enjoy provoking people, shocking them out of traditional views. Or this placement could express itself in an offbeat sex life. Somehow you often find yourself in unconventional situations. You enjoy being a leader of an active group, which pursues forward-looking studies, politics, or goals.

Mars in Pisces

This Mars is a good actor who knows just how to appeal to the sympathies of others. You create and project wonderful fantasies, or you use your sensitive antennae to crusade for those less fortunate. You get what you want through creating a veil of illusion and glamour. This is a good Mars for someone in the creative and imaginative fields—a dancer, performer, photographer, actor. Many famous film stars have this placement. Watch a tendency to manipulate by making others feel sorry for you.

Jupiter Piles the Plate High

In our recipe analogy, Jupiter would be the high-carb dish that can add on pounds. This big, bright, swirling mass of gases is associated with abundance, prosperity, and the kind of windfall you get without too much hard work. You're optimistic under Jupiter's influence, when anything seems possible. You'll travel, expand your mind with higher education, and publish to share your knowledge widely. On the other hand, Jupiter's influence is neither discriminating nor disciplined. It represents the principle of growth without judgment, and therefore could result in extravagance, weight gain, laziness, and carelessness, if not kept in check.

Be sure to look up your Jupiter in the tables in this book. When the current position of Jupiter is favorable, you may get that lucky break. This is a great time to try new things, take risks, travel, or get more education. Opportunities seem to open up easily, so take advantage of them.

Once a year, Jupiter changes signs. That means you are due for an expansive time every twelve years, when Jupiter travels through your sun sign. You'll also have up periods every four years, when Jupiter is in the same element as your sun sign.

Jupiter in Aries

You are the soul of enthusiasm and optimism. Your luckiest times are when you are getting started on an exciting project or selling an idea that you really believe in. You may have to watch a tendency to be arrogant with those who do not share your enthusiasm. You follow your impulses, often ignoring budget or other commonsense limitations. To produce real, solid benefits, you'll need patience and follow-through wherever this Jupiter falls in your horoscope.

Jupiter in Taurus

You'll spend on beautiful material things, especially those that come from nature—items made of rare woods, natural fabrics, or precious gems, for instance. You can't have too much comfort or too many sensual pleasures. Watch a tendency to overindulge in good food, or to overpamper yourself with nothing but the best. Spartan living is not for you! You may be especially lucky in matters of real estate.

Jupiter in Gemini

You are the great talker of the zodiac, and you may be a great writer, too. But restlessness could be your weak point. You jump around, talk too much, and could be a jack-of-all-trades. Keeping a secret is especially difficult, so you'll have to watch a tendency to spill the beans. Since you love to be at the center of a beehive of activity, you'll have a vibrant social life. Your best opportunities will come through your talent for language—speaking, writing, communicating, and selling.

Jupiter in Cancer

You are luckiest in situations where you can find emotional closeness or deal with basic security needs such as food, nurturing, or shelter. You may be a great collector. Or you may simply love to accumulate things—you are the one who stashes things away for a rainy day. You probably have a very good memory and love children. In fact, you may have many children to care for. The food, hotel, child-care, and shipping businesses hold good opportunities for you.

Jupiter in Leo

You are a natural showman who loves to live in a larger-than-life way. Yours is a personality full of color that always finds its way into the limelight. You can't have too much attention or applause. Showbiz is a natural place for you, and so is any area where you can play to a crowd. Exercising your flair for drama, your natural playfulness, and your romantic nature brings you good fortune. But watch a tendency to be overly extravagant or to monopolize center stage.

Jupiter in Virgo

You actually love those minute details others find boring. To you, they make all the difference between the perfect and the ordinary. You are the fine craftsman who spots every flaw. You expand your awareness by finding the most efficient methods and by being of service to others. Many of you will be drawn to medical or teaching fields. You'll also have luck in publishing, crafts, nutrition, and service professions. Watch out for a tendency to overwork.

Jupiter in Libra

This is an other-directed Jupiter that develops best with a partner. The stimulation of others helps you grow. You are also most comfortable in harmonious, beautiful situations and you work well with artistic people. You have a great sense of fair play and an ability to evaluate the pros and cons of a situation. You usually prefer to play the role of diplomat rather than adversary.

Jupiter in Scorpio

You love the feeling of power and control, of taking things to their limit. You can't resist a mystery. Your shrewd, penetrating mind sees right through to the heart of most situations and people. You have luck in work that provides for solutions to matters of life and death. You may be drawn to undercover work, behind-the-scenes intrigue, psychotherapy, the occult, and sex-related ventures. Your challenge will be to develop a sense of moderation and tolerance for other beliefs. This Jupiter can be fanatical. You may have luck in handling other people's money—insurance, taxes, and inheritance can bring you a windfall.

Jupiter in Sagittarius

Independent, outgoing, and idealistic, you'll shoot for the stars. This Jupiter compels you to travel far and wide, both physically and mentally, via higher education. You may have luck while traveling in an exotic place. You also have luck with outdoor ventures, exercise, and animals, particularly horses. Since you tend to be very open about your opinions, watch a tendency to be tactless and to exaggerate. Instead, use your wonderful sense of humor to make your point.

Jupiter in Capricorn

Jupiter is much more restrained in Capricorn, the sign of rules and authority. Here, Jupiter can make you overwork and heighten any ambition or sense of duty you may have.

You'll expand in areas that advance your position, putting you farther up the social or corporate ladder. You are lucky working within the establishment in a very structured situation where you can show off your ability to organize and reap rewards for your hard work.

Jupiter in Aquarius

This is another freedom-loving Jupiter, with great tolerance and originality. You are at your best when you are working for a humanitarian cause and in the company of many supporters. This is a good Jupiter for a political career. You'll relate to all kinds of people on all social levels. You have an abundance of original ideas, but you are best off away from routine and any situation that imposes rigid rules. You need mental stimulation!

Jupiter in Pisces

You are a giver whose feelings and pocketbook are easily touched by others, so choose your companions with care. You could be the original sucker for a hard-luck story. Better find a worthy hospital or a charity that will appreciate your selfless support. You have a great creative imagination. You may attract good fortune in fields related to oil, perfume, pharmaceuticals, petroleum, dance, footwear, and alcohol. But beware of overindulgence in alcohol—focus on a creative outlet instead.

Saturn Is a Disciplined Diet

Jupiter speeds you up with *lucky breaks* and quick energy. Then along comes Saturn to slow you down with the *disciplinary brakes* and slow-burning energy. It is the part of your planetary diet that helps you achieve lasting goals. Saturn has unfairly been called a malefic planet, one of the bad guys of the zodiac. On the contrary, Saturn is one of our best friends, the kind who tells you what you need to hear even if it's not good news. Under a Saturn transit, we grow up, take responsibility for our lives, and emerge from whatever test this planet has in store as far wiser, more capable and mature human beings. It is when we are under pressure that we grow stronger.

Look up your natal Saturn in the tables in this book for clues on where you need work.

Saturn in Aries

Saturn here puts the brakes on Aries' natural drive and enthusiasm. There is often an angry side to this placement. You don't let anyone push you around, and you know what's best for yourself. Following orders is not your strong point, and neither is diplomacy. You tend to be quick to go on the offensive in relationships, attacking first, before anyone attacks you. Because no one quite lives up to your standards, you often wind up doing everything yourself. You'll have to learn to cooperate and tone down self-centeredness. Both Pat Buchanan and Saddam Hussein have this Saturn.

Saturn in Taurus

A big issue is getting control of the cash flow. There will be lean periods that can be frightening, but you have the patience and endurance to stick them out and the methodical drive to prosper in the end. Learn to take a philosophical attitude, like Ben Franklin, who also had this placement and who said, "A penny saved is a penny earned."

Saturn in Gemini

You are a serious student of life, but you may have difficulty communicating or sharing your knowledge. You may be shy, speak slowly, or have fears about communicating, like Eleanor Roosevelt. You dwell in the realms of science, theory, or abstract analysis—even when you are dealing with the emotions, like Sigmund Freud, who also had this placement.

Saturn in Cancer

Your tests come with establishing a secure emotional base. In doing so, you may have to deal with some very basic fears centering on your early home environment. Most of your Saturn tests will have emotional roots in those early childhood experiences. You may have difficulty remaining objective in terms of what you try to achieve. So it will be especially important for you to deal with negative feelings such as guilt, paranoia, jealousy, resentment, and suspicion. Galileo and Michelangelo also navigated these murky waters.

Saturn in Leo

This is an authoritarian Saturn—a strict, demanding parent who may deny the pleasure principle in your zeal to see that rules are followed. Though you may feel guilty about taking the spotlight, you are very ambitious and loyal. You have to watch a tendency toward rigidity, also toward overwork and holding back affection. Joseph Kennedy and Billy Graham share this placement.

Saturn in Virgo

This is a cautious, exacting Saturn. You are intensely hard on yourself. Most of all, you give yourself the roughest time with your constant worries about every little detail, often making yourself sick. You may have difficulties setting priorities and getting the job done. Your tests will come in learning tolerance and understanding of others. Charles de Gaulle, Mae West, and Nathaniel Hawthorne had this meticulous Saturn.

Saturn in Libra

Saturn is exalted here, which makes this planet an ally. You may choose very serious, older partners in life, perhaps stemming from a fear of dependency. You need to learn to stand solidly on your own before you commit to another. You are extremely cautious as you deliberate every involvement—with good reason. It is best that you find an occupation that makes good use of your sense of duty and honor. Steer clear of fly-by-night situations. Both Khruschev and Mao Tse-tung had this placement.

Saturn in Scorpio

You have great staying power. This Saturn tests you in situations involving the control of others. You may feel drawn to some kind of intrigue or undercover work, like J. Edgar Hoover. Or there may be an air of mystery surrounding your life and death, like Marilyn Monroe and Robert Kennedy, who both had this placement. There are lessons to be learned from your sexual involvements. Often sex is used for manipulation or is somehow out of the ordinary. The Roman emperor Caligula and the transsexual Christine Jorgensen are extreme cases.

Saturn in Sagittarius

Your challenges and lessons will come from tests of your spiritual and philosophical values, as happened to Martin Luther King and Gandhi. You are high-minded and sincere with this reflective, moral placement. Uncompromising in your ethical standards, you could become a benevolent despot.

Saturn in Capricorn

With the help of Saturn at maximum strength, your judgment will improve with age. And like Spencer Tracy's screen image, you'll be the gray-haired hero with a strong sense of responsibility. You advance in life slowly but steadily, always with a strong hand at the helm and an eye for the advantageous situation. Like Pat Robertson, you're likely to stand for conservative values. Negatively, you may be a loner, prone to periods of melancholy.

Saturn in Aquarius

Your tests come from relationships with groups. Do you care too much about what others think? Do you feel like an outsider, like Greta Garbo? You may fear being different from others and therefore slight your own unique, forward-looking gifts. Or like Lord Byron and Howard Hughes, you may take the opposite tack and rebel in the extreme. You can apply discipline to accomplish great humanitarian goals, as Albert Schweitzer did.

Saturn in Pisces

Your fear of the unknown and the irrational may lead you to the safety and protection of an institution. You may go on the run like Jesse James, who had this placement, to avoid looking too deeply inside. Or you might go in the opposite, more positive direction and develop a disciplined psychoanalytic approach, which puts you more in control of your feelings. Some of you will take refuge in work with hospitals, charities, or religious institutions. Queen Victoria, who had this placement, symbolized an era when institutions of all kinds were sustained. Discipline applied to artistic work, especially poetry and dance, or to spiritual work, such as yoga or meditation, might be helpful.

How Uranus, Neptune, and Pluto Influence a Whole Generation

These three planets remain in signs such a long time that a whole generation bears the imprint of the sign. Mass movements, great sweeping changes, fads that characterize a generation, even the issues of the conflicts and wars of the time are influenced by these "outer three" planets. When one of those distant planets changes signs, there is a definite shift in the atmosphere, the feeling of the end of an era.

Since these planets are so far away from the sun—too distant to be seen by the naked eye—they pick up signals from the universe at large. These planetary receivers literally link the sun with distant energies, and then perform a similar function in your horoscope by linking your central character with intuitive, spiritual, transformative forces from the cosmos. Each planet has a special domain, and will reflect this in the area of your chart where it falls.

Uranus Is the Surprise Ingredient

In your cosmic recipe, Uranus is the unexpected ingredient that sets you and your generation apart. There is nothing ordinary about this quirky green planet that seems to be traveling on its side, surrounded by a swarm of moons. Is it any wonder that astrologers assigned it to Aquarius, the most eccentric and gregarious sign? Uranus seems to wend its way around the sun, marching to its own tune.

Significantly, Uranus follows Saturn, the planet of limitations and structures. Often we get caught up in the structures we have created to give ourselves a sense of security. However, if we lose contact with our spiritual roots, then Uranus is likely to jolt us out of our comfortable rut and wake us up.

Uranus energy is electrical, happening in sudden flashes. It is not influenced by karma or past events, nor does it regard tradition, sex, or sentiment. The Uranus key words are surprise and awakening. Suddenly, there's that flash of inspiration, that bright idea, that totally new approach to revolutionize whatever scheme you were undertaking. A Uranus event takes you by surprise; it happens from out of the blue, for better or for worse. The Uranus place in your life is where you awaken and become your own person, leaving the structures of Saturn behind. And it is probably the most unconventional place in your chart.

Look up the sign of Uranus at the time of your birth and see where you follow your own tune.

Uranus in Aries

Birth Dates:
March 31, 1927–November 4, 1927

January 13, 1928–June 6, 1934
October 10, 1934–March 28, 1935

Your generation is original, creative, pioneering. It developed the computer, the airplane, and the cyclotron. You let nothing hold you back from exploring the unknown, and you have a powerful mixture of fire and electricity behind you. Women of your generation were among the first to be liberated. You were the unforgettable style setters. You have a surprise in store for everyone. Like Yoko Ono, Grace Kelly, and Jacqueline Onassis, your life may be jolted by sudden and violent changes.

Uranus in Taurus

Birth Dates:
June 6, 1934–October 10, 1934
March 28, 1935–August 7, 1941
October 5, 1941–May 15, 1942

The great territorial shake-ups of World War II began during your generation. You are independent, probably self-employed or would like to be. You have original ideas about making money, and you brace yourself for sudden changes of fortune. This Uranus can cause shake-ups, particularly in finances, but it can also make you a born entrepreneur.

Uranus in Gemini

Birth Dates:
August 7, 1941–October 5, 1941
May 15, 1942–August 30, 1948
November 12, 1948–June 10, 1949

You were the first children to be influenced by television. Now, in your adult years, your generation stocks up on answering machines, cell phones, computers, and fax machines—any new way you can communicate. You have an inquiring mind, but your interests may be rather short-lived. This Uranus can be easily fragmented if there is no structure and focus.

Uranus in Cancer

Birth Dates:
  August 30, 1948–November 12, 1948
  June 10, 1949–August 24, 1955
  January 28, 1956–June 10, 1956

This generation came at a time when divorce was becoming commonplace, so your home image is unconventional. You may have an unusual relationship with your parents; you may have come from a broken home or an unconventional one. You'll have unorthodox ideas about parenting, intimacy, food, and shelter. You may also be interested in dreams, psychic phenomena, and memory work.

Uranus in Leo

Birth Dates:
  August 24, 1955–January 28, 1956
  June 10, 1956–November 1, 1961
  January 10, 1962–August 10, 1962

This generation understood how to use electronic media. Many of your group are now leaders in the high-tech industries, and you also understand how to use the new media to promote yourself. Like Isadora Duncan, you may have a very eccentric kind of charisma and a life that is sparked by unusual love affairs. Your children, too, may have traits that are out of the ordinary. Where this planet falls in your chart, you'll have a love of freedom, be a bit of an egomaniac, and show the full force of your personality in a unique way, like tennis great Martina Navratilova.

Uranus in Virgo

Birth Dates:
  November 1, 1961–January 10, 1962
  August 10, 1962–September 28, 1968
  May 20, 1969–June 24, 1969

You'll have highly individual work methods. Many of you will be finding newer, more practical ways to use computers. Like Einstein, who had this placement, you'll break the rules brilliantly. Your generation came at a time of student rebellions, the civil rights movement, and the general acceptance of health foods. Chances are, you're concerned about pollution and cleaning up the environment. You may also be involved with nontraditional healing methods.

Uranus in Libra

Birth Dates:
  September 28, 1968–May 20, 1969
  June 24, 1969–November 21, 1974
  May 1, 1975–September 8, 1975
Your generation will be always changing partners. Born during the era of women's liberation, you may have come from a broken home and have no clear image of what a marriage entails. There will be many sudden splits and experiments before you settle down. Your generation will be much involved in legal and political reforms and in changing artistic and fashion looks.

Uranus in Scorpio

Birth Dates:
  November 21, 1974–May 1, 1975
  September 8, 1975–February 17, 1981
  March 20, 1981–November 16, 1981
Interest in transformation, meditation, and life after death signaled the beginning of New Age consciousness. Your generation recognizes no boundaries, no limits, and no external controls. You'll have new attitudes toward death and dying, psychic phenomena, and the occult. Like Mae West and Casanova, you'll shock 'em sexually, too.

Uranus in Sagittarius

Birth Dates:
  February 17, 1981–March 20, 1981
  November 16, 1981–February 15, 1988
  May 27, 1988–December 2, 1988
Could this generation be the first to travel in outer space? An earlier generation with this placement included Charles Lindbergh and a time when the first zeppelins and

the Wright Brothers were conquering the skies. Uranus here forecasts great discoveries, mind expansion, and long-distance travel. Like Galileo and Martin Luther, those born in these years will generate new theories about the cosmos and mankind's relation to it.

Uranus in Capricorn

Birth Dates:
December 20, 1904–January 30, 1912
September 4, 1912–November 12, 1912
February 15, 1988–May 27, 1988
December 2, 1988–April 1, 1995
June 9, 1995–January 12, 1996

This generation, now growing up, will challenge traditions with the help of electronic gadgets. In these years, we got organized with the help of technology put to practical use. The Internet was born following the great economic boom of the 1990s. Great leaders who were movers and shakers of history, like Julius Caesar and Henry VIII, were born under this placement.

Uranus in Aquarius

Birth Dates:
January 30, 1912–September 4, 1912
November 12, 1912–April 1, 1919
August 16, 1919–January 22, 1920
April 1, 1995–June 9, 1995
January 12, 1996–March 10, 2003
September 15, 2003–December 30, 2003

Uranus in Aquarius is the strongest placement for this planet. Recently we've had the opportunity to witness the full force of its power of innovation, as well as its sudden wake-up calls and insistence on humanitarian values. This was a time of high-tech development, when home computers became as ubiquitous as television. It was a time of globalization, of surprise attacks (9/11), and underdeveloped countries demanding attention. The last generation with this placement produced great innovative minds such as Leonard Bernstein and Orson Welles. The next will become another radical breakthrough generation, much concerned with global issues that involve all humanity.

Uranus in Pisces

Birth Dates:
 April 1, 1919–August 16, 1919
 January 22, 1920–March 31, 1927
 November 4, 1927–January 12, 1928
 March 10, 2003–September 15, 2003
 December 20, 2003–May 28, 2010

Uranus is now in Pisces, ushering in a new generation. In the past century, Uranus in Pisces focused attention on the rise of electronic entertainment—radio and the cinema—and the secretiveness of Prohibition. This produced a generation of idealists exemplified by Judy Garland's theme "Somewhere over the Rainbow." Uranus in Pisces also hints at stealth activities, at hospital and prison reform, at high-tech drugs and medical experiments, at shake-ups and reforms in the Pisces-ruled petroleum industry. Issues regarding the water and oil supply, water-related storm damage, sudden hurricanes, and floods demand our attention.

Neptune Is the Magic Solvent

Neptune is the liquid in your horoscope recipe that dissolves other ingredients and creates a magical, inspired result. It is often maligned as the planet of illusions that dissolves reality, enabling you to escape the material world. Under Neptune's influence, you see what you want to see. But Neptune also encourages you to create. It embodies glamour, subtlety, mystery, and mysticism, and it governs anything that takes you beyond the mundane world, including out-of-body experiences.

Neptune acts to transcend your ordinary perceptions to take you to another level, where you experience either confusion or ecstasy. Its force can pull you off course only if you allow this to happen. Those who use Neptune wisely can translate their daydreams into poetry, theater, design, or inspired moves in the business world, avoiding the tricky "con artist" side of this planet.

Find your Neptune listed below.

Neptune in Cancer

Birth Dates:
  July 19, 1901–December 25, 1901
  May 21, 1902–September 23, 1914
  December 14, 1914–July 19, 1915
  March 19, 1916–May 2, 1916

Dreams of the homeland, idealistic patriotism, and glamorization of the nurturing assets of women characterized this time. You who were born here have unusual psychic ability and deep insights into basic needs of others.

Neptune in Leo

Birth Dates:
  September 23, 1914–December 14, 1914
  July 19, 1915–March 19, 1916
  May 2, 1916–September 21, 1928
  February 19, 1929–July 24, 1929

Neptune in Leo brought us the glamour and high living of the 1920s and the big spenders of that time. The Neptune temptations of gambling, seduction, theater, and lavish entertaining distracted from the realities of the age. Those born in that generation also made great advances in the arts.

Neptune in Virgo

Birth Dates:
  September 21, 1928–February 19, 1929
  July 24, 1929–October 3, 1942
  April 17, 1943–August 2, 1943

Neptune in Virgo encompassed the 1930s, the Great Depression, and the beginning of World War II, when a new order was born. There was a time of facing "what doesn't work." Many were unemployed and found solace at the movies, watching the great Virgo star Greta Garbo or the escapist dance films of Busby Berkeley. New public services were born. Those with Neptune in Virgo later spread the gospel of health and fitness. This generation's devotion to spending hours at the office inspired the term *workaholic*.

Neptune in Libra

Birth Dates:
October 3, 1942–April 17, 1943
August 2, 1943–December 24, 1955
March 12, 1956–October 19, 1956
June 15, 1957–August 6, 1957

This was the time of World War II and the postwar period, when the world regained balance and returned to relative stability. Neptune in Libra was the romantic generation who would later be concerned with relating. As this generation matured, there was a new trend toward marriage and commitment. Racial and sexual equality became important issues, as they redesigned traditional roles to suit modern times.

Neptune in Scorpio

Birth Dates:
December 24, 1955–March 12, 1956
October 19, 1956–June 15, 1957
August 6, 1957–January 4, 1970
May 3, 1970–November 6, 1970

Neptune in Scorpio brought in a generation that would become interested in transformative power. Born in an era that glamorized sex, drugs, rock and roll, and Eastern religion, they matured in a more sobering time of AIDS, cocaine abuse, and New Age spirituality. As they evolve, they will become active in healing the planet from the results of the abuse of power.

Neptune in Sagittarius

Birth Dates:
January 4, 1970–May 3, 1970
November 6, 1970–January 19, 1984

June 23, 1984–November 21, 1984

Neptune in Sagittarius was the time when space and astronaut travel became a reality. The Neptune influence glamorized new approaches to mysticism, religion, and mind expansion. This generation will take a new approach to spiritual life, with emphasis on visions, mysticism, and clairvoyance.

Neptune in Capricorn

Birth Dates:
January 19, 1984–June 23, 1984
November 21, 1984–January 29, 1998

Neptune in Capricorn brought a time when delusions about material power were glamorized in the mid–1980s and 1990s. There was a boom in the stock market, and the Internet era spawned young tycoons who later lost it all. It was also a time when the psychic and occult worlds spawned a new category of business enterprise, and sold services on television.

Neptune in Aquarius

Birth Dates:
January 29, 1998–April 4, 2011

This should continue to be a time of breakthroughs. Here the creative influence of Neptune reaches a universal audience. This is a time of dissolving barriers, of globalization—when we truly become one world. During this transit of high-tech Aquarius, new kinds of entertainment media reach across cultural differences. However, the transit of Neptune has also raised boundary issues between cultures, especially in Middle Eastern countries with Neptune-ruled oil fields. As Neptune raises issues of social and political structures not being as solid as they seem, this could continue to produce rebellion and chaos in the environment. However, by using imagination (Neptune) in partnership with a global view (Aquarius) we could reach creative solutions.

Those born with this placement should be true citizens of the world with a remarkable creative ability to transcend social and cultural barriers.

Pluto Can Transform You

Add a small touch of Pluto to your recipe and it will change the dish completely! Though it is a tiny planet, its influence is great. When Pluto zaps a strategic point in your horoscope, your life changes dramatically.

This little planet is the power behind the scenes; it affects you at deep levels of consciousness, causing events to come to the surface that will transform you and your generation. Nothing escapes, or is sacred, with this probing planet. Its purpose is to wipe out the past so something new can happen.

The Pluto place in your horoscope is where you have invisible power (Mars governs the visible power), where you can transform, heal, and affect the unconscious needs of the masses. Pluto tells lots about how your generation projects power, what makes it seem cool to others. And when Pluto changes signs, there is a whole new concept of what's cool. Pluto's strange elliptical orbit occasionally runs inside the orbit of neighboring Neptune. Because of its eccentric path, the length of time Pluto stays in any given sign can vary from thirteen to thirty-two years. It covered only seven signs in the last century.

Pluto in Gemini

Birth Dates:
  Late 1800s–May 26, 1914

This was a time of mass suggestion and breakthroughs in communications, a time when many brilliant writers such as Ernest Hemingway and F. Scott Fitzgerald were born. Henry Miller, D. H. Lawrence, and James Joyce scandalized society by using explicit sexual images and language in their literature. "Muckraking" journalists exposed corruption. Pluto-ruled Scorpio President Theodore Roosevelt said, "Speak softly, but carry a big stick." This generation had an intense need to communicate and made major breakthroughs in knowledge. A compulsive restlessness and a thirst for a variety of experiences characterized many of this generation.

Pluto in Cancer

Birth Dates:
May 26, 1914–June 14, 1939

Dictators and mass media arose to wield emotional power over the masses. Women's rights was a popular issue. Deep sentimental feelings, acquisitiveness, and possessiveness characterized these times and people. Most of the great stars of the Hollywood era that embodied the American image were born during this period: Grace Kelly, Esther Williams, Frank Sinatra, Lana Turner, to name a few.

Pluto in Leo

Birth Dates:
June 14, 1939–August, 19, 1957

The performing arts played on the emotions of the masses. Mick Jagger, John Lennon, and rock and roll were born at this time. So were "baby boomers" like Bill and Hillary Clinton. Those born here tend to be self-centered, powerful, and boisterous. This generation does its own thing, for better or for worse.

Pluto in Virgo

Birth Dates:
August 19, 1957–October 5, 1971
April 17, 1972–July 30, 1972

This is the "yuppie" generation that sparked a mass movement toward fitness, health, and career. It is a much more sober, serious, driven generation than the fun-loving Pluto in Leo. During this time, machines were invented to process detail work efficiently. Inventions took a practical turn with answering machines, fax machines, car phones, and home office equipment—all making the workplace far more efficient.

Pluto in Libra

Birth Dates:
October 5, 1971–April 17, 1972

July 30, 1972–November 5, 1983
May 18, 1984–August 27, 1984

A mellower generation, people born at this time are concerned with partnerships, working together, and finding diplomatic solutions to problems. Marriage is important to this generation, and they will define it by combining traditional values with equal partnership. This was a time of women's liberation, gay rights, ERA, and legal battles over abortion, all of which transformed our ideas about relationships.

Pluto in Scorpio

Birth Dates:
November 5, 1983–May 18, 1984
August 27, 1984–January 17, 1995

Pluto was in the sign it rules for a comparatively short period of time. However, this was a time of record achievements, destructive sexually transmitted diseases, nuclear power controversies, and explosive political issues. Pluto destroys in order to create new understanding—the phoenix rising from the ashes—which should be some consolation for those of you who felt Pluto's force before 1995. Sexual shockers were par for the course during these intense years when black clothing, transvestites, body piercing, tattoos, and sexually explicit advertising pushed the boundaries of good taste.

Pluto in Sagittarius

Birth Dates:
January 17, 1995–April 20, 1995
November 10, 1995–January 26, 2008

During our current Pluto transit, we are being pushed to expand our horizons, to find deeper spiritual meaning in life. Pluto's opposition with Saturn in 2001 brought an enormous conflict between traditional societies and the forces of change. It signals a time when religious convictions will exert more power in our political life as well.

Since Sagittarius is the sign that rules travel, there's a good possibility that Pluto, the planet of extremes, will make space travel a reality for some of us. Already, we are seeing wealthy adventurers paying for the privilege of travel on space shuttles. Discovery of life-forms on other planets could transform our ideas about where we came from.

New dimensions in electronic publishing, concern with animal rights and the environment, and an increasing emphasis on extreme forms of religion are other signs of these times. Look for charismatic religious leaders to arise now. We'll also be developing far-reaching philosophies designed to elevate our lives with a new sense of purpose.

VENUS SIGNS 1901–2007

	Aries	Taurus	Gemini	Cancer	Leo	Virgo
1901	3/29–4/22	4/22–5/17	5/17–6/10	6/10–7/5	7/5–7/29	7/29–8/23
1902	5/7–6/3	6/3–6/30	6/30–7/25	7/25–8/19	8/19–9/13	9/13–10/7
1903	2/28–3/24	3/24–4/18	4/18–5/13	5/13–6/9	6/9–7/7	7/7–8/17 9/6–11/8
1904	3/13–5/7	5/7–6/1	6/1–6/25	6/25–7/19	7/19–8/13	8/13–9/6
1905	2/3–3/6 4/9–5/28	3/6–4/9 5/28–7/8	7/8–8/6	8/6–9/1	9/1–9/27	9/27–10/21
1906	3/1–4/7	4/7–5/2	5/2–5/26	5/26–6/20	6/20–7/16	7/16–8/11
1907	4/27–5/22	5/22–6/16	6/16–7/11	7/11–8/4	8/4–8/29	8/29–9/22
1908	2/14–3/10	3/10–4/5	4/5–5/5	5/5–9/8	9/8–10/8	10/8–11/3
1909	3/29–4/22	4/22–5/16	5/16–6/10	6/10–7/4	7/4–7/29	7/29–8/23
1910	5/7–6/3	6/4–6/29	6/30–7/24	7/25–8/18	8/19–9/12	9/13–10/6
1911	2/28–3/23	3/24–4/17	4/18–5/12	5/13–6/8	6/9–7/7	7/8–11/18
1912	4/13–5/6	5/7–5/31	6/1–6/24	6/24–7/18	7/19–8/12	8/13–9/5
1913	2/3–3/6 5/2–5/30	3/7–5/1 5/31–7/7	7/8–8/5	8/6–8/31	9/1–9/26	9/27–10/20
1914	3/14–4/6	4/7–5/1	5/2–5/25	5/26–6/19	6/20–7/15	7/16–8/10
1915	4/27–5/21	5/22–6/15	6/16–7/10	7/11–8/3	8/4–8/28	8/29–9/21
1916	2/14–3/9	3/10–4/5	4/6–5/5	5/6–9/8	9/9–10/7	10/8–11/2
1917	3/29–4/21	4/22–5/15	5/16–6/9	6/10–7/3	7/4–7/28	7/29–8/21
1918	5/7–6/2	6/3–6/28	6/29–7/24	7/25–8/18	8/19–9/11	9/12–10/5
1919	2/27–3/22	3/23–4/16	4/17–5/12	5/13–6/7	6/8–7/7	7/8–11/8
1920	4/12–5/6	5/7–5/30	5/31–6/23	6/24–7/18	7/19–8/11	8/12–9/4
1921	2/3–3/6 4/26–6/1	3/7–4/25 6/2–7/7	7/8–8/5	8/6–8/31	9/1–9/25	9/26–10/20
1922	3/13–4/6	4/7–4/30	5/1–5/25	5/26–6/19	6/20–7/14	7/15–8/9
1923	4/27–5/21	5/22–6/14	6/15–7/9	7/10–8/3	8/4–8/27	8/28–9/20
1924	2/13–3/8	3/9–4/4	4/5–5/5	5/6–9/8	9/9–10/7	10/8–11/12
1925	3/28–4/20	4/21–5/15	5/16–6/8	6/9–7/3	7/4–7/27	7/28–8/21

Libra	Scorpio	Sagittarius	Capricorn	Aquarius	Pisces
8/23–9/17	9/17–10/12	10/12–1/16	1/16–2/9 11/7–12/5	2/9–3/5 12/5–1/11	3/5–3/29
10/7–10/31	10/31–11/24	11/24–12/18	12/18–1/11	2/6–4/4	1/11–2/6 4/4–5/7
8/17–9/6 11/8–12/9	12/9–1/5			1/11–2/4	2/4–2/28
9/6–9/30	9/30–10/25	1/5–1/30 10/25–11/18	1/30–2/24 11/18–12/13	2/24–3/19 12/13–1/7	3/19–4/13
10/21–11/14	11/14–12/8	12/8–1/1/06			1/7–2/3
8/11–9/7	9/7–10/9 12/15–12/25	10/9–12/15 12/25–2/6	1/1–1/25	1/25–2/18	2/18–3/14
9/22–10/16	10/16–11/9	11/9–12/3	2/6–3/6 12/3–12/27	3/6–4/2 12/27–1/20	4/2–4/27
11/3–11/28	11/28–12/22	12/22–1/15			1/20–2/4
8/23–9/17	9/17–10/12	10/12–11/17	1/15–2/9 11/17–12/5	2/9–3/5 12/5–1/15	3/5–3/29
10/7–10/30	10/31–11/23	11/24–12/17	12/18–12/31	1/1–1/15 1/29–4/4	1/16–1/28 4/5–5/6
11/19–12/8	12/9–12/31		1/1–1/10	1/11–2/2	2/3–2/27
9/6–9/30	1/1–1/4 10/1–10/24	1/5–1/29 10/25–11/17	1/30–2/23 11/18–12/12	2/24–3/18 12/13–12/31	3/19–4/12
10/21–11/13	11/14–12/7	12/8–12/31		1/1–1/6	1/7–2/2
8/11–9/6	9/7–10/9 12/6–12/30	10/10–12/5 12/31	1/1–1/24	1/25–2/17	2/18–3/13
9/22–10/15	10/16–11/8	1/1–2/6 11/9–12/2	2/7–3/6 12/3–12/26	3/7–4/1 12/27–12/31	4/2–4/26
11/3–11/27	11/28–12/21	12/22–12/31		1/1–1/19	1/20–2/13
8/22–9/16	9/17–10/11	1/1–1/14 10/12–11/6	1/15–2/7 11/7–12/5	2/8–3/4 12/6–12/31	3/5–3/28
10/6–10/29	10/30–11/22	11/23–12/16	12/17–12/31	1/1–4/5	4/6–5/6
11/9–12/8	12/9–12/31		1/1–1/9	1/10–2/2	2/3–2/26
9/5–9/30	1/1–1/3 9/31–10/23	1/4–1/28 10/24–11/17	1/29–2/22 11/18–12/11	2/23–3/18 12/12–12/31	3/19–4/11
10/21–11/13	11/14–12/7	12/8–12/31		1/1–1/6	1/7–2/2
8/10–9/6	9/7–10/10 11/29–12/31	10/11–11/28	1/1–1/24	1/25–2/16	2/17–3/12
9/21–10/14	1/1 10/15–11/7	1/2–2/6 11/8–12/1	2/7–3/5 12/2–12/25	3/6–3/31 12/26–12/31	4/1–4/26
11/13–11/26	11/27–12/21	12/22–12/31		1/1–1/19	1/20–2/12
8/22–9/15	9/16–10/11	1/1–1/14 10/12–11/6	1/15–2/7 11/7–12/5	2/8–3/3 12/6–12/31	3/4–3/27

VENUS SIGNS 1901–2007

	Aries	Taurus	Gemini	Cancer	Leo	Virgo
1926	5/7–6/2	6/3–6/28	6/29–7/23	7/24–8/17	8/18–9/11	9/12–10/5
1927	2/27–3/22	3/23–4/16	4/17–5/11	5/12–6/7	6/8–7/7	7/8–11/9
1928	4/12–5/5	5/6–5/29	5/30–6/23	6/24–7/17	7/18–8/11	8/12–9/4
1929	2/3–3/7 4/20–6/2	3/8–4/19 6/3–7/7	7/8–8/4	8/5–8/30	8/31–9/25	9/26–10/19
1930	3/13–4/5	4/6–4/30	5/1–5/24	5/25–6/18	6/19–7/14	7/15–8/9
1931	4/26–5/20	5/21–6/13	6/14–7/8	7/9–8/2	8/3–8/26	8/27–9/19
1932	2/12–3/8	3/9–4/3	4/4–5/5 7/13–7/27	5/6–7/12 7/28–9/8	9/9–10/6	10/7–11/1
1933	3/27–4/19	4/20–5/28	5/29–6/8	6/9–7/2	7/3–7/26	7/27–8/20
1934	5/6–6/1	6/2–6/27	6/28–7/22	7/23–8/16	8/17–9/10	9/11–10/4
1935	2/26–3/21	3/22–4/15	4/16–5/10	5/11–6/6	6/7–7/6	7/7–11/8
1936	4/11–5/4	5/5–5/28	5/29–6/22	6/23–7/16	7/17–8/10	8/11–9/4
1937	2/2–3/8 4/14–6/3	3/9–4/13 6/4–7/6	7/7–8/3	8/4–8/29	8/30–9/24	9/25–10/18
1938	3/12–4/4	4/5–4/28	4/29–5/23	5/24–6/18	6/19–7/13	7/14–8/8
1939	4/25–5/19	5/20–6/13	6/14–7/8	7/9–8/1	8/2–8/25	8/26–9/19
1940	2/12–3/7	3/8–4/3	4/4–5/5 7/5–7/31	5/6–7/4 8/1–9/8	9/9–10/5	10/6–10/31
1941	3/27–4/19	4/20–5/13	5/14–6/6	6/7–7/1	7/2–7/26	7/27–8/20
1942	5/6–6/1	6/2–6/26	6/27–7/22	7/23–8/16	8/17–9/9	9/10–10/3
1943	2/25–3/20	3/21–4/14	4/15–5/10	5/11–6/6	6/7–7/6	7/7–11/8
1944	4/10–5/3	5/4–5/28	5/29–6/21	6/22–7/16	7/17–8/9	8/10–9/2
1945	2/2–3/10 4/7–6/3	3/11–4/6 6/4–7/6	7/7–8/3	8/4–8/29	8/30–9/23	9/24–10/18
1946	3/11–4/4	4/5–4/28	4/29–5/23	5/24–6/17	6/18–7/12	7/13–8/8
1947	4/25–5/19	5/20–6/12	6/13–7/7	7/8–8/1	8/2–8/25	8/26–9/18
1948	2/11–3/7	3/8–4/3	4/4–5/6 6/29–8/2	5/7–6/28 8/3–9/7	9/8–10/5	10/6–10/31
1949	3/26–4/19	4/20–5/13	5/14–6/6	6/7–6/30	7/1–7/25	7/26–8/19
1950	5/5–5/31	6/1–6/26	6/27–7/21	7/22–8/15	8/16–9/9	9/10–10/3
1951	2/25–3/21	3/22–4/15	4/16–5/10	5/11–6/6	6/7–7/7	7/8–11/9

Libra	Scorpio	Sagittarius	Capricorn	Aquarius	Pisces
10/6–10/29	10/30–11/22	11/23–12/16	12/17–12/31	1/1–4/5	4/6–5/6
11/10–12/8	12/9–12/31	1/1–1/7	1/8	1/9–2/1	2/2–2/26
9/5–9/28	1/1–1/3	1/4–1/28	1/29–2/22	2/23–3/17	3/18–4/11
	9/29–10/23	10/24–11/16	11/17–12/11	12/12–12/31	
10/20–11/12	11/13–12/6	12/7–12/30	12/31	1/1–1/5	1/6–2/2
8/10–9/6	9/7–10/11	10/12–11/21	1/1–1/23	1/24–2/16	2/17–3/12
	11/22–12/31				
9/20–10/13	1/1–1/3	1/4–2/6	2/7–3/4	3/5–3/31	4/1–4/25
	10/14–11/6	11/7–11/30	12/1–12/24	12/25–12/31	
11/2–11/25	11/26–12/20	12/21–12/31		1/1–1/18	1/19–2/11
8/21–9/14	9/15–10/10	1/1–1/13	1/14–2/6	2/7–3/2	3/3–3/26
		10/11–11/5	11/6–12/4	12/5–12/31	
10/5–10/28	10/29–11/21	11/22–12/15	12/16–12/31	1/1–4/5	4/6–5/5
11/9–12/7	12/8–12/31		1/1–1/7	1/8–1/31	2/1–2/25
9/5–9/27	1/1–1/2	1/3–1/27	1/28–2/21	2/22–3/16	3/17–4/10
	9/28–10/22	10/23–11/15	11/16–12/10	12/11–12/31	
10/19–11/11	11/12–12/5	12/6–12/29	12/30–12/31	1/1–1/5	1/6–2/1
8/9–9/6	9/7–10/13	10/14–11/14	1/1–1/22	1/23–2/15	2/16–3/11
	11/15–12/31				
9/20–10/13	1/1–1/3	1/4–2/5	2/6–3/4	3/5–3/30	3/31–4/24
	10/14–11/6	11/7–11/30	12/1–12/24	12/25–12/31	
11/1–11/25	11/26–12/19	12/20–12/31		1/1–1/18	1/19–2/11
8/21–9/14	9/15–10/9	1/1–1/12	1/13–2/5	2/6–3/1	3/2–3/26
		10/10–11/5	11/6–12/4	12/5–12/31	
10/4–10/27	10/28–11/20	11/21–12/14	12/15–12/31	1/1–4/5	4/6–5/5
11/9–12/7	12/8–12/31		1/1–1/7	1/8–1/31	2/1–2/24
9/3–9/27	1/1–1/2	1/3–1/27	1/28–2/20	2/21–3/16	3/17–4/9
	9/28–10/21	10/22–11/15	11/16–12/10	12/11–12/31	
10/19–11/11	11/12–12/5	12/6–12/29	12/30–12/31	1/1–1/4	1/5–2/1
8/9–9/6	9/7–10/15	10/16–11/7	1/1–1/21	1/22–2/14	2/15–3/10
	11/8–12/31				
9/19–10/12	1/1–1/4	1/5–2/5	2/6–3/4	3/5–3/29	3/30–4/24
	10/13–11/5	11/6–11/29	11/30–12/23	12/24–12/31	
11/1–11/25	11/26–12/19	12/20–12/31		1/1–1/17	1/18–2/10
8/20–9/14	9/15–10/9	1/1–1/12	1/13–2/5	2/6–3/1	3/2–3/25
		10/10–11/5	11/6–12/5	12/6–12/31	
10/4–10/27	10/28–11/20	11/21–12/13	12/14–12/31	1/1–4/5	4/6–5/4
11/10–12/7	12/8–12/31		1/1–1/7	1/8–1/31	2/1–2/24

VENUS SIGNS 1901–2007

	Aries	Taurus	Gemini	Cancer	Leo	Virgo
1952	4/10–5/4	5/5–5/28	5/29–6/21	6/22–7/16	7/17–8/9	8/10–9/3
1953	2/2–3/3	3/4–3/31	7/8–8/3	8/4–8/29	8/30–9/24	9/25–10/18
	4/1–6/5	6/6–7/7				
1954	3/12–4/4	4/5–4/28	4/29–5/23	5/24–6/17	6/18–7/13	7/14–8/8
1955	4/25–5/19	5/20–6/13	6/14–7/7	7/8–8/1	8/2–8/25	8/26–9/18
1956	2/12–3/7	3/8–4/4	4/5–5/7	5/8–6/23	9/9–10/5	10/6–10/31
			6/24–8/4	8/5–9/8		
1957	3/26–4/19	4/20–5/13	5/14–6/6	6/7–7/1	7/2–7/26	7/27–8/19
1958	5/6–5/31	6/1–6/26	6/27–7/22	7/23–8/15	8/16–9/9	9/10–10/3
1959	2/25–3/20	3/21–4/14	4/15–5/10	5/11–6/6	6/7–7/8	7/9–9/20
					9/21–9/24	9/25–11/9
1960	4/10–5/3	5/4–5/28	5/29–6/21	6/22–7/15	7/16–8/9	8/10–9/2
1961	2/3–6/5	6/6–7/7	7/8–8/3	8/4–8/29	8/30–9/23	9/24–10/17
1962	3/11–4/3	4/4–4/28	4/29–5/23	5/23–6/17	6/18–7/12	7/13–8/8
1963	4/24–5/18	5/19–6/12	6/13–7/7	7/8–7/31	8/1–8/25	8/26–9/18
1964	2/11–3/7	3/8–4/4	4/5–5/9	5/10–6/17	9/9–10/5	10/6–10/31
			6/18–8/5	8/6–9/8		
1965	3/26–4/18	4/19–5/12	5/13–6/6	6/7–6/30	7/1–7/25	7/26–8/19
1966	5/6–6/31	6/1–6/26	6/27–7/21	7/22–8/15	8/16–9/8	9/9–10/2
1967	2/24–3/20	3/21–4/14	4/15–5/10	5/11–6/6	6/7–7/8	7/9–9/9
					9/10–10/1	10/2–11/9
1968	4/9–5/3	5/4–5/27	5/28–6/20	6/21–7/15	7/16–8/8	8/9–9/2
1969	2/3–6/6	6/7–7/6	7/7–8/3	8/4–8/28	8/29–9/22	9/23–10/17
1970	3/11–4/3	4/4–4/27	4/28–5/22	5/23–6/16	6/17–7/12	7/13–8/8
1971	4/24–5/18	5/19–6/12	6/13–7/6	7/7–7/31	8/1–8/24	8/25–9/17
1972	2/11–3/7	3/8–4/3	4/4–5/10	5/11–6/11		
			6/12–8/6	8/7–9/8	9/9–10/5	10/6–10/30
1973	3/25–4/18	4/18–5/12	5/13–6/5	6/6–6/29	7/1–7/25	7/26–8/19
1974	5/5–5/31	6/1–6/25	6/26–7/21	7/22–8/14	8/15–9/8	9/9–10/2
1975	2/24–3/20	3/21–4/13	4/14–5/9	5/10–6/6	6/7–7/9	7/10–9/2
					9/3–10/4	10/5–11/9

Libra	Scorpio	Sagittarius	Capricorn	Aquarius	Pisces
9/4–9/27	1/1–1/2	1/3–1/27	1/28–2/20	2/21–3/16	3/17–4/9
	9/28–10/21	10/22–11/15	11/16–12/10	12/11–12/31	
10/19–11/11	11/12–12/5	12/6–12/29	12/30–12/31	1/1–1/5	1/6–2/1
8/9–9/6	9/7–10/22	10/23–10/27	1/1–1/22	1/23–2/15	2/16–3/11
	10/28–12/31				
9/19–10/13	1/1–1/6	1/7–2/5	2/6–3/4	3/5–3/30	3/31–4/24
	10/14–11/5	11/6–11/30	12/1–12/24	12/25–12/31	
11/1–11/25	11/26–12/19	12/20–12/31		1/1–1/17	1/18–2/11
8/20–9/14	9/15–10/9	1/1–1/12	1/13–2/5	2/6–3/1	3/2–3/25
		10/10–11/5	11/6–12/6	12/7–12/31	
10/4–10/27	10/28–11/20	11/21–12/14	12/15–12/31	1/1–4/6	4/7–5/5
11/10–12/7	12/8–12/31		1/1–1/7	1/8–1/31	2/1–2/24
9/3–9/26	1/1–1/2	1/3–1/27	1/28–2/20	2/21–3/15	3/16–4/9
	9/27–10/21	10/22–11/15	11/16–12/10	12/11–12/31	
10/18–11/11	11/12–12/4	12/5–12/28	12/29–12/31	1/1–1/5	1/6–2/2
8/9–9/6	9/7–12/31		1/1–1/21	1/22–2/14	2/15–3/10
9/19–10/12	1/1–1/6	1/7–2/5	2/6–3/4	3/5–3/29	3/30–4/23
	10/13–11/5	11/6–11/29	11/30–12/23	12/24–12/31	
11/1–11/24	11/25–12/19	12/20–12/31		1/1–1/16	1/17–2/10
8/20–9/13	9/14–10/9	1/1–1/12	1/13–2/5	2/6–3/1	3/2–3/25
		10/10–11/5	11/6–12/7	12/8–12/31	
10/3–10/26	10/27–11/19	11/20–12/13	2/7–2/25	1/1–2/6	4/7–5/5
			12/14–12/31	2/26–4/6	
11/10–12/7	12/8–12/31		1/1–1/6	1/7–1/30	1/31–2/23
9/3–9/26	1/1	1/2–1/26	1/27–2/20	2/21–3/15	3/16–4/8
	9/27–10/21	10/22–11/14	11/15–12/9	12/10–12/31	
10/18–11/10	11/11–12/4	12/5–12/28	12/29–12/31	1/1–1/4	1/5–2/2
8/9–9/7	9/8–12/31		1/1–1/21	1/22–2/14	2/15–3/10
9/18–10/11	1/1–1/7	1/8–2/5	2/6–3/4	3/5–3/29	3/30–4/23
	10/12–11/5	11/6–11/29	11/30–12/23	12/24–12/31	
	11/25–12/18	12/19–12/31		1/1–1/16	1/17–2/10
10/31–11/24					
8/20–9/13	9/14–10/8	1/1–1/12	1/13–2/4	2/5–2/28	3/1–3/24
		10/9–11/5	11/6–12/7	12/8–12/31	
			1/30–2/28	1/1–1/29	
10/3–10/26	10/27–11/19	11/20–12/13	12/14–12/31	3/1–4/6	4/7–5/4
11/10–12/7	12/8–12/31		1/1–1/6	1/7–1/30	1/31–2/23

VENUS SIGNS 1901–2007

	Aries	Taurus	Gemini	Cancer	Leo	Virgo
1976	4/8–5/2	5/2–5/27	5/27–6/20	6/20–7/14	7/14–8/8	8/8–9/1
1977	2/2–6/6	6/6–7/6	7/6–8/2	8/2–8/28	8/28–9/22	9/22–10/17
1978	3/9–4/2	4/2–4/27	4/27–5/22	5/22–6/16	6/16–7/12	7/12–8/6
1979	4/23–5/18	5/18–6/11	6/11–7/6	7/6–7/30	7/30–8/24	8/24–9/17
1980	2/9–3/6	3/6–4/3	4/3–5/12 6/5–8/6	5/12–6/5 8/6–9/7	9/7–10/4	10/4–10/30
1981	3/24–4/17	4/17–5/11	5/11–6/5	6/5–6/29	6/29–7/24	7/24–8/18
1982	5/4–5/30	5/30–6/25	6/25–7/20	7/20–8/14	8/14–9/7	9/7–10/2
1983	2/22–3/19	3/19–4/13	4/13–5/9	5/9–6/6	6/6–7/10 8/27–10/5	7/10–8/27 10/5–11/9
1984	4/7–5/2	5/2–5/26	5/26–6/20	6/20–7/14	7/14–8/7	8/7–9/1
1985	2/2–6/6	6/7–7/6	7/6–8/2	8/2–8/28	8/28–9/22	9/22–10/16
1986	3/9–4/2	4/2–4/26	4/26–5/21	5/21–6/15	6/15–7/11	7/11–8/7
1987	4/22–5/17	5/17–6/11	6/11–7/5	7/5–7/30	7/30–8/23	8/23–9/16
1988	2/9–3/6	3/6–4/3	4/3–5/17 5/27–8/6	5/17–5/27 8/28–9/22	9/7–10/4 9/22–10/16	10/4–10/29
1989	3/23–4/16	4/16–5/11	5/11–6/4	6/4–6/29	6/29–7/24	7/24–8/18
1990	5/4–5/30	5/30–6/25	6/25–7/20	7/20–8/13	8/13–9/7	9/7–10/1
1991	2/22–3/18	3/18–4/13	4/13–5/9	5/9–6/6	6/6–7/11 8/21–10/6	7/11–8/21 10/6–11/9
1992	4/7–5/1	5/1–5/26	5/26–6/19	6/19–7/13	7/13–8/7	8/7–8/31
1993	2/2–6/6	6/6–7/6	7/6–8/1	8/1–8/27	8/27–9/21	9/21–10/16
1994	3/8–4/1	4/1–4/26	4/26–5/21	5/21–6/15	6/15–7/11	7/11–8/7
1995	4/22–5/16	5/16–6/10	6/10–7/5	7/5–7/29	7/29–8/23	8/23–9/16
1996	2/9–3/6	3/6–4/3	4/3–8/7	8/7–9/7	9/7–10/4	10/4–10/29
1997	3/23–4/16	4/16–5/10	5/10–6/4	6/4–6/28	6/28–7/23	7/23–8/17
1998	5/3–5/29	5/29–6/24	6/24–7/19	7/19–8/13	8/13–9/6	9/6–9/30
1999	2/21–3/18	3/18–4/12	4/12–5/8	5/8–6/5	6/5–7/12 8/15–10/7	7/12–8/15 10/7–11/9
2000	4/6–5/1	5/1–5/25	5/25–6/13	6/13–7/13	7/13–8/6	8/6–8/31
2001	2/2–6/6	6/6–7/5	7/5–8/1	8/1–8/26	8/26–9/20	9/20–10/15
2002	3/7–4/1	4/1–4/25	4/25–5/20	5/20–6/14	6/14–7/10	7/10–8/7
2003	4/21–5/16	5/16–6/9	6/9–7/4	7/4–7/29	7/29–8/22	8/22–9/15
2004	2/8–3/5	3/5–4/3	4/3–8/7	8/7–9/6	9/6–10/3	10/3–10/28
2005	3/22–4/15	4/15–5/10	5/10–6/3	6/3–6/28	6/28–7/23	7/23–8/17
2006	5/3–5/29	5/29–6/24	6/24–7/19	7/19–8/12	8/12–9/6	9/6–9/30
2007	2/21–3/16	3/17–4/10	4/11–5/7	5/8–6/4	6/5–7/13 8/8–10/6	7/14–8/7 10/7–11/7

Libra	Scorpio	Sagittarius	Capricorn	Aquarius	Pisces
9/1–9/26	9/26–10/20	1/1–1/26	1/26–2/19	2/19–3/15	3/15–4/8
10/17–11/10	11/10–12/4	12/4–12/27	12/27–1/20/78		1/4–2/2
8/6–9/7	9/7–1/7			1/20–2/13	2/13–3/9
9/17–10/11	10/11–11/4	1/7–2/5	2/5–3/3	3/3–3/29	3/29–4/23
		11/4–11/28	11/28–12/22	12/22–1/16/80	
10/30–11/24	11/24–12/18	12/18–1/11/81			1/16–2/9
8/18–9/12	9/12–10/9	10/9–11/5	1/11–2/4	2/4–2/28	2/28–3/24
			11/5–12/8	12/8–1/23/82	
10/2–10/26	10/26–11/18	11/18–12/12	1/23–3/2	3/2–4/6	4/6–5/4
			12/12–1/5/83		
11/9–12/6	12/6–1/1/84			1/5–1/29	1/29–2/22
9/1–9/25	9/25–10/20	1/1–1/25	1/25–2/19	2/19–3/14	3/14–4/7
		10/20–11/13	11/13–12/9	12/10–1/4	
10/16–11/9	11/9–12/3	12/3–12/27	12/28–1/19		1/4–2/2
8/7–9/7	9/7–1/7			1/20–2/13	2/13–3/9
9/16–10/10	10/10–11/3	1/7–2/5	2/5–3/3	3/3–3/28	3/28–4/22
		11/3–11/28	11/28–12/22	12/22–1/15	
10/29–11/23	11/23–12/17	12/17–1/10			1/15–2/9
8/18–9/12	9/12–10/8	10/8–11/5	1/10–2/3	2/3–2/27	2/27–3/23
			11/5–12/10	12/10–1/16/90	
10/1–10/25	10/25–11/18	11/18–12/12	1/16–3/3	3/3–4/6	4/6–5/4
			12/12–1/5		
11/9–12/6	12/6–12/31	12/31–1/25/92		1/5–1/29	1/29–2/22
8/31–9/25	9/25–10/19	10/19–11/13	1/25–2/18	2/18–3/13	3/13–4/7
			11/13–12/8	12/8–1/3/93	
10/16–11/9	11/9–12/2	12/2–12/26	12/26–1/19		1/3–2/2
8/7–9/7	9/7–1/7			1/19–2/12	2/12–3/8
9/16–10/10	10/10–11/13	1/7–2/4	2/4–3/2	3/2–3/28	3/28–4/22
		11/3–11/27	11/27–12/21	12/21–1/15	
10/29–11/23	11/23–12/17	12/17–1/10/97			1/15–2/9
8/17–9/12	9/12–10/8	10/8–11/5	1/10–2/3	2/3–2/27	2/27–3/23
			11/5–12/12	12/12–1/9	
9/30–10/24	10/24–11/17	11/17–12/11	1/9–3/4	3/4–4/6	4/6–5/3
11/9–12/5	12/5–12/31	12/31–1/24		1/4–1/28	1/28–2/21
8/31–9/24	9/24–10/19	10/19–11/13	1/24–2/18	2/18–3/12	3/13–4/6
			11/13–12/8	12/8	
10/15–11/8	11/8–12/2	12/2–12/26	12/26/01–1/18/02	12/8/00–1/3/01	1/3–2/2
8/7–9/7	9/7–1/7/03		12/26/01–1/18	1/18–2/11	2/11–3/7
9/15–10/9	10/9–11/2	1/7–2/4	2/4–3/2	3/2–3/27	3/27–4/21
		11/2–11/26	11/26–12/21	12/21–1/14/04	
10/28–11/22	11/22–12/16	12/16–1/9/05		1/1–1/14	1/14–2/8
8/17–9/11	9/11–10/8	10/8–11/15	1/9–2/2	2/2–2/26	2/26–3/22
			11/5–12/15	12/15–1/1/06	
9/30–10/24	10/24–11/17	11/17–12/11	1/1–3/5	3/5–4/6	4/6–5/3
11/8–12/4	12/5–12/29	12/30–1/24/08		1/3–1/26	1/27–2/20

How to Use the Mars, Jupiter, and Saturn Tables

Find the year of your birth on the left side of each column. The dates when the planet entered each sign are listed on the right side of each column. (Signs are abbreviated to three letters.) Your birthday should fall on or between each date listed, and your planetary placement should correspond to the earlier sign of that period.

All planet changes are calculated for the Greenwich Mean Time zone.

MARS SIGNS 1901–2007

Year	Date	Sign		Year	Date	Sign
1901	MAR 1	Leo			OCT 1	Vir
	MAY 11	Vir			NOV 20	Lib
	JUL 13	Lib		1905	JAN 13	Scp
	AUG 31	Scp			AUG 21	Sag
	OCT 14	Sag			OCT 8	Cap
	NOV 24	Cap			NOV 18	Aqu
1902	JAN 1	Aqu			DEC 27	Pic
	FEB 8	Pic		1906	FEB 4	Ari
	MAR 19	Ari			MAR 17	Tau
	APR 27	Tau			APR 28	Gem
	JUN 7	Gem			JUN 11	Can
	JUL 20	Can			JUL 27	Leo
	SEP 4	Leo			SEP 12	Vir
	OCT 23	Vir			OCT 30	Lib
	DEC 20	Lib			DEC 17	Scp
1903	APR 19	Vir		1907	FEB 5	Sag
	MAY 30	Lib			APR 1	Cap
	AUG 6	Scp			OCT 13	Aqu
	SEP 22	Sag			NOV 29	Pic
	NOV 3	Cap		1908	JAN 11	Ari
	DEC 12	Aqu			FEB 23	Tau
1904	JAN 19	Pic			APR 7	Gem
	FEB 27	Ari			MAY 22	Can
	APR 6	Tau			JUL 8	Leo
	MAY 18	Gem			AUG 24	Vir
	JUN 30	Can			OCT 10	Lib
	AUG 15	Leo			NOV 25	Scp

Year	Month	Day	Sign		Year	Month	Day	Sign
1909	JAN	10	Sag			MAR	9	Pic
	FEB	24	Cap			APR	16	Ari
	APR	9	Aqu			MAY	26	Tau
	MAY	25	Pic			JUL	6	Gem
	JUL	21	Ari			AUG	19	Can
	SEP	26	Pic			OCT	7	Leo
	NOV	20	Ari		1916	MAY	28	Vir
1910	JAN	23	Tau			JUL	23	Lib
	MAR	14	Gem			SEP	8	Scp
	MAY	1	Can			OCT	22	Sag
	JUN	19	Leo			DEC	1	Cap
	AUG	6	Vir		1917	JAN	9	Aqu
	SEP	22	Lib			FEB	16	Pic
	NOV	6	Scp			MAR	26	Ari
	DEC	20	Sag			MAY	4	Tau
1911	JAN	31	Cap			JUN	14	Gem
	MAR	14	Aqu			JUL	28	Can
	APR	23	Pic			SEP	12	Leo
	JUN	2	Ari			NOV	2	Vir
	JUL	15	Tau		1918	JAN	11	Lib
	SEP	5	Gem			FEB	25	Vir
	NOV	30	Tau			JUN	23	Lib
1912	JAN	30	Gem			AUG	17	Scp
	APR	5	Can			OCT	1	Sag
	MAY	28	Leo			NOV	11	Cap
	JUL	17	Vir			DEC	20	Aqu
	SEP	2	Lib		1919	JAN	27	Pic
	OCT	18	Scp			MAR	6	Ari
	NOV	30	Sag			APR	15	Tau
1913	JAN	10	Cap			MAY	26	Gem
	FEB	19	Aqu			JUL	8	Can
	MAR	30	Pic			AUG	23	Leo
	MAY	8	Ari			OCT	10	Vir
	JUN	17	Tau			NOV	30	Lib
	JUL	29	Gem		1920	JAN	31	Scp
	SEP	15	Can			APR	23	Lib
1914	MAY	1	Leo			JUL	10	Scp
	JUN	26	Vir			SEP	4	Sag
	AUG	14	Lib			OCT	18	Cap
	SEP	29	Scp			NOV	27	Aqu
	NOV	11	Sag		1921	JAN	5	Pic
	DEC	22	Cap			FEB	13	Ari
1915	JAN	30	Aqu			MAR	25	Tau

	MAY	6	Gem		OCT	26	Scp
	JUN	18	Can		DEC	8	Sag
	AUG	3	Leo	1928	JAN	19	Cap
	SEP	19	Vir		FEB	28	Aqu
	NOV	6	Lib		APR	7	Pic
	DEC	26	Scp		MAY	16	Ari
1922	FEB	18	Sag		JUN	26	Tau
	SEP	13	Cap		AUG	9	Gem
	OCT	30	Aqu		OCT	3	Can
	DEC	11	Pic		DEC	20	Gem
1923	JAN	21	Ari	1929	MAR	10	Can
	MAR	4	Tau		MAY	13	Leo
	APR	16	Gem		JUL	4	Vir
	MAY	30	Can		AUG	21	Lib
	JUL	16	Leo		OCT	6	Scp
	SEP	1	Vir		NOV	18	Sag
	OCT	18	Lib		DEC	29	Cap
	DEC	4	Scp	1930	FEB	6	Aqu
1924	JAN	19	Sag		MAR	17	Pic
	MAR	6	Cap		APR	24	Ari
	APR	24	Aqu		JUN	3	Tau
	JUN	24	Pic		JUL	14	Gem
	AUG	24	Aqu		AUG	28	Can
	OCT	19	Pic		OCT	20	Leo
	DEC	19	Ari	1931	FEB	16	Can
1925	FEB	5	Tau		MAR	30	Leo
	MAR	24	Gem		JUN	10	Vir
	MAY	9	Can		AUG	1	Lib
	JUN	26	Leo		SEP	17	Scp
	AUG	12	Vir		OCT	30	Sag
	SEP	28	Lib		DEC	10	Cap
	NOV	13	Scp	1932	JAN	18	Aqu
	DEC	28	Sag		FEB	25	Pic
1926	FEB	9	Cap		APR	3	Ari
	MAR	23	Aqu		MAY	12	Tau
	MAY	3	Pic		JUN	22	Gem
	JUN	15	Ari		AUG	4	Can
	AUG	1	Tau		SEP	20	Leo
1927	FEB	22	Gem		NOV	13	Vir
	APR	17	Can	1933	JUL	6	Lib
	JUN	6	Leo		AUG	26	Scp
	JUL	25	Vir		OCT	9	Sag
	SEP	10	Lib		NOV	19	Cap

	DEC	28	Aqu		FEB	17	Tau
1934	FEB	4	Pic		APR	1	Gem
	MAR	14	Ari		MAY	17	Can
	APR	22	Tau		JUL	3	Leo
	JUN	2	Gem		AUG	19	Vir
	JUL	15	Can		OCT	5	Lib
	AUG	30	Leo		NOV	20	Scp
	OCT	18	Vir	1941	JAN	4	Sag
	DEC	11	Lib		FEB	17	Cap
1935	JUL	29	Scp		APR	2	Aqu
	SEP	16	Sag		MAY	16	Pic
	OCT	28	Cap		JUL	2	Ari
	DEC	7	Aqu	1942	JAN	11	Tau
1936	JAN	14	Pic		MAR	7	Gem
	FEB	22	Ari		APR	26	Can
	APR	1	Tau		JUN	14	Leo
	MAY	13	Gem		AUG	1	Vir
	JUN	25	Can		SEP	17	Lib
	AUG	10	Leo		NOV	1	Scp
	SEP	26	Vir		DEC	15	Sag
	NOV	14	Lib	1943	JAN	26	Cap
1937	JAN	5	Scp		MAR	8	Aqu
	MAR	13	Sag		APR	17	Pic
	MAY	14	Scp		MAY	27	Ari
	AUG	8	Sag		JUL	7	Tau
	SEP	30	Cap		AUG	23	Gem
	NOV	11	Aqu	1944	MAR	28	Can
	DEC	21	Pic		MAY	22	Leo
1938	JAN	30	Ari		JUL	12	Vir
	MAR	12	Tau		AUG	29	Lib
	APR	23	Gem		OCT	13	Scp
	JUN	7	Can		NOV	25	Sag
	JUL	22	Leo	1945	JAN	5	Cap
	SEP	7	Vir		FEB	14	Aqu
	OCT	25	Lib		MAR	25	Pic
	DEC	11	Scp		MAY	2	Ari
1939	JAN	29	Sag		JUN	11	Tau
	MAR	21	Cap		JUL	23	Gem
	MAY	25	Aqu		SEP	7	Can
	JUL	21	Cap		NOV	11	Leo
	SEP	24	Aqu		DEC	26	Can
	NOV	19	Pic	1946	APR	22	Leo
1940	JAN	4	Ari		JUN	20	Vir

	AUG	9	Lib		OCT	12	Cap
	SEP	24	Scp		NOV	21	Aqu
	NOV	6	Sag		DEC	30	Pic
	DEC	17	Cap	1953	FEB	8	Ari
1947	JAN	25	Aqu		MAR	20	Tau
	MAR	4	Pic		MAY	1	Gem
	APR	11	Ari		JUN	14	Can
	MAY	21	Tau		JUL	29	Leo
	JUL	1	Gem		SEP	14	Vir
	AUG	13	Can		NOV	1	Lib
	OCT	1	Leo		DEC	20	Scp
	DEC	1	Vir	1954	FEB	9	Sag
1948	FEB	12	Leo		APR	12	Cap
	MAY	18	Vir		JUL	3	Sag
	JUL	17	Lib		AUG	24	Cap
	SEP	3	Scp		OCT	21	Aqu
	OCT	17	Sag		DEC	4	Pic
	NOV	26	Cap	1955	JAN	15	Ari
1949	JAN	4	Aqu		FEB	26	Tau
	FEB	11	Pic		APR	10	Gem
	MAR	21	Ari		MAY	26	Can
	APR	30	Tau		JUL	11	Leo
	JUN	10	Gem		AUG	27	Vir
	JUL	23	Can		OCT	13	Lib
	SEP	7	Leo		NOV	29	Scp
	OCT	27	Vir	1956	JAN	14	Sag
	DEC	26	Lib		FEB	28	Cap
1950	MAR	28	Vir		APR	14	Aqu
	JUN	11	Lib		JUN	3	Pic
	AUG	10	Scp		DEC	6	Ari
	SEP	25	Sag	1957	JAN	28	Tau
	NOV	6	Cap		MAR	17	Gem
	DEC	15	Aqu		MAY	4	Can
1951	JAN	22	Pic		JUN	21	Leo
	MAR	1	Ari		AUG	8	Vir
	APR	10	Tau		SEP	24	Lib
	MAY	21	Gem		NOV	8	Scp
	JUL	3	Can		DEC	23	Sag
	AUG	18	Leo	1958	FEB	3	Cap
	OCT	5	Vir		MAR	17	Aqu
	NOV	24	Lib		APR	27	Pic
1952	JAN	20	Scp		JUN	7	Ari
	AUG	27	Sag		JUL	21	Tau

	SEP	21	Gem		NOV	6	Vir
	OCT	29	Tau	1965	JUN	29	Lib
1959	FEB	10	Gem		AUG	20	Scp
	APR	10	Can		OCT	4	Sag
	JUN	1	Leo		NOV	14	Cap
	JUL	20	Vir		DEC	23	Aqu
	SEP	5	Lib	1966	JAN	30	Pic
	OCT	21	Scp		MAR	9	Ari
	DEC	3	Sag		APR	17	Tau
1960	JAN	14	Cap		MAY	28	Gem
	FEB	23	Aqu		JUL	11	Can
	APR	2	Pic		AUG	25	Leo
	MAY	11	Ari		OCT	12	Vir
	JUN	20	Tau		DEC	4	Lib
	AUG	2	Gem	1967	FEB	12	Scp
	SEP	21	Can		MAR	31	Lib
1961	FEB	5	Gem		JUL	19	Scp
	FEB	7	Can		SEP	10	Sag
	MAY	6	Leo		OCT	23	Cap
	JUN	28	Vir		DEC	1	Aqu
	AUG	17	Lib	1968	JAN	9	Pic
	OCT	1	Scp		FEB	17	Ari
	NOV	13	Sag		MAR	27	Tau
	DEC	24	Cap		MAY	8	Gem
1962	FEB	1	Aqu		JUN	21	Can
	MAR	12	Pic		AUG	5	Leo
	APR	19	Ari		SEP	21	Vir
	MAY	28	Tau		NOV	9	Lib
	JUL	9	Gem		DEC	29	Scp
	AUG	22	Can	1969	FEB	25	Sag
	OCT	11	Leo		SEP	21	Cap
1963	JUN	3	Vir		NOV	4	Aqu
	JUL	27	Lib		DEC	15	Pic
	SEP	12	Scp	1970	JAN	24	Ari
	OCT	25	Sag		MAR	7	Tau
	DEC	5	Cap		APR	18	Gem
1964	JAN	13	Aqu		JUN	2	Can
	FEB	20	Pic		JUL	18	Leo
	MAR	29	Ari		SEP	3	Vir
	MAY	7	Tau		OCT	20	Lib
	JUN	17	Gem		DEC	6	Scp
	JUL	30	Can	1971	JAN	23	Sag
	SEP	15	Leo		MAR	12	Cap

	MAY	3	Aqu		JUN	6	Tau
	NOV	6	Pic		JUL	17	Gem
	DEC	26	Ari		SEP	1	Can
1972	FEB	10	Tau		OCT	26	Leo
	MAR	27	Gem	1978	JAN	26	Can
	MAY	12	Can		APR	10	Leo
	JUN	28	Leo		JUN	14	Vir
	AUG	15	Vir		AUG	4	Lib
	SEP	30	Lib		SEP	19	Scp
	NOV	15	Scp		NOV	2	Sag
	DEC	30	Sag		DEC	12	Cap
1973	FEB	12	Cap	1979	JAN	20	Aqu
	MAR	26	Aqu		FEB	27	Pic
	MAY	8	Pic		APR	7	Ari
	JUN	20	Ari		MAY	16	Tau
	AUG	12	Tau		JUN	26	Gem
	OCT	29	Ari		AUG	8	Can
	DEC	24	Tau		SEP	24	Leo
1974	FEB	27	Gem		NOV	19	Vir
	APR	20	Can	1980	MAR	11	Leo
	JUN	9	Leo		MAY	4	Vir
	JUL	27	Vir		JUL	10	Lib
	SEP	12	Lib		AUG	29	Scp
	OCT	28	Scp		OCT	12	Sag
	DEC	10	Sag		NOV	22	Cap
1975	JAN	21	Cap		DEC	30	Aqu
	MAR	3	Aqu	1981	FEB	6	Pic
	APR	11	Pic		MAR	17	Ari
	MAY	21	Ari		APR	25	Tau
	JUL	1	Tau		JUN	5	Gem
	AUG	14	Gem		JUL	18	Can
	OCT	17	Can		SEP	2	Leo
	NOV	25	Gem		OCT	21	Vir
1976	MAR	18	Can		DEC	16	Lib
	MAY	16	Leo	1982	AUG	3	Scp
	JUL	6	Vir		SEP	20	Sag
	AUG	24	Lib		OCT	31	Cap
	OCT	8	Scp		DEC	10	Aqu
	NOV	20	Sag	1983	JAN	17	Pic
1977	JAN	1	Cap		FEB	25	Ari
	FEB	9	Aqu		APR	5	Tau
	MAR	20	Pic		MAY	16	Gem
	APR	27	Ari		JUN	29	Can

	AUG	13	Leo	1990	JAN	29	Cap
	SEP	30	Vir		MAR	11	Aqu
	NOV	18	Lib		APR	20	Pic
1984	JAN	11	Scp		MAY	31	Ari
	AUG	17	Sag		JUL	12	Tau
	OCT	5	Cap		AUG	31	Gem
	NOV	15	Aqu		DEC	14	Tau
	DEC	25	Pic	1991	JAN	21	Gem
1985	FEB	2	Ari		APR	3	Can
	MAR	15	Tau		MAY	26	Leo
	APR	26	Gem		JUL	15	Vir
	JUN	9	Can		SEP	1	Lib
	JUL	25	Leo		OCT	16	Scp
	SEP	10	Vir		NOV	29	Sag
	OCT	27	Lib	1992	JAN	9	Cap
	DEC	14	Scp		FEB	18	Aqu
1986	FEB	2	Sag		MAR	28	Pic
	MAR	28	Cap		MAY	5	Ari
	OCT	9	Aqu		JUN	14	Tau
	NOV	26	Pic		JUL	26	Gem
1987	JAN	8	Ari		SEP	12	Can
	FEB	20	Tau	1993	APR	27	Leo
	APR	5	Gem		JUN	23	Vir
	MAY	21	Can		AUG	12	Lib
	JUL	6	Leo		SEP	27	Scp
	AUG	22	Vir		NOV	9	Sag
	OCT	8	Lib		DEC	20	Cap
	NOV	24	Scp	1994	JAN	28	Aqu
1988	JAN	8	Sag		MAR	7	Pic
	FEB	22	Cap		APR	14	Ari
	APR	6	Aqu		MAY	23	Tau
	MAY	22	Pic		JUL	3	Gem
	JUL	13	Ari		AUG	16	Can
	OCT	23	Pic		OCT	4	Leo
	NOV	1	Ari		DEC	12	Vir
1989	JAN	19	Tau	1995	JAN	22	Leo
	MAR	11	Gem		MAY	25	Vir
	APR	29	Can		JUL	21	Lib
	JUN	16	Leo		SEP	7	Scp
	AUG	3	Vir		OCT	20	Sag
	SEP	19	Lib		NOV	30	Cap
	NOV	4	Scp	1996	JAN	8	Aqu
	DEC	18	Sag		FEB	15	Pic

	MAR	24	Ari		MAR	1	Tau
	MAY	2	Tau		APR	13	Gem
	JUN	12	Gem		MAY	28	Can
	JUL	25	Can		JUL	13	Leo
	SEP	9	Leo		AUG	29	Vir
	OCT	30	Vir		OCT	15	Lib
1997	JAN	3	Lib		DEC	1	Scp
	MAR	8	Vir	2003	JAN	17	Sag
	JUN	19	Lib		MAR	4	Cap
	AUG	14	Scp		APR	21	Aqu
	SEP	28	Sag		JUN	17	Pic
	NOV	9	Cap		DEC	16	Ari
	DEC	18	Aqu	2004	FEB	3	Tau
1998	JAN	25	Pic		MAR	21	Gem
	MAR	4	Ari		MAY	7	Can
	APR	13	Tau		JUN	23	Leo
	MAY	24	Gem		AUG	10	Vir
	JUL	6	Can		SEP	26	Lib
	AUG	20	Leo		NOV	11	Sep
	OCT	7	Vir		DEC	25	Sag
	NOV	27	Lib	2005	FEB	6	Cap
1999	JAN	26	Scp		MAR	20	Aqu
	MAY	5	Lib		MAY	1	Pic
	JUL	5	Scp		JUN	12	Ari
	SEP	2	Sag		JUL	28	Tau
	OCT	17	Cap	2006	FEB	17	Gem
	NOV	26	Aqu		APR	14	Can
2000	JAN	4	Pic		JUN	3	Leo
	FEB	12	Ari		JUL	22	Vir
	MAR	23	Tau		SEP	8	Lib
	MAY	3	Gem		OCT	23	Scp
	JUN	16	Can		DEC	6	Sag
	AUG	1	Leo	2007	JAN	16	Cap
	SEP	17	Vir		FEB	25	Aqu
	NOV	4	Lib		APR	6	Pic
	DEC	23	Scp		MAY	15	Ari
2001	FEB	14	Sag		JUNE	24	Tau
	SEP	8	Cap		AUG	7	Gem
	OCT	27	Aqu		SEP	28	Can
	DEC	8	Pic		DEC	31	Gem*
2002	JAN	18	Ari				

*Repeat means planet is retrograde.

JUPITER SIGNS 1901–2007

Year	Month	Day	Sign		Year	Month	Day	Sign
1901	JAN	19	Cap		1930	JUN	26	Can
1902	FEB	6	Aqu		1931	JUL	17	Leo
1903	FEB	20	Pic		1932	AUG	11	Vir
1904	MAR	1	Ari		1933	SEP	10	Lib
	AUG	8	Tau		1934	OCT	11	Scp
	AUG	31	Ari		1935	NOV	9	Sag
1905	MAR	7	Tau		1936	DEC	2	Cap
	JUL	21	Gem		1937	DEC	20	Aqu
	DEC	4	Tau		1938	MAY	14	Pic
1906	MAR	9	Gem			JUL	30	Aqu
	JUL	30	Can			DEC	29	Pic
1907	AUG	18	Leo		1939	MAY	11	Ari
1908	SEP	12	Vir			OCT	30	Pic
1909	OCT	11	Lib			DEC	20	Ari
1910	NOV	11	Scp		1940	MAY	16	Tau
1911	DEC	10	Sag		1941	MAY	26	Gem
1913	JAN	2	Cap		1942	JUN	10	Can
1914	JAN	21	Aqu		1943	JUN	30	Leo
1915	FEB	4	Pic		1944	JUL	26	Vir
1916	FEB	12	Ari		1945	AUG	25	Lib
	JUN	26	Tau		1946	SEP	25	Scp
	OCT	26	Ari		1947	OCT	24	Sag
1917	FEB	12	Tau		1948	NOV	15	Cap
	JUN	29	Gem		1949	APR	12	Aqu
1918	JUL	13	Can			JUN	27	Cap
1919	AUG	2	Leo			NOV	30	Aqu
1920	AUG	27	Vir		1950	APR	15	Pic
1921	SEP	25	Lib			SEP	15	Aqu
1922	OCT	26	Scp			DEC	1	Pic
1923	NOV	24	Sag		1951	APR	21	Ari
1924	DEC	18	Cap		1952	APR	28	Tau
1926	JAN	6	Aqu		1953	MAY	9	Gem
1927	JAN	18	Pic		1954	MAY	24	Can
	JUN	6	Ari		1955	JUN	13	Leo
	SEP	11	Pic			NOV	17	Vir
1928	JAN	23	Ari		1956	JAN	18	Leo
	JUN	4	Tau			JUL	7	Vir
1929	JUN	12	Gem			DEC	13	Lib

Year	Month	Day	Sign	Year	Month	Day	Sign
1957	FEB	19	Vir	1974	MAR	8	Pic
	AUG	7	Lib	1975	MAR	18	Ari
1958	JAN	13	Scp	1976	MAR	26	Tau
	MAR	20	Lib		AUG	23	Gem
	SEP	7	Scp		OCT	16	Tau
1959	FEB	10	Sag	1977	APR	3	Gem
	APR	24	Scp		AUG	20	Can
	OCT	5	Sag		DEC	30	Gem
1960	MAR	1	Cap	1978	APR	12	Can
	JUN	10	Sag		SEP	5	Leo
	OCT	26	Cap	1979	FEB	28	Can
1961	MAR	15	Aqu		APR	20	Leo
	AUG	12	Cap		SEP	29	Vir
	NOV	4	Aqu	1980	OCT	27	Lib
1962	MAR	25	Pic	1981	NOV	27	Scp
1963	APR	4	Ari	1982	DEC	26	Sag
1964	APR	12	Tau	1984	JAN	19	Cap
1965	APR	22	Gem	1985	FEB	6	Aqu
	SEP	21	Can	1986	FEB	20	Pic
	NOV	17	Gem	1987	MAR	2	Ari
1966	MAY	5	Can	1988	MAR	8	Tau
	SEP	27	Leo		JUL	22	Gem
1967	JAN	16	Can		NOV	30	Tau
	MAY	23	Leo	1989	MAR	11	Gem
	OCT	19	Vir		JUL	30	Can
1968	FEB	27	Leo	1990	AUG	18	Leo
	JUN	15	Vir	1991	SEP	12	Vir
	NOV	15	Lib	1992	OCT	10	Lib
1969	MAR	30	Vir	1993	NOV	10	Scp
	JUL	15	Lib	1994	DEC	9	Sag
	DEC	16	Scp	1996	JAN	3	Cap
1970	APR	30	Lib	1997	JAN	21	Aqu
	AUG	15	Scp	1998	FEB	4	Pic
1971	JAN	14	Sag	1999	FEB	13	Ari
	JUN	5	Scp		JUN	28	Tau
	SEP	11	Sag		OCT	23	Ari
1972	FEB	6	Cap	2000	FEB	14	Tau
	JUL	24	Sag		JUN	30	Gem
	SEP	25	Cap	2001	JUL	14	Can
1973	FEB	23	Aqu	2002	AUG	1	Leo

2003	AUG	27	Vir	2006	NOV	24	Sag
2004	SEP	24	Lib	2007	DEC	17	Cap
2005	OCT	26	Scp				

SATURN SIGNS 1903–2007

1903	JAN	19	Aqu		SEP	22	Ari
1905	APR	13	Pic	1940	MAR	20	Tau
	AUG	17	Aqu	1942	MAY	8	Gem
1906	JAN	8	Pic	1944	JUN	20	Can
1908	MAR	19	Ari	1946	AUG	2	Leo
1910	MAY	17	Tau	1948	SEP	19	Vir
	DEC	14	Ari	1949	APR	3	Leo
1911	JAN	20	Tau		MAY	29	Vir
1912	JUL	7	Gem	1950	NOV	20	Lib
	NOV	30	Tau	1951	MAR	7	Vir
1913	MAR	26	Gem		AUG	13	Lib
1914	AUG	24	Can	1953	OCT	22	Scp
	DEC	7	Gem	1956	JAN	12	Sag
1915	MAY	11	Can		MAY	14	Scp
1916	OCT	17	Leo		OCT	10	Sag
	DEC	7	Can	1959	JAN	5	Cap
1917	JUN	24	Leo	1962	JAN	3	Aqu
1919	AUG	12	Vir	1964	MAR	24	Pic
1921	OCT	7	Lib		SEP	16	Aqu
1923	DEC	20	Scp		DEC	16	Pic
1924	APR	6	Lib	1967	MAR	3	Ari
	SEP	13	Scp	1969	APR	29	Tau
1926	DEC	2	Sag	1971	JUN	18	Gem
1929	MAR	15	Cap	1972	JAN	10	Tau
	MAY	5	Sag		FEB	21	Gem
	NOV	30	Cap	1973	AUG	1	Can
1932	FEB	24	Aqu	1974	JAN	7	Gem
	AUG	13	Cap		APR	18	Can
	NOV	20	Aqu	1975	SEP	17	Leo
1935	FEB	14	Pic	1976	JAN	14	Can
1937	APR	25	Ari		JUN	5	Leo
	OCT	18	Pic	1977	NOV	17	Vir
1938	JAN	14	Ari	1978	JAN	5	Leo
1939	JUL	6	Tau		JUL	26	Vir

1980	SEP	21	Lib	1994	JAN	28	Pic
1982	NOV	29	Scp	1996	APR	7	Ari
1983	MAY	6	Lib	1998	JUN	9	Tau
	AUG	24	Scp		OCT	25	Ari
1985	NOV	17	Sag	1999	MAR	1	Tau
1988	FEB	13	Cap	2000	AUG	10	Gem
	JUN	10	Sag		OCT	16	Tau
	NOV	12	Cap	2001	APR	21	Gem
1991	FEB	6	Aqu	2003	JUN	3	Can
1993	MAY	21	Pic	2005	JUL	16	Leo
	JUN	30	Aqu	2007	SEP	2	Vir

CHAPTER 7

Your Rising Sign Tells Where the Action Is

You can learn much about a person by the signs and interactions of the sun, moon, and planets in the horoscope, but you can't tell where in that person's life the activity will take place. Knowing the rising sign, which is based on the exact moment in time of an event such as a birth, will provide information that enables the astrologer to make predictions. For example, you might know that a person has Mars in Aries, which will describe that person's dynamic fiery energy. But if you also know that the person has a Capricorn rising sign, this Mars will fall in the fourth house of home and family, so you know where that energy will operate.

Your rising sign is the degree of the zodiac ascending over the eastern horizon when you were born. (That's why it's often called the ascendant.) It marks the first point in the horoscope, the beginning of the first house, one of twelve divisions of the horoscope, each of which represents a different area of your life. After the rising sign sets up the first house, the other houses parade around the chart in sequence, with the following sign on the house cusp. Due to the earth's rotation, the rising sign changes every two hours, which means that other babies, who may have been born later or earlier on the same day in the same hospital as you were (and will be sure to have most planets in the same signs as you do) may not have the same rising sign and their planets may fall in different houses in the chart.

For instance, if Mars is in Gemini and your rising sign is Taurus, Mars will most likely be active in the second or financial house of your chart. Someone born later in the day when the rising sign is Virgo would have Mars positioned at the top of the chart, energizing the tenth house of career.

Most astrologers insist on knowing the exact time of a client's birth before analyzing a chart. The more accurate your birth time, the more accurately an astrologer can position the planets in your chart. Without a valid rising sign, your collection of planets would have no homes. One would have no idea which area of your life would be influenced by a particular planet.

How Your Rising Sign Can Influence Your Sun Sign

Your rising sign has an important relationship with your sun sign. Some will complement the sun sign; others hide it under a totally different mask, as if playing an entirely different role, making it difficult to guess the person's sun sign from outer appearances. This may be the reason why you might not look or act like your sun sign's archetype. For example, a Leo with a conservative Capricorn ascendant would come across as much more serious than a Leo with a fiery Aries or Sagittarius ascendant.

Though the rising sign usually creates the first impression you make, there are exceptions. When the sun sign is reinforced by other planets in the same sign, this might overpower the impression of the rising sign. For instance, a Leo sun plus a Leo Venus and Leo Jupiter would counteract the more conservative image that would otherwise be conveyed by the person's Capricorn ascendant.

Those born early in the morning when the sun was on the horizon will be most likely to project the image of their sun sign. These people are often called a "double Aries" or a "double Virgo" because the same sun sign and ascendant reinforce each other.

Find Your Rising Sign

Look up your rising sign from the chart at the end of this chapter. Since rising signs change every two hours, it is important to know your birth time as close to the minute as possible. Even a few minutes' difference could change the rising sign and therefore the setup of your chart. If you are unsure about the exact time, but know within a few hours, check the following descriptions to see which is most like the personality you project.

Aries Rising: Alpha Energy

You are the most aggressive version of your sun sign, with boundless energy that can be used productively if it's channeled in the right direction. Watch a tendency to overreact emotionally and blow your top. You come across as openly competitive, a positive asset in business or sports. Be on guard against impatience, which could lead to head injuries. Your walk and bearing could have the telltale head-forward Aries posture. You may wear more bright colors, especially red, than others of your sign. You may also have a tendency to drive your car faster.

Can you see the alpha Aries tendency in Barbra Streisand (a sun-sign Taurus) and Bette Midler (a sun-sign Sagittarius)?

Taurus Rising: Down to Earth

You're slow-moving, with a beautiful (or distinctive) speaking or singing voice that can be especially soothing or melodious. You probably surround yourself with comfort, good food, luxurious environments, and other sensual pleasures. You prefer welcoming others into your home to gadding about. You may have a talent for business, especially in trading, appraising, and real estate. A Taurus ascendant gives a well-padded physique that gains weight easily, like Liza Minnelli. This ascendant can also endow females with a curvaceous beauty.

Gemini Rising: A Way with Words

You're naturally sociable, with lighter, more ethereal mannerisms than others of your sign, especially if you're female.

You love to communicate with people, and express your ideas and feelings easily, like British prime minister Tony Blair. You may have a talent for writing or public speaking. You thrive on variety, a constantly changing scene, and a lively social life. However, you may relate to others at a deeper level than might be suspected. And you will be far more sympathetic and caring than you project. You will probably travel widely, changing partners and jobs several times (or juggle two at once). Physically, your nerves are quite sensitive. Occasionally, you would benefit from a calm, tranquil atmosphere away from your usual social scene.

Cancer Rising: Nurturing Instincts

You are naturally acquisitive, possessive, private, a moneymaker, like Bill Gates or Michael Bloomberg. You easily pick up on others' needs and feelings—a great gift in business, the arts, and personal relationships. But you must guard against overreacting or taking things too personally, especially during full moon periods. Find creative outlets for your natural nurturing gifts, such as helping the less fortunate, particularly children. Your insights would be helpful in psychology. Your desire to feed and care for others would be useful in the restaurant, hotel, or child-care industries. You may be especially fond of wearing romantic old clothes, collecting antiques, and, of course, dining on exquisite food. Since your body may retain fluids, pay attention to your diet. To relax, escape to places near water.

Leo Rising: Diva Dazzle

You may come across as more poised than you really feel. However, you play it to the hilt, projecting a proud royal presence. A Leo ascendant gives you a natural flair for drama, like Marilyn Monroe, and you might be accused of stealing the spotlight. You'll also project a much more outgoing, optimistic, sunny personality than others of your sign. You take care to please your public by always projecting your best star quality, probably tossing a luxuriant mane of hair, sporting a striking hairstyle, or dressing to impress. Females often dazzle with spectacular jewelry. Since you may have a strong parental nature, you could well be the regal family matriarch or patriarch, like George W. Bush.

Virgo Rising: High Standards

Virgo rising masks your inner nature with a practical, analytical outer image. You seem neat, orderly, more particular than others of your sign. Others in your life may feel they must live up to your high standards. Though at times you may be openly critical, this masks a well-meaning desire to have only the best for loved ones. Your sharp eye for details could be used in the financial world, or your literary skills could draw you to teaching or publishing. The healing arts, health care, and service-oriented professions attract many with a Virgo ascendant. You're likely to take good care of yourself, with great attention to health, diet, and exercise, like Madonna. You might even show some hypochondriac tendencies, like Woody Allen. Physically, you may have a very sensitive digestive system.

Libra Rising: The Charmer

Libra rising gives you a charming, social public persona, like Bill Clinton. You tend to avoid confrontations in relationships, preferring to smooth the way or negotiate diplomatically rather than give in to an emotional reaction. Because you are interested in all aspects of a situation, you may be slow to reach decisions. Physically, you'll have good proportions and symmetry. You will move with natural grace and balance. You're likely to have pleasing, if not beautiful, facial features, with a winning smile, like Cary Grant. You'll show natural good taste and harmony in your clothes and home decor. Legal, diplomatic, or public relations professions could draw your interest.

Scorpio Rising: An Air of Mystery

You project an intriguing air of mystery with this ascendant, as the Scorpio secretiveness and sense of underlying power combines with your sun sign. As with Jackie O, there's more to you than meets the eye. You seem like someone who is always in control and who can move comfortably in the world of power. Your physical look comes across as intense. Many of you have remarkable eyes, with a direct, penetrating gaze. But you'll never reveal your private agenda, and you tend to keep your true feelings under wraps (watch a tendency toward paranoia). You may have an interesting romantic history with secret love affairs, like Grace Kelly. Many of you heighten your air of mystery by wearing black. You're happiest near water and should provide yourself with a seaside retreat.

Sagittarius Rising: The Explorer

You travel with this ascendant. You may also be a more outdoor, sportive type, with an athletic, casual, outgoing air. Your moods are camouflaged with cheerful optimism or a philosophical attitude. Though you don't hesitate to speak your mind, like Ted Turner, who was called the Mouth of the South, you can also laugh at your troubles or crack a joke more easily than others of your sign. A Sagittarius ascendant can also draw you to the field of higher education or to spiritual life. You'll seem to have less attachment to things and people, and may explore the globe. Your strong, fast legs are a physical bonus.

Capricorn Rising: Serious Business

This rising sign makes you come across as serious, goal-oriented, disciplined, and careful with cash. You are not one of the zodiac's big spenders, though you might splurge occasionally on items with good investment value. You're the traditional, conservative type in dress and environment, and you might come across as quite normal and businesslike, like Rupert Murdoch. You'll function well in a structured or corporate environment where you can climb to the top. (You are always aware of who's the boss.) In your personal life, you could be a loner or a single parent who is "father and mother" to your children.

Aquarius Rising: One of a Kind

You come across as less concerned about what others think and could even be a bit eccentric. You're more at ease with groups of people than others in your sign, and you may be attracted to public life, like Jay Leno. Your appearance may be unique, either unconventional or unimportant to you. Those of you whose sun is in a water sign (Cancer, Scorpio, Pisces) may exercise your nurturing qualities with a large group, an extended family, or a day-care or community center.

Pisces Rising: Romantic Roles

Your creative, nurturing talents are heightened and so is your ability to project emotional drama. And, like Antonio Banderas, your dreamy eyes and poetic air bring out the protective instinct in others. You could be attracted to the arts, especially theater, dance, film, and photography, or to psychology, spiritual practice, and charity work. You are happiest when you are using your creative ability to help others. Since you are vulnerable to mood swings, it is especially important for you to find interesting, creative work where you can express your talents and heighten your self-esteem. Accentuate the positive. Be wary of escapist tendencies, particularly involving alcohol or drugs to which you are supersensitive, like Whitney Houston.

RISING SIGNS—A.M. BIRTHS

	1 AM	2 AM	3 AM	4 AM	5 AM	6 AM	7 AM	8 AM	9 AM	10 AM	11 AM	12 NOON
Jan 1	Lib	Sc	Sc	Sc	Sag	Sag	Cap	Cap	Aq	Aq	Pis	Ar
Jan 9	Lib	Sc	Sc	Sag	Sag	Sag	Cap	Cap	Aq	Pis	Ar	Tau
Jan 17	Sc	Sc	Sc	Sag	Sag	Cap	Cap	Aq	Aq	Pis	Ar	Tau
Jan 25	Sc	Sc	Sag	Sag	Sag	Cap	Cap	Aq	Pis	Ar	Tau	Tau
Feb 2	Sc	Sc	Sag	Sag	Cap	Cap	Aq	Pis	Pis	Ar	Tau	Gem
Feb 10	Sc	Sag	Sag	Sag	Cap	Cap	Aq	Pis	Ar	Tau	Tau	Gem
Feb 18	Sc	Sag	Sag	Cap	Cap	Aq	Pis	Pis	Ar	Tau	Gem	Gem
Feb 26	Sag	Sag	Sag	Cap	Aq	Aq	Pis	Ar	Tau	Tau	Gem	Gem
Mar 6	Sag	Sag	Cap	Cap	Aq	Pis	Pis	Ar	Tau	Gem	Gem	Can
Mar 14	Sag	Cap	Cap	Aq	Aq	Pis	Ar	Tau	Tau	Gem	Gem	Can
Mar 22	Sag	Cap	Cap	Aq	Pis	Ar	Ar	Tau	Gem	Gem	Can	Can
Mar 30	Cap	Cap	Aq	Pis	Pis	Ar	Tau	Tau	Gem	Can	Can	Can
Apr 7	Cap	Cap	Aq	Pis	Ar	Ar	Tau	Gem	Gem	Can	Can	Leo
Apr 14	Cap	Aq	Aq	Pis	Ar	Tau	Tau	Gem	Gem	Can	Can	Leo
Apr 22	Cap	Aq	Pis	Ar	Ar	Tau	Gem	Gem	Gem	Can	Leo	Leo
Apr 30	Aq	Aq	Pis	Ar	Tau	Tau	Gem	Can	Can	Can	Leo	Leo
May 8	Aq	Pis	Ar	Ar	Tau	Gem	Gem	Can	Can	Leo	Leo	Leo
May 16	Aq	Pis	Ar	Tau	Gem	Gem	Can	Can	Can	Leo	Leo	Vir
May 24	Pis	Ar	Ar	Tau	Gem	Gem	Can	Can	Leo	Leo	Leo	Vir
June 1	Pis	Ar	Tau	Gem	Gem	Can	Can	Can	Leo	Leo	Vir	Vir
June 9	Ar	Ar	Tau	Gem	Gem	Can	Can	Leo	Leo	Leo	Vir	Vir
June 17	Ar	Tau	Gem	Gem	Can	Can	Can	Leo	Leo	Vir	Vir	Vir
June 25	Tau	Tau	Gem	Gem	Can	Can	Leo	Leo	Leo	Vir	Vir	Lib
July 3	Tau	Gem	Gem	Can	Can	Can	Leo	Leo	Vir	Vir	Vir	Lib
July 11	Tau	Gem	Gem	Can	Can	Leo	Leo	Leo	Vir	Vir	Lib	Lib
July 18	Gem	Gem	Can	Can	Can	Leo	Leo	Vir	Vir	Vir	Lib	Lib
July 26	Gem	Gem	Can	Can	Leo	Leo	Vir	Vir	Vir	Lib	Lib	Lib
Aug 3	Gem	Can	Can	Can	Leo	Leo	Vir	Vir	Vir	Lib	Lib	Sc
Aug 11	Gem	Can	Can	Leo	Leo	Vir	Vir	Vir	Lib	Lib	Lib	Sc
Aug 18	Can	Can	Can	Leo	Leo	Vir	Vir	Vir	Lib	Lib	Sc	Sc
Aug 27	Can	Can	Leo	Leo	Leo	Vir	Vir	Lib	Lib	Lib	Sc	Sc
Sept 4	Can	Can	Leo	Leo	Vir	Vir	Vir	Lib	Lib	Sc	Sc	Sc
Sept 12	Can	Leo	Leo	Leo	Vir	Vir	Lib	Lib	Lib	Sc	Sc	Sag
Sept 20	Leo	Leo	Leo	Vir	Vir	Vir	Lib	Lib	Sc	Sc	Sc	Sag
Sept 28	Leo	Leo	Leo	Vir	Vir	Lib	Lib	Lib	Sc	Sc	Sag	Sag
Oct 6	Leo	Leo	Vir	Vir	Vir	Lib	Lib	Sc	Sc	Sc	Sag	Sag
Oct 14	Leo	Vir	Vir	Vir	Lib	Lib	Lib	Sc	Sc	Sag	Sag	Cap
Oct 22	Leo	Vir	Vir	Lib	Lib	Lib	Sc	Sc	Sc	Sag	Sag	Cap
Oct 30	Vir	Vir	Vir	Lib	Lib	Sc	Sc	Sc	Sag	Sag	Cap	Cap
Nov 7	Vir	Vir	Lib	Lib	Lib	Sc	Sc	Sc	Sag	Sag	Cap	Cap
Nov 15	Vir	Vir	Lib	Lib	Sc	Sc	Sc	Sag	Sag	Cap	Cap	Aq
Nov 23	Vir	Lib	Lib	Lib	Sc	Sc	Sag	Sag	Sag	Cap	Cap	Aq
Dec 1	Vir	Lib	Lib	Sc	Sc	Sc	Sag	Sag	Cap	Cap	Aq	Aq
Dec 9	Lib	Lib	Lib	Sc	Sc	Sag	Sag	Sag	Cap	Cap	Aq	Pis
Dec 18	Lib	Lib	Sc	Sc	Sc	Sag	Sag	Cap	Cap	Aq	Aq	Pis
Dec 28	Lib	Lib	Sc	Sc	Sag	Sag	Sag	Cap	Aq	Aq	Pis	Ar

RISING SIGNS—P.M. BIRTHS

	1 PM	2 PM	3 PM	4 PM	5 PM	6 PM	7 PM	8 PM	9 PM	10 PM	11 PM	12 MIDNIGHT
Jan 1	Tau	Gem	Gem	Can	Can	Can	Leo	Leo	Vir	Vir	Vir	Lib
Jan 9	Tau	Gem	Gem	Can	Can	Leo	Leo	Leo	Vir	Vir	Vir	Lib
Jan 17	Gem	Gem	Can	Can	Can	Leo	Leo	Vir	Vir	Vir	Lib	Lib
Jan 25	Gem	Gem	Can	Can	Leo	Leo	Leo	Vir	Vir	Lib	Lib	Lib
Feb 2	Gem	Can	Can	Can	Leo	Leo	Vir	Vir	Vir	Lib	Lib	Sc
Feb 10	Gem	Can	Can	Leo	Leo	Leo	Vir	Vir	Lib	Lib	Lib	Sc
Feb 18	Can	Can	Can	Leo	Leo	Vir	Vir	Vir	Lib	Lib	Sc	Sc
Feb 26	Can	Can	Leo	Leo	Vir	Vir	Vir	Lib	Lib	Lib	Sc	Sc
Mar 6	Can	Leo	Leo	Leo	Vir	Vir	Lib	Lib	Lib	Sc	Sc	Sc
Mar 14	Can	Leo	Leo	Vir	Vir	Vir	Lib	Lib	Sc	Sc	Sc	Sag
Mar 22	Leo	Leo	Leo	Vir	Vir	Lib	Lib	Lib	Sc	Sc	Sc	Sag
Mar 30	Leo	Leo	Vir	Vir	Vir	Lib	Lib	Sc	Sc	Sc	Sag	Sag
Apr 7	Leo	Leo	Vir	Vir	Lib	Lib	Lib	Sc	Sc	Sc	Sag	Sag
Apr 14	Leo	Vir	Vir	Vir	Lib	Lib	Sc	Sc	Sc	Sag	Sag	Cap
Apr 22	Leo	Vir	Vir	Lib	Lib	Lib	Sc	Sc	Sc	Sag	Sag	Cap
Apr 30	Vir	Vir	Vir	Lib	Lib	Sc	Sc	Sc	Sag	Sag	Cap	Cap
May 8	Vir	Vir	Lib	Lib	Lib	Sc	Sc	Sag	Sag	Sag	Cap	Cap
May 16	Vir	Vir	Lib	Lib	Sc	Sc	Sc	Sag	Sag	Cap	Cap	Aq
May 24	Vir	Lib	Lib	Lib	Sc	Sc	Sag	Sag	Sag	Cap	Cap	Aq
June 1	Vir	Lib	Lib	Sc	Sc	Sc	Sag	Sag	Cap	Cap	Aq	Aq
June 9	Lib	Lib	Lib	Sc	Sc	Sag	Sag	Sag	Cap	Cap	Aq	Pis
June 17	Lib	Lib	Sc	Sc	Sc	Sag	Sag	Cap	Cap	Aq	Aq	Pis
June 25	Lib	Lib	Sc	Sc	Sag	Sag	Sag	Cap	Cap	Aq	Pis	Ar
July 3	Lib	Sc	Sc	Sc	Sag	Sag	Cap	Cap	Aq	Aq	Pis	Ar
July 11	Lib	Sc	Sc	Sag	Sag	Sag	Cap	Cap	Aq	Pis	Ar	Tau
July 18	Sc	Sc	Sc	Sag	Sag	Cap	Cap	Aq	Aq	Pis	Ar	Tau
July 26	Sc	Sc	Sag	Sag	Sag	Cap	Cap	Aq	Pis	Ar	Tau	Tau
Aug 3	Sc	Sc	Sag	Sag	Cap	Cap	Aq	Aq	Pis	Ar	Tau	Gem
Aug 11	Sc	Sag	Sag	Sag	Cap	Cap	Aq	Pis	Ar	Tau	Tau	Gem
Aug 18	Sc	Sag	Sag	Cap	Cap	Aq	Pis	Pis	Ar	Tau	Gem	Gem
Aug 27	Sag	Sag	Sag	Cap	Cap	Aq	Pis	Ar	Tau	Tau	Gem	Gem
Sept 4	Sag	Sag	Cap	Cap	Aq	Pis	Pis	Ar	Tau	Gem	Gem	Can
Sept 12	Sag	Sag	Cap	Aq	Aq	Pis	Ar	Tau	Tau	Gem	Gem	Can
Sept 20	Sag	Cap	Cap	Aq	Pis	Pis	Ar	Tau	Gem	Gem	Can	Can
Sept 28	Cap	Cap	Aq	Aq	Pis	Ar	Tau	Tau	Gem	Gem	Can	Can
Oct 6	Cap	Cap	Aq	Pis	Ar	Ar	Tau	Gem	Gem	Can	Can	Leo
Oct 14	Cap	Aq	Aq	Pis	Ar	Tau	Tau	Gem	Gem	Can	Can	Leo
Oct 22	Cap	Aq	Pis	Ar	Ar	Tau	Gem	Gem	Can	Can	Leo	Leo
Oct 30	Aq	Aq	Pis	Ar	Tau	Tau	Gem	Gem	Can	Can	Leo	Leo
Nov 7	Aq	Aq	Pis	Ar	Tau	Tau	Gem	Can	Can	Leo	Leo	Leo
Nov 15	Aq	Pis	Ar	Tau	Gem	Gem	Can	Can	Can	Leo	Leo	Vir
Nov 23	Pis	Ar	Ar	Tau	Gem	Gem	Can	Can	Leo	Leo	Leo	Vir
Dec 1	Pis	Ar	Tau	Gem	Gem	Can	Can	Can	Leo	Leo	Vir	Vir
Dec 9	Ar	Tau	Tau	Gem	Gem	Can	Can	Leo	Leo	Leo	Vir	Vir
Dec 18	Ar	Tau	Gem	Gem	Can	Can	Can	Leo	Leo	Vir	Vir	Vir
Dec 28	Tau	Tau	Gem	Gem	Can	Can	Leo	Leo	Vir	Vir	Vir	Lib

CHAPTER 8

Learn the Glyphs and Read Your Own Chart!

If you get to a certain point in astrology, you'll want to read your own chart (or someone else's). Or perhaps you'll have a reading and be given a copy of your chart by an astrologer. In either case, you'll be confronted by a circular chart covered with mysterious symbols—unreadable except by someone who has learned these glyphs.

Breaking into astrology requires cracking the ancient code that is a type of picture writing universally understood by astrologers. It's well worth the effort to learn these symbols. You'll not only be able to read a chart, but you will be able to make use of free charts available on any number of Internet sites and astrology software programs. This year, you can even take astrology with you on your PDA and read a chart on the go. But almost none of these programs show the planetary positions written in plain English, so you'll miss out if you don't learn the glyphs.

Each little symbol has built-in clues to help you decipher not only which sign or planet it represents, but what the object means in a more esoteric sense. Actually the physical act of writing the symbol is a mystical experience in itself, a way to invoke the deeper meaning of the sign or planet through age-old visual elements that have been with us since time began.

Since there are only twelve signs and ten planets (not counting a few asteroids and other space objects some astrologers use), it's a lot easier than learning to read a foreign language. Here's a code cracker for the glyphs, beginning with the glyphs for the planets. To those who already know their glyphs, don't just skim over the chapter.

These familiar graphics have hidden meanings you will discover!

The Glyphs for the Planets

The glyphs for the planets are easy to learn. They're simple combinations of the most basic visual elements: the circle, the semicircle or arc, and the cross. However, each component of a glyph has a special meaning in relation to the other parts of the symbol.

The circle, which has no beginning or end, is one of the oldest symbols of spirit or spiritual forces. Early diagrams of the heavens—spiritual territory—are shown in circular form. The never-ending line of the circle is the perfect symbol for eternity. The semicircle or arc is an incomplete circle, symbolizing the receptive, finite soul, which contains spiritual potential in the curving line.

The vertical line of the cross symbolizes movement from heaven to earth. The horizontal line describes temporal movement, here and now, in time and space. Combined in a cross, the vertical and horizontal planes symbolize manifestation in the material world.

The Sun Glyph ☉

The sun is always shown by this powerful solar symbol, a circle with a point in the center. The center point is you, your spiritual center, and the symbol represents your infinite personality incarnating (the point) into the finite cycles of birth and death.

The sun has been represented by a circle or disk since ancient Egyptian times when the solar disk represented the sun god, Ra. Some archaeologists believe the great stone circles found in England were centers of sun worship. This particular version of the symbol was brought into common use in the sixteenth century after German occultist and scholar Cornelius Agrippa (1486–1535) wrote a book called *Die Occulta Philosophia,* which became accepted as the authority in the field. Agrippa collected many medieval astrological and magical symbols in this book, which have been used by astrologers since then.

The Moon Glyph ☽

The moon glyph is the most recognizable symbol on a chart, a left-facing arc stylized into the crescent moon. As part of a circle, the arc symbolizes the potential fulfillment of the entire circle, the life force that is still incomplete. Therefore, it is the ideal representation of the reactive, receptive, emotional nature of the moon.

The Mercury Glyph ☿

Mercury contains all three elemental symbols: the crescent, the circle, and the cross in vertical order. This is the "Venus with a hat" glyph (compare with the symbol of Venus). With another stretch of the imagination, can't you see the winged cap of Mercury the messenger? Think of the upturned crescent as antennae that tune in and transmit messages from the sun, reminding you that Mercury is the way you communicate, the way your mind works. The upturned arc is receiving energy into the spirit or solar circle, which will later be translated into action on the material plane, symbolized by the cross. All the elements are equally sized because Mercury is neutral; it doesn't play favorites! This planet symbolizes objective, detached, unemotional thinking.

The Venus Glyph ♀

Here the relationship is between two components: the circle of spirit and the cross of matter. Spirit is elevated over matter, pulling it upward. Venus asks, "What is beautiful? What do you like best? What do you love to have done to you?" Consequently, Venus determines both your ideal of beauty and what feels good sensually. It governs your own allure and power to attract, as well as what attracts and pleases you.

The Mars Glyph ♂

In this glyph, the cross of matter is stylized into an arrowhead pointed up and outward, propelled by the circle of spirit. With a little imagination, you can visualize it as the shield and spear of Mars, the ancient god of war. You can deduce that Mars embodies your spiritual energy projected into the outer world. It's your assertiveness, your initiative, your aggressive drive, what you like to do to others, your temper. If you know someone's Mars, you know whether they'll blow up when angry or do a slow burn. Your task is to use your outgoing Mars energy wisely and well.

The Jupiter Glyph ♃

Jupiter is the basic cross of matter, with a large stylized crescent perched on the left side of the horizontal, temporal plane. You might think of the crescent as an open hand, because one meaning of Jupiter is "luck," what's handed to you. You don't have to work for what you get from Jupiter; it comes to you, if you're open to it.

The Jupiter glyph might also remind you of a jumbo jet plane, with a huge tail fin, about to take off. This is the planet of travel, mental and spiritual, of expanding your horizons via new ideas, new spiritual dimensions, and new places. Jupiter embodies the optimism and enthusiasm of the traveler about to embark on an exciting adventure.

The Saturn Glyph ♄

Flip Jupiter over, and you've got Saturn. This might not be immediately apparent because Saturn is usually stylized into an "h" form like the one shown here. The principle it expresses is the opposite of Jupiter's expansive tendencies. Saturn pulls you back to earth: the receptive arc is pushed down underneath the cross of matter. Before there are any rewards or expansion, the duties and obligations of the material world must be considered. Saturn says, "Stop, wait, finish your chores before you take off!"

Saturn's glyph also resembles the sickle of old "Father Time." Saturn was first known as Chronos, the Greek god of time, for time brings all matter to an end. When it was the most distant planet (before the discovery of Uranus), Saturn was believed to be the place where time stopped. After the soul departed from earth, it journeyed back to the outer reaches of the universe and finally stopped at Saturn, or at "the end of time."

The Uranus Glyph ♅

The glyph for Uranus is often stylized to form a capital *H* after Sir William Herschel, who discovered the planet. But the more esoteric version curves the two pillars of the H into crescent antennae, or "ears," like satellite disks receiving signals from space. These are perched on the horizontal material line of the cross of matter and pushed from below by the circle of the spirit. To many sci-fi fans, Uranus looks like an orbiting satellite.

Uranus channels the highest energy of all, the white electrical light of the universal spiritual force that holds the cosmos together. This pure electrical energy is gathered from all over the universe. Because Uranus energy doesn't follow any ordinary celestial drumbeat, it can't be controlled or predicted (which is also true of those who are strongly influenced by this eccentric planet). In the symbol, this energy is manifested through the balance of polarities (the two opposite arms of the glyph) like the two polarized wires of a lightbulb.

The Neptune Glyph ♆

Neptune's glyph is usually stylized to look like a trident, the weapon of the Roman god Neptune. However, on a more esoteric level, it shows the large upturned crescent of the soul pierced through by the cross of matter. Neptune nails down, or materializes, soul energy, bringing impulses from the soul level into manifestation. That is why Neptune is associated with imagination or "imagining in," making an image of the soul. Neptune works through feelings, sensitivity, and the mystical capacity to bring the divine into the earthly realm.

The Pluto Glyph ♀

Pluto is written two ways. One is a composite of the letters *PL*, the first two letters of the word Pluto and coincidentally the initials of Percival Lowell, one of the planet's discovers. The other, more esoteric symbol is a small circle above a large open crescent that surmounts the cross of matter. This depicts Pluto's power to regenerate. Imagine a new little spirit emerging from the sheltering cup of the soul. Pluto rules the forces of life and death. After this planet has passed a sensitive point in your chart, you are transformed, reborn in some way.

Sci-fi fans might visualize this glyph as a small satellite (the circle) being launched. It was shortly after Pluto's discovery that we learned how to harness the nuclear forces that made space exploration possible. Pluto rules the transformative power of atomic energy, which totally changed our lives and from which there is no turning back.

The Glyphs for the Signs

On an astrology chart, the glyph for the sign will appear after that of the planet. For example, when you see the moon glyph followed first by a number and then by another glyph representing the sign, this means that the moon was passing over a certain degree of that astrological sign at the time of the chart. On the dividing lines between the houses on your chart, you'll find the symbol for the sign that rules the house.

Because sun sign symbols do not contain the same basic geometric components of the planetary glyphs, we must look elsewhere for clues to their meanings. Many have been passed down from ancient Egyptian and Chaldean civilizations with few modifications. Others have been adapted over the centuries.

In deciphering many of the glyphs, you'll often find that the symbols reveal a dual nature of the sign, which is not always apparent in the usual sun sign descriptions. For instance, the Gemini glyph is similar to the Roman numeral for two, and reveals this sign's longing to discover a twin soul. The Cancer glyph may be interpreted as resembling either the nurturing breasts or the self-protective claws of a crab, both symbols associated with the contrasting qualities of this sign. Libra's glyph embodies the duality of the spirit balanced with material reality. The Sagittarius glyph shows that the aspirant must also carry along the earthly animal nature in his quest. The Capricorn sea goat is another symbol with dual emphasis. The goat climbs high, yet is always pulled back by the deep waters of the unconscious. Aquarius embodies the double waves of mental detachment, balanced by the desire for connection with others, in a friendly way. Finally, the two fishes of Pisces, which are forever tied together, show the duality of the soul and the spirit that must be reconciled.

The Aries Glyph ♈

Since the symbol for Aries is the Ram, this glyph is obviously associated with a ram's horns, which characterize one aspect of the Aries personality—an aggressive, me-first, leaping-headfirst attitude. But the symbol can be interpreted in other ways as well. Some astrologers liken it to a fountain of energy, which Aries people also embody. The first sign of the zodiac bursts on the scene eagerly, ready to go. Another analogy is to the eyebrows and nose of the human head, which Aries rules, and the thinking power that is initiated by the brain.

One theory of this symbol links it to the Egyptian god Amun, represented by a ram in ancient times. As Amun-Ra, this god was believed to embody the creator of the universe, the leader of all the other gods. This relates easily to the position of Aries as the leader (or first sign) of the zodiac, which begins at the spring equinox, a time of the year when nature is renewed.

The Taurus Glyph ♉

This is another easy glyph to draw and identify. It takes little imagination to decipher the bull's head with long curving horns. Like its symbol the Bull, the archetypal Taurus is slow to anger but ferocious when provoked, as well as stubborn, steady, and sensual. Another association is the larynx (and thyroid) of the throat area (ruled by Taurus) and the eustachian tubes running up to the ears, which coincides with the relationship of Taurus to the voice, song, and music. Many famous singers, musicians, and composers have prominent Taurus influences.

Many ancient religions involved a bull as the central figure in fertility rites or initiations, usually symbolizing the victory of man over his animal nature. Another possible origin is in the sacred bull of Egypt, who embodied the incarnate form of Osiris, god of death and resurrection. In early Christian imagery, the Taurus Bull represented St. Luke.

The Gemini Glyph ♊

The standard glyph immediately calls to mind the Roman numeral for two (II) and the Twins symbol, as it is called, for Gemini. In almost all drawings and images used for this sign, the relationship between two persons is emphasized. Usually one twin will be touching the other, which signifies communication, human contact, the desire to share.

The top line of the Gemini glyph indicates mental communication, while the bottom line indicates shared physical space.

The most famous Gemini legend is that of the twin sons, Castor and Pollux, one of whom had a mortal father while the other was the son of Zeus, king of the gods. When it came time for the mortal twin to die, his grief-stricken brother pleaded with Zeus, who agreed to let them spend half the year on earth in mortal form and half in immortal life, with the gods on Mount Olympus. This reflects a basic duality of humankind, which possesses an immortal soul yet is also subject to the limits of mortality.

The Cancer Glyph ♋

Two convenient images relate to the Cancer glyph. It is easiest to decode the curving claws of the Cancer symbol, the Crab. Like the crab's, Cancer's element is water. This sensitive sign also has a hard protective shell to protect its tender interior. The crab must be wily to escape predators, scampering sideways and hiding under rocks. The crab also responds to the cycles of the moon, as do all shellfish. The other image is that of two female breasts, which Cancer rules, showing that this is a sign that nurtures and protects others as well as itself.

In ancient Egypt, Cancer was also represented by the scarab beetle, a symbol of regeneration and eternal life.

The Leo Glyph ♌

Notice that the Leo glyph seems to be an extension of Cancer's glyph, with a significant difference. In the Cancer glyph, the lines curve inward protectively. The Leo glyph expresses energy outwardly. And there is no duality in the symbol, the Lion, or in Leo, the sign.

Lions have belonged to the sign of Leo since earliest times. It is not difficult to imagine the king of beasts with his sweeping mane and curling tail from this glyph. The upward sweep of the glyph easily describes the positive energy of Leo: the flourishing tail, their flamboyant qualities. Anther analogy, perhaps a stretch of the imagination, is that of a heart leaping up with joy and enthusiasm, also very typical of Leo, which also rules the heart. In early Christian imagery, the Leo Lion represented St. Mark.

The Virgo Glyph ♍

You can read much into this mysterious glyph. For instance, it could represent the initials of "Mary Virgin," or a young woman holding a staff of wheat, or stylized female genitalia, all common interpretations. The M shape might also remind you that Virgo is ruled by Mercury. The cross beneath the symbol reveals the grounded, practical nature of this earth sign.

The earliest zodiacs link Virgo with the Egyptian goddess Isis, who gave birth to the god Horus after her husband Osiris had been killed, in the archetype of a miraculous conception. There are many ancient statues of Isis nursing her baby son, which are reminiscent of medieval Virgin and Child motifs. This sign has also been associated with the image of the Holy Grail, when the Virgo symbol was substituted with a chalice.

The Libra Glyph ♎

It is not difficult to read the standard image for Libra, the Scales, into this glyph. There is another meaning, however, that is equally relevant: the setting sun as it descends over the horizon. Libra's natural position on the zodiac wheel is the descendant, or sunset position (as the Aries natural position is the ascendant, or rising sign). Both images relate to Libra's personality. Libra is always weighing pros and cons for a balanced decision. In the sunset image, the sun (male) hovers over the horizontal earth (female) before setting. Libra is the space between these lines, harmonizing yin and yang, spiritual and material, male and female, ideal and real worlds. The glyph has also been linked to the kidneys, which are ruled by Libra.

The Scorpio Glyph ♏

With its barbed tail, this glyph is easy to identify as the Scorpion for the sign of Scorpio. It also represents the male sexual parts, over which the sign rules. From the arrowhead, you can draw the conclusion that Mars was once its ruler. Some earlier Egyptian glyphs for Scorpio represent it as an erect serpent, so the Serpent is an alternate symbol.

Another symbol for Scorpio, which is not identifiable in this glyph, is the Eagle. Scorpios can go to extremes, either in soaring like the eagle or self-destructing like the scorpion. In early Christian imagery, which often used zodiacal symbols, the Scorpio Eagle was chosen to symbolize the intense apostle St. John the Evangelist.

The Sagittarius Glyph ♐

This is one of the easiest to spot and draw: an upward pointing arrow lifting up a cross. The arrow is pointing skyward, while the cross represents the four elements of the material world, which the arrow must convey. Elevating materiality into spirituality is an important Sagittarius quality, which explains why this sign is associated with higher learning, religion, philosophy, travel—the aspiring professions. Sagittarius can also send barbed arrows of frankness in the pursuit of truth, so the Archer symbol for Sagittarius is apt. (Sagittarius is also the sign of the supersalesman.)

Sagittarius is symbolically represented by the centaur, a mythological creature who is half man, half horse, aiming his arrow toward the skies. Though Sagittarius is motivated by spiritual aspiration, it also must balance the powerful appetites of the animal nature. The centaur Chiron, a figure in Greek mythology, became a wise teacher who, after many adventures and world travels, was killed by a poisoned arrow.

The Capricorn Glyph ♑

One of the most difficult symbols to draw, this glyph may take some practice. It is a representation of the sea goat: a mythical animal that is a goat with a curving fish's tail. The goat part of Capricorn wants to leave the waters of the emotions and climb to the elevated areas of life. But the fish tail is the unconscious, the deep chaotic psychic level that draws the goat back. Capricorn is often trying to escape the deep, feeling part of life by submerging himself in work, steadily ascending to the top. To some people, the glyph represents a seated figure with a bent knee, a reminder that Capricorn governs the knee area of the body.

An interesting aspect of this glyph is the contrast of the sharp pointed horns—which represent the penetrating, shrewd, conscious side of Capricorn—with the swishing tail—which represents its serpentine, unconscious, emotional force. One Capricorn legend, which dates from Roman times, tells of the earthy fertility god, Pan, who tried to save himself from uncontrollable sexual desires by jumping into the Nile. His upper body then turned into a goat, while the lower part became a fish. Later, Jupiter gave him a safe haven as a constellation in the skies.

The Aquarius Glyph ♒

This ancient water symbol can be traced back to an Egyptian hieroglyph representing streams of life force. Symbolized by the Water Bearer, Aquarius is distributor of the waters of life—the magic liquid of regeneration. The two waves can also be linked to the positive and negative charges of the electrical energy that Aquarius rules, a sort of universal wavelength. Aquarius is tuned in intuitively to higher forces via this electrical force. The duality of the glyph could also refer to the dual nature of Aquarius, a sign that runs hot and cold and that is friendly but also detached in the mental world of air signs.

In Greek legends, Aquarius is represented by Ganymede, who was carried to heaven by an eagle in order to become the cupbearer of Zeus and to supervise the annual flooding of the Nile. The sign later became associated with aviation and notions of flight.

The Pisces Glyph)(

Here is an abstraction of the familiar image of Pisces, two Fishes swimming in opposite directions yet bound together by a cord. The Fishes represent the spirit—which yearns for the freedom of heaven—and the soul—which remains attached to the desires of the temporal world. During life on earth, the spirit and the soul are bound together. When they complement each other, instead of pulling in opposite directions, they facilitate the Pisces creativity. The ancient version of this glyph, taken from the Egyptians, had no connecting line, which was added in the fourteenth century.

In another interpretation, it is said that the left fish indicates the direction of involution or the beginning of a cycle, while the right fish signifies the direction of evolution, the way to completion of a cycle. It's an appropriate grand finale for Pisces, the last sign of the zodiac.

CHAPTER 9

Astrology on Your Computer: Where to Find Software That Suits Your Budget and Ability

Once you've learned the basics of astrology, you'll be ready to practice reading charts. It's great fun to start out by analyzing the charts of friends and family so you can see how the planets manifest in real life. If you have a computer, there's no easier way than to use astrology software, which can calculate a chart in seconds and even help you interpret it.

When it comes to astrology software, there are endless options. How do you make the right choice? First, define your goals. Do you want to do charts of friends and family, study celebrity charts, or check the aspects every day on your Palm Pilot? Do you want to invest in a more comprehensive program that adapts to your changing needs as you learn astrology?

The good news is that there's a program for every level of interest in all price points—starting with free. For the dabbler, there are the affordable Winstar Express and the Astroscan shareware. For the serious student, there are Astrolog (free), Solar Fire, Kepler, Winstar Plus—software that does every technique on planets and gives you beautiful chart printouts. You can do a chart of someone you've just met on your PDA with Astracadabra. If you're a Mac user, you'll be satisfied with the wonderful IO and Time Passages software.

However, since all the programs use the astrology symbols, or glyphs, for planets and signs, rather than written words, you should learn the glyphs before you purchase your software. Our chapter on the glyphs in this book will help you do just that. Here are some software options for you to explore.

Easy for Beginners

Time Passages

Designed for either a Macintosh or Windows computer, Time Passages is straightforward and easy to use. It allows you to generate charts and interpretation reports for yourself or friends and loved ones at the touch of a button. If you haven't yet learned the astrology symbols, this might be the program for you; just roll your mouse over any symbol of the planets, signs, or house cusps, and you'll be shown a description in plain English below the chart. Then click on the planet, sign, or house cusp and up pops a detailed interpretation. It couldn't be easier. A new basic edition, under fifty dollars at this writing, is bargain priced and ideal for beginners.

Time Passages
(866) 772-7876 (866-77-ASTRO)
Web site: www.astrograph.com

Growth Opportunities

Astrolabe

Astrolabe is one of the top astrology software resources. Check out the latest version of their powerful Solar Fire software for Windows. A breeze to use, it will grow with your increasing knowledge of astrology to the most sophisticated levels. This company also markets a variety of programs for all levels of expertise and a wide selection of computer-generated astrology readings. This is a good resource for innovative software as well as applications for older computers.

The Astrolabe Web site is a great place to start your astrology tour of the Internet. Visitors to the site are greeted with a chart of the time you log on. And you can get your chart calculated, also free, with an interpretation e-mailed to you.

Astrolabe
Box 1750-R
Brewster, MA 02631
Phone: (800) 843-6682
Web site: www.alabe.com

Matrix Software

You'll find a wide variety of software at student and advanced levels in all price ranges, demo disks, and lots of interesting readings. Check out Winstar Express, a powerful but reasonably priced program suitable for all skill levels. The Matrix Web site offers lots of fun activities for Web surfers, such as free readings from the *I Ching,* the runes, and the tarot. There are many free desktop backgrounds with astrology themes. Go here to connect with news groups and online discussions. Their online almanac helps you schedule the best day to sign on the dotted line, ask for a raise, or plant your tomatoes.

Matrix Software
126 South Michigan Ave.
Big Rapids, MI 49307
Phone: (800) 752-6387
Web site: www.astrologysoftware.com

Astro Communications Services (ACS)

Books, software for Mac and IBM compatibles, individual charts, and telephone readings are offered by this California company. Their freebies include astrology greeting cards and new moon reports. Find technical astrology materials here, such as *The American Ephemeris* and PC atlases. ACS will calculate and send charts to you, a valuable service if you do not have a computer.

ACS Publications
P.O. box 1646
El Cajon, CA 72022-1646
Phone: (800) 514-5070
Fax: (619) 631-0185
Web site: www.astrocom.com

Air Software

Here you'll find powerful, creative astrology software, and current stock market analysis. Financial astrology programs for stock market traders are a specialty. There are some interesting freebies at this site; check out the maps of eclipse paths for any year and a free astrology clock program.

Air Software
115 Caya Avenue
West Hartford, CT 06110
Phone: (800) 659-1247
Web site: www.alphee.com

Kepler: State of the Art

Here's a program that has everything. Gorgeous graphic images, audio-visual effects, and myriad sophisticated chart options are built into this fascinating software. It's even got an astrological encyclopedia, plus diagrams and images to help you understand advanced concepts. This program is expensive, but if you're serious about learning astrology, it's an investment that will grow with you! There's a cheaper scaled-down version called Pegasus for those who don't want all the features. Check out its features at www.astrologysoftwareshop.com.

Time Cycles Research: For Mac Users

Here's where Mac users can find astrology software that's as sophisticated as it gets. If you have a Mac, you'll love their beautiful graphic IO Series programs.

Time Cycles Research
P.O. Box 797
Waterford, CT 06385
Web site: www.timecycles.com

Shareware and Freeware: The Price Is Right!

Halloran Software: A Super Shareware Program

Check out Halloran Software's Web site (www.halloran.com), which offers several levels of Windows astrology software. Beginners should consider their Astrology for Windows shareware program, which is available in unregistered demo form as a free download and in registered form for a very reasonable price.

Astrolog

If you're computer-savvy, you can't go wrong with Walter Pullen's amazingly complete Astrolog program, which is offered absolutely free at the site. The Web address is www.astrolog.org/astrolog.htm.

Astrolog is an ultrasophisticated program with all the features of much more expensive programs. It comes in versions for all formats—DOS, Windows, Mac, UNIX—and has some cool features, such as a revolving globe and a constellation map. If you are looking for astrology software with bells and whistles that doesn't cost big bucks, this program has it all!

Astroscan

Surf to www.astroscan.ca for a free program called Astroscan. Stunning graphics and ease of use make this basic program a winner. Astroscan has a fun list of celebrity charts you can call up with a few clicks.

Programs for the Pocket PDA and Palm Pilot

Would you like to have astrology at your fingertips everywhere you go? No need to drag along your laptop. You can check the chart of the moment or of someone you've just met on your pocket PDA or Palm Pilot. As with most other programs, you'll need to know the astrological symbols in order to read the charts.

For the pocket PC that has the Microsoft Pocket PC 2002 or the Microsoft Windows Mobile 2003 operating system, there is the versatile Astracadabra, which can interchange charts with the popular Solar Fire software. It can be ordered at www.leelehman.com or www.astrologysoftwareshop.com.

For the Palm OS5 and compatible handheld devices, there is Astropocket from www.yves.robert.org/features.html. This is a shareware program, which allows you to use all the features free. However, you cannot store more than one chart at a time until you pay a mere twenty-eight-dollar registration fee for the complete version.

CHAPTER 10

How to Connect with Astrology Fans Around the Globe

Are you interested in connecting with other astrology fans? How about expanding your knowledge by studying with a famous astrologer or by attending international lectures and conferences, even astrological workshops in exotic places? The astrological community is ready to welcome you.

You need only type the word astrology into any Internet search engine and watch hundreds of listings of astrology-related sites pop up. There are local meetings and international conferences where you can connect with other astrologers, and books and tapes to help you study at home.

To help you sort out the variety of options available, here are our top picks of the Internet and the astrological community at large.

Nationwide Astrology Organizations and Conferences

National Council for Geocosmic Research (NCGR)

Whether you'd like to know more about such specialties as financial astrology or techniques for timing events, or if you'd prefer the psychological or mythological approach, you'll meet the top astrologers at conferences sponsored by the National Council for Geocosmic Research. NCGR is dedicated to providing quality education, bringing astrologers and astrology fans together at conferences, and promoting fellowship. Their course structure provides a systematized study of the many facets of astrology. The organization sponsors educational workshops, taped lectures, conferences, and a directory of professional astrologers. For an annual membership fee, you get their excellent publications and newsletters, plus the opportunity to network with other astrology buffs at local chapter events. (At this writing there are chapters in twenty-six states and four countries.)

To join NCGR for the latest information on upcoming events and chapters in your city, consult their Web site: www.geocosmic.org.

American Federation of Astrologers (AFA)

Established in 1938, this is one of the oldest astrological organizations in the United States. AFA offers conferences, conventions, and a thorough correspondence course. If you are looking for a reading, their interesting Web site will refer you to an accredited AFA astrologer.

AFA
P.O. Box 22040
Tempe, AZ 85285-2040
Phone: (888) 301-7630 or (480) 838-1751
Fax: (480) 838-8293
Web site: www.astrologers.com

Association for Astrological Networking (AFAN)

Did you know that astrologers are still being harassed for practicing astrology? AFAN provides support and legal information and works toward improving the public image of astrology. AFAN's network of local astrologers links with the international astrological community. Here are the people who will go to bat for astrology when it is attacked in the media. Everyone who cares about astrology should join!

AFAN
8306 Wilshire Boulevard
PMB 537
Beverly Hills, CA 90211
Phone: (800) 578-2326
E-mail: info@afan.org
Web site: www.afan.org

International Society for Astrology Research (ISAR)

An international organization of professional astrologers dedicated to encouraging the highest standards of quality in the field of astrology with an emphasis on research. Among ISAR's benefits are a quarterly journal, a weekly e-mail newsletter, frequent conferences, and a free membership directory.

ISAR
P.O. Box 38613
Los Angeles, CA 90038
Fax: (805) 933-0301
Web site: www.isarastrology.com

Astrology Magazines

In addition to articles by top astrologers, most of these have listings of astrology conferences, events, and local happenings.

Horoscope Guide
Kappa Publishing Group
Dept. 4
P.O. Box 2085
Marion, OH 43306-8121

Dell Horoscope
P.O. Box 54097
Boulder, CO 80322-4907

The Mountain Astrologer

A favorite magazine of astrology fans! *The Mountain Astrologer* also has an interesting Web site featuring the latest news from an astrological point of view, plus feature articles from the magazine.

The Mountain Astrologer
P.O. Box 970
Cedar Ridge, CA 95924
Phone: (800) 247-4828
Web site: www.mountainastrologer.com

Astrology College

Kepler College of Astrological Arts and Sciences

A degree-granting college, which is also a center of astrology, has long been the dream of the astrological community and is a giant step forward in providing credibility to the profession. Therefore, the opening of Kepler College in 2000 was a historical event for astrology. It is the only college in the western hemisphere authorized to issue B.A. and M.A. degrees in Astrological Studies. Here is where to study with the best scholars, teachers, and communicators in the field. A long-distance study program is available for those interested.

For more information, contact:

Kepler College of Astrological Arts and Sciences
4630 200th Street SW
Suite A-1
Lynnwood, WA 98036
Phone: (425) 673-4292
Fax: (425) 673-4983
Web site: www.kepler.edu

Our Favorite Web Sites

Of the thousands of astrological Web sites that come and go on the Internet, these have stood the test of time and are likely to still be operating when this book is published.

Astrodienst (www.astro.com)

Don't miss this fabulous international site that has long been one of the best astrology resources on the Internet. It's also a great place to view and download your own astrology chart. The world atlas on this site will give you the accurate longitude and latitude of your birthplace for setting up your horoscope. Then you can print out your free chart in a range of easy-to-read formats. Other attractions: a list of famous people born on your birth date, a feature that helps you choose the best vacation spot, plus articles by world-famous astrologers.

AstroDatabank (www.astrodatabank.com)

When the news is breaking, you can bet this site will be the first to get accurate birthdays of the headliners. The late astrologer Lois Rodden was a stickler for factual information and her meticulous research is being continued, much to the benefit of the astrological community. The Web site specializes in charts of current newsmakers, political figures, and international celebrities. You can also participate in discussions and analysis of the charts and see what some of the world's best astrologers have to say about them. Their AstroDatabank program, which you can purchase at the site, provides thousands of verified birthdays sorted into categories. It's an excellent research tool.

StarIQ (www.stariq.com)

Find out how top astrologers view the latest headlines at the must-see StarIQ site. Many of the best minds in astrology comment on the latest news, stock market ups and downs, political contenders. You can sign up to receive e-mail forecasts at the most important times keyed to your individual chart. (This is one of the best of the many online forecasts.)

Astrology Books (www.astroamerica.com)

The Astrology Center of America sells a wide selection of books on all aspects of astrology, from the basics to the most advanced, at this online bookstore. Also available are many hard-to-find and recycled books.

Astrology Scholars' Sites

See what one of astrology's great teachers, Robert Hand, has to offer on his site: www.robhand.com. A leading expert on the history of astrology, he's on the cutting edge of the latest research.

The Project Hindsight group of astrologers is devoted to restoring the astrology of the Hellenistic period, the primary source for all later Western astrology. There are fascinating articles for astrology fans on this site, www.projecthindsight.com.

Financial Astrology Sites

Financial astrology is a hot specialty, with many tipsters, players, and theorists. There are online columns, newsletters, specialized financial astrology software, and mutual funds run by astrology seers. One of the more respected financial astrologers is Ray Merriman, whose column on www.stariq.com is a must read for those following the bulls and bears. Other top financial astrologers offer tips and forecasts at the www.afund.com and www.alphee.com sites.

CHAPTER 11

Got a Big Question? A Personal Reading Might Give You the Answer

Life can sometimes leave you feeling bewitched, bothered, and bewildered, as the song goes. Whether you're faced with a seemingly insurmountable problem or would simply like an objective opinion, it might be helpful to consult a professional astrologer who will take all the facets of your astrological chart into consideration. A good reading can give you peace of mind by confirming those mysterious intuitive feelings that you can't quite identify. It can give you insights on your situation that will lead you to better choices, perhaps ones that have been blocked by a blind spot.

A reading can answer some very practical questions as well, such as setting the perfect date for a wedding, a crucial job interview, or a real estate closing. If a partnership is turning sour, insights from a reading might help you put the relationship back on track. Or, after a reading, you might understand the compromises and adjustments needed to make it work. For example, one astrologically minded business team has charts done to help them work well together. Charts for family members might be done to help improve home life or figure out some complicated family dynamics.

Another good reason for a reading is to improve your personal knowledge of astrology by consulting someone who has years of experience analyzing charts. You might choose someone with a special technique that intrigues you. Armed with the knowledge of your chart that you have acquired so far, you can learn to interpret subtle nuances or gain perspective on your talents and abilities.

But what kind of reading should you have? Besides one-on-one readings with a professional astrologer, there are personal readings by mail, telephone, Internet, and tape. Well-advertised computer-generated reports and celebrity-sponsored readings are sure to attract your attention.

Done by a qualified astrologer, the personal reading can be an empowering experience if you want to reach your full potential, size up a lover or business situation, or find out what the future has in store. There are astrologers who are specialists in certain areas such as finance or medical astrology. And, unfortunately, there are many questionable practitioners who range from streetwise gypsy fortune-tellers to unscrupulous scam artists.

The following basic guidelines can help you sort out your options to find the reading that's right for you.

One-on-One Consultations with a Professional Astrologer

Nothing compares to a one-on-one consultation with a professional astrologer who has analyzed thousands of charts and can pinpoint the potential in yours. During your reading, you can get your specific questions answered. For instance, how to get along better with your mate or coworker. There are many astrologers who now combine their skills with training in psychology and are well-suited to help you examine your alternatives.

To give you an accurate reading, an astrologer needs certain information from you: the date, time, and place where you were born. (A horoscope can be cast about anyone or anything that has a specific time and place.) Most astrologers will then enter this information into a computer, which will calculate a chart in seconds. From the resulting chart, the astrologer will do an interpretation.

If you don't know your exact birth time, you can usually locate it at the Bureau of Vital Statistics at the city hall or county seat of the state where you were born. If you still have no success in getting your time of birth, some astrologers can estimate an approximate birth time by using past events in your life to determine the chart. This technique is called *rectification*.

How to Find an Astrologer

Choose your astrologer with the same care as you would any trusted adviser such as a doctor, lawyer, or banker. Unfortunately, anyone can claim to be an astrologer—to date, there is no licensing of astrologers or universally established professional criteria. However, there are nationwide organizations of serious, committed astrologers that can help you in your search.

Good places to start your investigation are organizations such as the American Federation of Astrologers (AFA) or the National Council for Geocosmic Research (NCGR), which offer a program of study and certification. If you live near a major city, there is sure to be an active NCGR chapter or astrology club in your area; many are listed in astrology magazines available at your local newsstand. In response to many requests for referrals, both the AFA and the NCGR have directories of professional astrologers listed on their Web sites; these directories include a glossary of terms and an explanation of specialties within the astrological field. Contact the NCGR and AFA headquarters for information (see chapter 10 in this book).

Warning Signals

As a potentially lucrative freelance business, astrology has always attracted self-styled experts who may not have the knowledge or the counseling experience to give a helpful reading. These astrologers can range from the well-meaning amateur to the charlatan or street-corner gypsy who has for many years given astrology a bad name. Be very wary of astrologers who claim to have occult powers or who make pretentious claims of celebrated clients or miraculous achievements. You can often tell from the initial phone conversation if the astrologer is legitimate. He or she should ask for your birthday time and place, then conduct the conversation in a professional manner. Any astrologer who gives a reading based only on your sun sign is highly suspect.

When you arrive at the reading, the astrologer should be prepared. The consultation should be conducted in a private, quiet place. The astrologer should be interested in your problems of the moment. A good reading involves feedback on your part. So if the reading is not relating to your concerns, you should let the astrologer know. You should feel free to ask questions and get clarifications of technical terms. The more you actively participate, rather than expecting the astrologer to carry the reading or come forth with oracular predictions, the more meaningful your experience will be. An astrologer should help you validate your current experience and be frank about possible negative happenings, but also suggest a positive course of action.

In their approach to a reading, some astrologers may be more literal, others more intuitive. Those who have had counseling training may take a more psychological approach. Though some astrologers may seem to have an almost psychic ability, extrasensory perception or any other parapsychological talent is not essential. A very accurate picture can be drawn from the data in your horoscope chart.

An astrologer may do several charts for each client, including one for the time of birth and a *progressed chart,* showing the evolution from birth to the present time. According to your individual needs, there are many other possibilities, such as a chart for a different location if you are contemplating a change of place. Relationships between any two people, things, or events can be interpreted with a chart that compares one partner's horoscope with the other's. A composite chart, which uses the midpoint between planets in two individual charts to describe the relationship, is another commonly used device.

An astrologer will be particularly interested in transits, those times when cycling planets activate the planets or sensitive points in your birth chart. These indicate important events in your life.

Many astrologers offer tape-recorded readings, another option to consider, especially if the astrologer you choose lives at a distance. In this case, you'll be mailed a taped reading based on your birth chart. This type of reading is more personal than a computer printout and can give you valuable insights, though it is not equivalent to a live dialogue with the astrologer when you can discuss your specific interests and issues of the moment.

The Telephone Reading

Telephone readings come in two varieties: a dial-in taped reading, usually recorded in advance by an astrologer, or a live consultation with an "astrologer" on the other end of the line. The taped readings are general daily or weekly forecasts, applied to all members of your sign and charged by the minute. The quality depends on the astrologer. One caution: Be aware that these readings can run up quite a telephone bill, especially if you get into the habit of calling every day. Be sure that you are aware of the per-minute cost of each call beforehand.

Live telephone readings also vary with the expertise of the astrologer. Ideally, the astrologer at the other end of the line enters your birth date into a computer, which then quickly calculates your chart. This chart will be referred to during the consultation. The advantage of a live telephone reading is that your individual chart is used and you can ask about a specific problem. However, before you invest in any reading, be sure that your astrologer is qualified and that you fully understand in advance how much you will be charged. There should be no unpleasant financial surprises later.

Computer-Generated Reports

Companies that offer computer programs (such as ACS, Matrix, Astrolabe) also offer a variety of computer-generated horoscope readings. These can be quite comprehensive, offering a beautiful printout of the chart plus many pages of detailed information about each planet and aspect of the chart. You can then study it at your convenience. Of course, the interpretations will be general, since there is no personal input from you, and may not cover your immediate concerns. Since computer-generated horoscopes are much lower in cost than live consultations, you might consider one as either a supplement or a preparation for an eventual live reading. You'll then be more familiar with your chart and able to plan specific questions in advance. They also make terrific gifts for astrology fans. There are several companies, listed in chapter 9, that offer computerized readings prepared by reputable astrologers.

Whichever option you decide to pursue, may your reading be an empowering one!

CHAPTER 12

Your Pet-scope for 2007: How to Choose Your Best Friend for Life

With both Jupiter, the planet of luck and expansion, and powerful Pluto in the animal-loving sign of Sagittarius, this is sure to be a year of pets and a great time to bring joy into your life by adopting an animal friend. At this writing, 63 percent of all American households have at least one pet, according to a recent survey by the American Pet Product Manufacturers Association. And we spend billions of dollars on the care and feeding of our beloved pets. Our pets are counted as part of the family, often sharing our beds and accompanying us on trips.

Whether you choose to adopt an animal from a local shelter or buy a thoroughbred from a breeder, try for an optimal time of adoption and the sun sign of your new friend. If you're rescuing an animal, however, it's difficult to know the sun sign of the animal, but you can adopt on a day when the moon is compatible with yours, which should bless the emotional relationship. Using the moon signs listed in the daily forecasts in this book, choose a day when the moon is in your sign, a sign of the same element, or a compatible element. This means fire and air signs should go for a day when the moon is in fire signs—Aries, Leo, Sagittarius—or air signs—Gemini, Libra, or Aquarius. Water and earth signs should choose a day when the moon is in water signs—Cancer, Scorpio or Pisces—or earth signs—Taurus, Virgo, or Capricorn. If possible, aim for a new moon, good for beginning a new relationship.

Here are some sign-specific tips for adopting an animal that will become your best friend for life.

Aries: The Rescuer

Aries gets special pleasure from rescuing animals in distress and rehabing them, so check your local shelters if you're thinking of adopting an animal. As an active fire sign, you'd be happiest with a lively animal, and you might do well with a rescue animal, such as a German shepherd or Labrador retriever. You'd also enjoy training such an animal. Otherwise look for intelligence, alertness, playfulness, and obedience in your friend. Since Aries tend to have an active life, look for a sleek, low-maintenance coat on your dog or cat. Cat lovers would enjoy the more active breeds such as the Siamese or Abyssinian.

An Aries sun-sign dog or cat would be ideal. Aries animals have a brave, energetic, rather combative nature. They can be mischievous, so the kittens and puppies should be monitored for safety. They'll dare to jump higher, run faster, and chase more animals than their peers. They may require stronger words and more obedience training than other signs. Give them plenty of toys and play active games with them often.

Taurus: The Toucher

Taurus is a touchy-feely sign; this tendency extends to your animal relationships. Look for a dog or cat that enjoys being petted and groomed, is affectionate, and adapts well to family life. As one of the great animal-loving signs, Taurus is likely to have several pets, so it is important that they all get along together. Give each one its own special safe space to minimize turf wars.

Taurus animals are calm and even tempered, but do not like being teased and could retaliate, so be sure to instruct children how to handle and play with their pet. Since this sign has strong appetites and tends to put on weight easily, be careful not to overindulge the animals in high-calorie treats and table snacks.

Taurus female animals are excellent mothers and make good breeders. They tend to be clean and less destructive of home furnishings than other animals.

Gemini: The Companion

A bright, quick-witted sign like yours requires an equally interesting and communicative pet. Choose a social animal that adapts well to different environments, since you may travel or have homes in different locations.

Gemini animals can put up with noise, telephones, music, and people coming and going. They'll want to be part of the action, so place a pillow or roost in a public place. They do not like being left alone. If you will be away for long periods, find them an animal companion to play with. You might consider adopting two Gemini pets from the same litter.

Animals born under this sign are easy to teach and some enjoy doing tricks or retrieving. They may be more vocal than other animals, especially if they are confined without companionship.

Cancer: The Nurturer

Cancer enjoys a devoted, obedient animal who demonstrates loyalty to its master. An affectionate home-loving dog or cat that welcomes you and sits on your lap would be ideal. The emotional connection with your pet is most important; therefore, you may depend on your powerful psychic powers when choosing an animal. Wait until you feel a strong bond of psychic communication. The moon sign of the day you adopt is very important for moon-ruled Cancer, so choose a water sign, if possible.

Cancer animals need a feeling of security; they don't like changes of environment or too much chaos at home. If you intend to breed your animal, the Cancer pet makes a wonderful and fertile mother.

Leo: The Prideful Owner

The Leo owner may choose a pet that reminds you of your own physical characteristics, such as similar coloring or build. You will be proud of your pet, will keep the animal groomed to perfection, and will choose the most spectacular example of the breed. Noble animals with a regal attitude, beautiful fur, or striking markings are often preferred, such as the Himalayan or the red tabby Persian cat, the standard poodle or the chow chow. An attention getter is a must.

Under the sign of the king of beasts, Leo-born animals have proud noble natures. They usually have a cheerful, magnanimous disposition and rule their domains regardless of their breed, holding their heads with pride and walking with great authority. They enjoy being groomed, like to show off, and enjoy the attention of fans. Leo animals thrive in the spotlight.

Virgo: The Caregiver

Virgo owners will be very particular about their pets, paying special attention to requirements for care and maintenance. You need a pet who is clean, obedient, intelligent, yet rather quiet. A highly active, barking or meowing pet that might get on your nerves is a no-no.

Cats are usually very good pets for Virgo. Choose one of the calm breeds, such as a Persian. Though this is a high-maintenance cat, its beauty and personality will be rewarding. You are compassionate with animals in need, and you might find it rewarding to volunteer at a local shelter or veterinary clinic or to train service dogs.

Virgo animals can be fussy eaters and very particular about their environment. They are gentle and intelligent; they respond to kind words and quiet commands, never harsh treatment. Virgo is an excellent sign for dogs that are trained to do service work, since they seem to enjoy being useful and are intelligent enough to be easily trained.

Libra: The Beautifier

The Libra owner responds to beauty and elegance in your pet. You require a well-mannered, but social companion, who can be displayed in all of nature's finery. An exotic variety such as a graceful curly-haired Devon Rex cat would be a show stopper. Libra often prefers the smaller varieties, such as a miniature schnauzer, a mini greyhound, or a teacup poodle.

Pets born under Libra are usually charming and well-mannered. They tend to be more careful than those of other signs. They'll avoid confrontations and harsh sounds, but respond to words of love and gentle corrections.

Scorpio: The Powerful

Scorpios enjoy a powerful animal with a strong character. They enjoy training animals and do well with service dogs, guard dogs, or police animals. Some Scorpios enjoy exotic, edgy pets, such as hairless Sphynx cats or Chinese Chin dogs. Rescuing animals in dire circumstances and finding them new homes are especially rewarding for Scorpios, as Matthew McConaughey did during Hurricane Katrina.

Animals born under this sign tend to be one-person pets, very strongly attached to their owners and extremely loyal and possessive. They are natural guard animals that will take extreme risks to protect their owners. They are best ruled by love and with consistent behavior training. They need to respect their owners and will return their love with great devotion.

Sagittarius: The Jovial Freedom Lover

Sagittarius is a traveler and one of the great animal lovers of the zodiac. The horse is especially associated with your sign, and you could well be a horse whisperer. You generally respond most to large, active animals. If a small animal, like a chihuahua, steals your heart, be sure it's one that travels well or tolerates your absence. Outdoor dogs like hunting dogs, retrievers, and border collies would be good companions on your outdoor adventures.

Sagittarius animals are freedom-loving, jovial, happy-go-lucky types. They may be wanderers, however, so be sure they have the proper identification tags and consider embedded microchip identification. These animals tend to be openly affectionate, companionable, and untemperamental. They enjoy socializing and playing with humans and other animals and are especially good with active children.

Capricorn: The Thoroughbred

Capricorn is a discriminating owner, with a great sense of responsibility toward your animal. You will be concerned with maintenance and care; you will rarely neglect or overlook any health issues with your pet. You will also discipline your pet wisely, not tolerating any destructive or outrageous antics. You will be attracted to good breeding, good manners, and deep loyalty from your pet.

The Capricorn pet tends to be more quiet and serious than other pets, perhaps a lone wolf who prefers the company of its owner rather than a sociable or mischievous type. This is another good sign for a working dog, such as a herder, because Capricorn animals enjoy this outlet for their energy.

Aquarius: The Independent Original

Aquarius owners tend to lead active, busy lives and need an animal who can either accompany them cheerfully or who won't make waves. Demanding or high-maintenance dogs are not for you. You might prefer unusual or oddball pets, such as dressed-up chihuahuas that travel in your tote bag or scene-stealing, rather shocking hairless cats. Or you will acquire a group of animals that can play with one another when you are pursuing outside activities. You can relate to the independence of cats.

Aquarius animals are not loners. They enjoy the companionship of humans or groups of other animals. They tend to be more independent and may require more training to follow the house rules.

Pisces: The Soul-Mate

This is the sign that can talk to the animals. Pisces owners enjoy deep communication with their pets, love having their animals accompany them, sleep with them, and show affection. Pisces will often rescue an animal in distress or adopt an animal from a shelter. Tropical fish are often recommended as a Pisces pet, and they seem to have a natural tranquilizing effect on this sign. However, Pisces may require an animal that shows more affection than do their fish friends.

Pisces animals are creative types; they can be sensually seductive and mysterious, mischievous and theatrical. They make fine house pets, do not usually like to roam far from their owners, and have winning personalities, especially with the adults in the home. Naturally sensitive and seldom vicious, they should be treated gently and given much praise and encouragement.

CHAPTER 13

Your Baby-scope: Children Born in 2007

Will the babies born this year be easy to raise or will they require a time-out mat or supernanny? Astrology answers these questions by looking beyond sun signs to the planets that describe a whole generation.

Children born this year will belong to one of the most spiritual generations in history. The three outer planets—Uranus, Neptune, and Pluto, which stay in a sign for at least seven years—are the ones that most affect each generation. Now passing through Pisces, Aquarius, and Sagittarius respectively, the three most visionary signs are sure to imprint the children of 2007.

In the past century, Uranus in Pisces coincided with enormous creativity, which should impact this year's children. Neptune in Aquarius and Pluto in Sagittarius are bringing a time of dissolving barriers, of globalization, of interest in religion and spirituality . . . breaking away from the materialism of the last century. In contrast, the members of this generation will truly be children of the world, searching for deeper meanings to existence.

Astrology can be an especially helpful tool that can be used to design an environment that will enhance and encourage each child's positive qualities. Some parents start before conception, planning the birth of their child as far as possible to harmonize with the signs of other family members. However, each baby has its own schedule, so if yours arrives a week early or late, or elects a different sign than you'd planned, recognize that the new sign may be more in line with the mission your child is here to accomplish. In other words, if you were hoping for a Libra child and he arrives during Virgo, that Virgo energy may be just what is needed to stimulate or complement your family. Remember that there are many astrological elements besides the sun sign that indicate strong family ties. Usually each child will share a particular planetary placement, an emphasis on a particular sign or house, or a certain chart configuration with his parents and other family members. Often there is a significant planetary angle that will define the parent-child relationship, such as family sun signs that form a T-square or a triangle.

One important thing you can do is to be sure the exact moment of birth is recorded. This will be essential in calculating an accurate astrological chart. The following descriptions can be applied to the sun or moon sign (if known) of a child—the sun sign will describe basic personality and the moon sign indicates the child's emotional needs.

The Aries Child

Baby Aries is quite a handful! This energetic child will walk—and run—as soon as possible and perform daring feats of exploration. Caregivers should be vigilant. Little Aries seems to know no fear (and is especially vulnerable to head injuries). Many Aries children, in their rush to get on with life, seem hyperactive and are easily frustrated when they can't get their own way. Violent temper tantrums and dramatic physical displays are par for the course with these children, necessitating a time-out chair.

The very young Aries should be monitored carefully, since he is prone to take risks and may injure himself. An Aries loves to take things apart and may break toys easily, but with encouragement, the child will develop formidable coordination. Aries's bossy tendencies should be molded into leadership qualities, rather than bullying. Otherwise, the me-first Aries will have many clashes with other strong-willed youngsters. Encourage these children to take out aggressions and frustrations in active, competitive sports, where they usually excel. When a young Aries learns to focus his energies long enough to master a subject and learns consideration for others, the indomitable Aries spirit will rise to the head of the class.

Aries born in 2007 will benefit from the jovial rays of Jupiter in Sagittarius until December of that year, which should give this child a sunny, optimistic personality.

The Taurus Child

This is a cuddly, affectionate child who eagerly explores the world of the senses, especially the senses of taste and touch. The Taurus child can be a big eater and will put on weight easily if not encouraged to exercise. Since this child likes comfort and gravitates to beauty, try coaxing little Taurus to exercise to music or take him outdoors for hikes or long walks. Though Taurus may be a slow learner, this sign has an excellent retentive memory and generally masters a subject thoroughly. Taurus is interested in results and will see each project patiently through to completion, continuing long after others have given up.

Choose Taurus toys carefully to help develop innate talents. Construction toys, such as blocks or erector sets, appeal to their love of building. Paints or crayons develop their sense of color. Many Taurus have musical talents and love to sing, which is apparent at a young age.

This year's Taurus will want a pet or two and a few plants of his own. Give little Taurus a minigarden and watch the natural green thumb develop. This child has a strong sense of acquisition and an early grasp of material value. After filling a piggy bank, Taurus graduates to a savings account, before other children have started to learn the value of money. Jupiter in their house of joint ventures this year should give Taurus another edge in financial matters.

The Gemini Child

Little Gemini will talk as soon as possible, filing the air with questions and chatter. This is a friendly child who enjoys social contact, seems to require company, and adapts quickly to different surroundings. Geminis have quick minds that easily grasp the use of words, books, and telephones and will probably learn to talk and read at an earlier age than most. Though they are fast learners, Gemini may have a short attention span, darting from subject to subject. Projects and games that help focus the mind could be used to help them concentrate. Musical instruments, typewriters, and computers help older Gemini children combine mental with manual dexterity. Geminis should be encouraged to finish what they start before they go on to another project. Otherwise, they can become jack-of-all-trade types who have trouble completing anything they do. Their dispositions are usually cheerful and witty, making these children popular with their peers and delightful company at home.

This year's Gemini baby should go to the head of the class. Uranus in Pisces could inspire Gemini to make an unusual career choice, perhaps in a high-tech field. When he grows up, this year's Gemini may change fields several times before he finds a job that satisfies his need for stimulation and variety.

The Cancer Child

This emotional, sensitive child is especially influenced by patterns set early in life. Young Cancers cling to their first memories as well as their childhood possessions. They thrive in calm emotional waters, with a loving, protective mother, and usually remain close to her (even if their relationship with her was difficult) throughout their lives. Divorce, death—anything that disturbs the safe family unit—are devastating to Cancers, who may need extra support and reassurance during a family crisis.

They sometimes need a firm hand to push the positive, creative side of their personality and discourage them from getting swept away by emotional moods or resorting to emotional manipulation to get their way. Praised and encouraged to find creative expression, Cancer will be able to express his positive side consistently on a firm, secure foundation.

This year's Cancer child should be more grounded and practical, thanks to Jupiter in Sagittarius. This also brings the blessing of good health!

The Leo Child

Leo children love the limelight and will plot to get the lion's share of attention. These children assert themselves with flair and drama and can behave like tiny tyrants to get their way. But in general, they have sunny, positive dispositions and are rarely subject to blue moods. At school, they're the ones who are voted most popular, head cheerleader, or homecoming queen. Leo is sure to be noticed for personality, if not for stunning looks or academic work; the homely Leo will be a class clown and the unhappy Leo may be the class bully.

Above all, a Leo child cannot tolerate being ignored for long. Drama or performing-arts classes, sports, and school politics are healthy ways for Leo to be a star. But Leos must learn to take lesser roles occasionally, or they will have some painful put-downs in store. Usually, the popularity of Leos is well earned; they are hard workers who try to measure up to their own high standards—and usually succeed.

The Leo baby born this year is likely to be more serious than the typical Leo, thanks to the taskmaster planet Saturn finishing up its two-year stay in Leo. This endows the child with self-discipline and the ability to function well in structured situations. With enhanced focusing ability, little Leo can be a high achiever.

The Virgo Child

The young Virgo can be a quiet, rather serious child, with a quick, intelligent mind. Early on, little Virgo shows far more attention to detail and concern with small things than other children do. Little Virgo has a built-in sense of order and a fascination with how things work. It is important for these children to have a place of their own, which they can order as they wish and where they can read or busy themselves with crafts and hobbies.

This child's personality can be very sensitive. Little Virgo may get hyper and overreact to seemingly small irritations, which can take the form of stomach upsets or delicate digestive systems. But this child will flourish where there is mental stimulation and a sense of order. Virgos thrive in school, especially in writing or language skills, and seem truly happy when buried in books. Chances are, young Virgo will learn to read ahead of classmates. Hobbies that involve detail work or that develop fine craftsmanship are especially suited to young Virgos.

Baby Virgo of 2007 is likely to be an especially active, intelligent child, since there are at least five planets in mutable signs during this period. With Saturn, also in Virgo beginning on September 2, he should respond to discipline. However, there should be plenty of mental and social stimulation in his environment to tame his restless nature.

The Libra Child

The Libra child learns early about the power of charm and appearance. This is often a very physically appealing child with an enchanting dimpled smile, who is naturally sociable and enjoys the company of both children and adults. It is a rare Libra child who is a discipline problem, but when their behavior is unacceptable, they respond better to calm discussion than displays of emotion, especially if the discussion revolves around fairness. Because young Libras without a strong direction tend to drift with the mood of the group, these children should be encouraged to develop their unique talents and powers of discrimination so they can later stand on their own.

In school, this child is usually popular and will often have to choose between social invitations and studies. In the teen years, social pressures mount as the young Libra begins to look for a partner. This is the sign of best friends, so Libra's choice of companions can have a strong effect on his future direction. Beautiful Libra girls may be tempted to go steady or have an unwise early marriage. Chances are, both sexes will fall in and out of love several times in their search for the ideal partner.

Little Libra of 2007 should have a way with words, thanks to Jupiter and Pluto in Sagittarius, which will enhance verbal and communications skills. This is an especially social, talkative child, who gets along well with siblings and classmates. Later in life, this Libra could choose a career in writing or the communication field.

The Scorpio Child

The Scorpio child may seem quiet and shy, but will surprise others with intense feelings and formidable willpower. Scorpio children are single-minded when they want something and intensely passionate about whatever they do. One of a caregiver's tasks is to teach this child to balance activities and emotions, yet at the same time to make the most of his or her great concentration and intense commitment.

Since young Scorpios do not show their depth of feelings easily, parents will have to learn to read almost imperceptible signs that troubles are brewing beneath the surface. Both Scorpio boys and girls enjoy games of power and control on or off the playground. Scorpio girls may take an early interest in the opposite sex, masquerading as tomboys, while Scorpio boys may be intensely competitive and loners. When their powerful energies are directed into work, sports, or challenging studies, Scorpio is a superachiever, focused on a goal. With trusted friends, young Scorpio is devoted and caring—the proverbial friend through thick and thin, loyal for life.

Jupiter and Pluto in Sagittarius should give this year's baby Scorpio a more carefree personality plus a flair for finance. There's lots of water in their horoscope, with Pisces and Cancer planets endowing these babies with plenty of imagination and creativity to be developed. Mars in Cancer will ignite a spirit of adventure and a love of water sports. Long journeys could be in the future.

The Sagittarius Child

This restless, athletic child will be out of the playpen and off on adventures as soon as possible. Little Sagittarius is remarkably well-coordinated, attempting daredevil feats on any wheeled vehicle from scooters to skateboards. These natural athletes need little encouragement to channel their energies into sports. Their cheerful, friendly dispositions earn them popularity in school, and once they have found a subject where their talent and imagination can soar, they will do well academically. They love animals, especially horses, and will be sure to have a pet or two, if not a home zoo. When they are old enough to take care of themselves, they'll clamor to be off on adventures of their own, away from home, if possible.

This child loves to travel, will not get homesick at summer camp, and may sign up to be a foreign-exchange student or spend summers abroad. Outdoor adventure appeals to little Sagittarius, especially if it involves an active sport, such as skiing, cycling, or mountain climbing. Give them enough space and encouragement, and their fiery spirit will propel them to achieve high goals.

Baby Sagittarius of 2007 is a freedom-loving child with a bonanza of luck and charisma, thanks to potent Pluto and lucky Jupiter in Sagittarius. This child has a natural generosity of spirit and an optimistic, expansive nature. He may need reality checks from time to time, since he may also be a big risk taker. He will also demand a great deal of freedom.

The Capricorn Child

These purposeful, goal-oriented children will work to capacity if they feel this will bring results. They're not ones who enjoy work for its own sake—there must be an end in sight. Authority figures can do much to motivate these children, but once set on an upward path, young Capricorns will mobilize energy and talent and work harder, and with more perseverance, then any other sign. Capricorn has built-in self-discipline that can achieve remarkable results, even if lacking the flashy personality, quick brain power, or penetrating insight of others. Once involved, young Capricorn will stick to a task until it is mastered. These children also know how to use others to their advantage and may well become team captains or class presidents.

A wise parent will set realistic goals for the Capricorn child, paving the way for the early thrill of achievement. Youngsters should be encouraged to express their caring, feeling side to others, as well as their natural aptitude for leadership. Capricorn children may be especially fond of grandparents and older relatives and will enjoy spending time with them and learning from them. It is not uncommon for young Capricorns to have an older mentor or teacher who guides them. With their great respect for authority, Capricorn children will take this influence very much to heart.

The Capricorn born in 2007 will have serious and responsible alliances, thanks to Saturn in the house of mutual ventures. This placement also hints at financial savvy—so give the child a savings account early on. Jupiter in Sagittarius promises a deep inner life and a generous nature.

The Aquarius Child

The Aquarius child has an innovative, well-focused mind that often streaks so far ahead of those of peers that this child seems like an oddball. Routine studies never hold the restless youngster for long; he will look for another, more experimental place to try out his ideas and develop his inventions. Life is a laboratory to the inquiring Aquarius mind. School politics, sports, science, and the arts offer scope for such talents. But if there is no room for expression within approved social limits, Aquarius is sure to rebel. Questioning institutions and religions comes naturally, so these children may find an outlet elsewhere, becoming rebels with a cause. It is better not to force this child to conform, but rather to channel forward-thinking young minds into constructive group activities.

This year's Aquarius will have far-out glamour as well as

charisma, thanks to his ruler, Uranus, in a friendly bond with Neptune. This child could be a rock star, a statesman, or a scientist.

The Pisces Child

Give young Pisces praise, applause, and a gentle, but firm, push in the right direction. Lovable Pisces children may be abundantly talented, but may be hesitant to express themselves, because they are quite sensitive and easily hurt. It is a parent's challenge to help them gain self-esteem and self-confidence. However, this same sensitivity makes them trusted friends who'll have many confidants as they develop socially. It also endows many Pisces with spectacular creative talent.

Pisces adores drama and theatrics of all sorts; therefore, encourage them to channel their creativity into art forms rather than indulging in emotional dramas. Understand that they may need more solitude than other children, as they develop their creative ideas. But though daydreaming can be creative, it is important that these natural dreamers not dwell too long in the world of fantasy. Teach them practical coping skills for the real world. Since Pisces are physically sensitive, parents should help them build strong bodies with proper diet and regular exercise. Young Pisces may gravitate to more individual sports, such as swimming, sailing, and skiing, rather than to team sports. Or they may prefer more artistic physical activities like dance or ice skating.

Born givers, these children are often drawn to the underdog (they fall quickly for sob stories) and attract those who might take advantage of their emphatic nature. Teach them to choose friends wisely and to set boundaries in relationships, to protect their emotional vulnerability—invaluable lessons in later life.

With the planet Uranus now in Pisces, the 2007 baby belongs to a generation of Pisces movers and shakers. This child may have a rebellious streak that rattles the status quo. But this generation also has a visionary nature, which will be much concerned with the welfare of the world at large.

CHAPTER 14

Is This the Right Time to Fall in Love?

Astrology gives you a power tool for discovering why you are attracted to a certain person and how that person might act or react toward you. It also gives you the times when you are at your most attractive to the opposite sex. Although astrology can't guarantee that you'll have a problem-free relationship, it can give you a romantic timetable and road map to guide you over the rough spots and reveal what you might expect in the future with your partner, after the initial glow has given way to day-to-day reality. Working in your favor is the fact that no one totally embodies any one sign; we're a combination of all the signs in different proportions. So there will always be some naturally compatible (as well as incompatible) aspects between two people's charts.

The Right Time to Reunite with an Old Lover or Reignite Passion in Your Current Relationship

An old love might resurface in your life when the planet Mercury, which rules communications, is in retrograde motion, about three times each year. (Check this information in chapter 2.) This planet often brings back people from the past, as well as old issues that should be resolved. It's an ideal time to troubleshoot existing relationships in which passion has cooled and to take action to reignite the flame of love. Heart-to-heart talks about what went wrong could help you understand each other better. Retrograde Venus is another good time to set a relationship back on course; it happens briefly in Virgo this year, from July 27 until September 8, when it turns direct in Leo. Those especially affected will have the sun or moon in Leo or Virgo. It is not a good idea to begin a new romantic relationship when either Venus or Mercury is retrograding.

Take a Chance on Love

Jupiter, the planet of risk, is in the risk-taking sign Sagittarius, which it rules this year. This could inspire fire signs (Aries, Leo, Sagittarius), in particular, to take a chance on love, perhaps choosing someone from a distant land or different culture. The mood of love is adventurous, exciting, daring, flirtatious. You could be swept off your feet, but this is not necessarily a time for long-term monogamous relationships. Jupiter encourages exploration in all areas!

Make the First Move

Venus is the planet that makes others respond favorably to you. When it's in your sun sign or a favorable sign, you have a terrific opportunity to attract the opposite sex, so turn on the charm. Ideally both the sun and Venus in your sun sign make you catnip to others.

Go Out and Meet Someone New

New activities of all kinds are favored during the new moon, especially if it's the new moon in your sun sign (or a sign in the same or complementary element). You'll also want a favorable Mercury (not retrograde) to give you the right words and a good Venus so that hot new prospect gets your message.

When to Break Up

Breaking up may be easier to do during a waning moon, in the last quarter, when we're gearing up for a new cycle. However, some planetary aspects such as eclipses could force emotional issues out into the open and thus cause a breakup. As Mars transits your sun sign, you may become impatient with long-standing irritations in a relationship and be tempted to move on. Check the Mars tables after chapter 6 and the new and full moon list in chapter 2.

Is This Person the Right One?

Here's a three-step technique for determining if your lover is the right one for a lasting relationship.

How to Predict Your Romantic Success

Consider the other planets in your lover's chart, not just the sun sign (you can look up most of them using the charts in this book). Venus will tell what attracts you both. Mars reveals your temper and sex drive, Mercury how you'll communicate, and the moon your emotional nature. (For the moon and Mercury signs, consult one of the free charts available on the Internet. See chapter 10.)

Step One: Size Up the Overall Relationship

To do an instant take on your relationship, compare the elements of the sun, moon, Mercury, Mars, and Venus—each a key planet in compatibility, in both charts. The interaction of elements (earth, air, fire, water) is the fastest way to size up a relationship. Planets of the same element will have the smoothest chemistry.

Earth element: Taurus Virgo, Capricorn
Air element: Gemini, Libra, Aquarius

Fire element: Aries, Leo, Sagittarius
Water element: Cancer, Scorpio, Pisces

When your partner has the same planet in the same element as your planet in question, the energy will flow freely. Complementary elements (fire signs with air signs or earth signs with water signs) also get along easily.

What if many planets are in other combinations? That's where you'll probably have to work at the relationship. There is tension and possible combustion between fire and water signs or earth and air signs. Take the analogies literally. Fire brings water to a boil; earth and air create a dust storm or tornado. If both your Venus signs are clashing, you will probably have very different tastes, something that could adversely affect a long-term relationship. However, challenges can be stimulating as well, adding spice to a relationship, especially when planets of sexual attraction—Mars relating to Venus—are involved.

Step Two: Find Out How the Individual Planets Relate

Find out and compare how each planet operates in both your horoscopes (sun, moon, Mercury, Venus, and Mars) by comparing its quality or mode. Planets in cardinal signs are active, assertive; planets in fixed signs are tenacious, stubborn; planets in mutable signs are adaptable, easily changeable. Two planets of the same quality (but different signs) do not easily relate—there is usually a conflict of interests—but they can challenge each other to be more flexible or they can open up new areas in each other's lives. This is where you have to make compromises to reconcile different points of view. You'll have to be flexible or give in often.

Cardinal signs (active): Aries, Cancer, Libra, Capricorn
Fixed signs (static): Taurus, Leo, Scorpio, Aquarius
Mutable signs (changeable): Gemini, Virgo, Pisces, Sagittarius

Step Three: Rate Your Overall Compatibility

The planets closest to the earth (sun, moon, Mercury, Mars, Venus) are those most likely to affect close relationships. Where possible, look up your planets and those of your partner in this book and grade them as follows. (The more A's and B's, the better! Y's and Z's indicate where you'll have to compromise to work things out.)

Grade A: for the same element (earth, air, fire, water)
Grade B: for complementary elements (air with fire, earth with water)
Grade Y: for challenging elements (air with water, earth with fire)
Grade Z: for the same quality, but different signs

By now, you should have a good idea where your relationship stands astrologically. A further check of the individual planets can answer some all-important questions.

Here's what the individual planets in your charts can reveal about your relationship:

Are you basically attracted? Compare sun signs.

The sun sign gives the big picture. Though it is not the whole story, and can be modified by other factors, the sun sign will always have an overall effect.

Are you emotionally compatible? Check your moon signs.

Emotional compatibility is strong enough to offset many other stressful factors in your horoscopes. Compare moon and sun signs too. There is an especially strong bond if your partner's moon is in your sun sign or vice versa.

How well do you communicate? Check Mercury.

Mercury in the same quality (cardinal, fixed, or mutable) could give you mental stimulation or irritation. Mercury in the same sign or element could be a meeting of minds.

Do you have similar tastes? Check Venus.

An incompatible Venus relationship can be very difficult over the long run, if other factors do not balance this out, because it has so much to do with the kind of atmosphere that makes you happy. One of you likes modern; the other likes traditional. One of you has an elegant style; the other is casual. It can be difficult to find the middle ground where you both win. Sometimes you just don't want to compromise that much.

Sexually sizzling or fizzling? Check Mars.

It is also useful to compare both Mars and Venus signs. Mars and Venus in the same sign or element is strong chemistry. Your partner's Mars or Venus in your sun sign is another big plus. Sometimes if Mars and Venus are in different modes, it can add sizzle to the relationship.

Will your partner be faithful?

Some sun signs tend to more monogamous than others. Fixed signs like a steady relationship and tend not to have multiple lovers. However, if a person with a fixed sign is unhappy, he will tend to have lovers on the side. The chief culprit here is Leo, which needs to be treated like royalty or else it will exercise royal rights elsewhere. Mutable signs tend to be the least monogamous. Gemini, Sagittarius, and Pisces are difficult to tie down and more difficult to hold. Sharing common interests and providing a stable home base can be a big help here, especially with Gemini.

Where can you meet the sign of your dreams?

If you have a sun sign in mind, here are places where they are likely to be (and like to go):

Aries: Try a sports event, martial arts display, action movie, cooking school, adventure sports vacation, the trendy new hot spot in town, the jogging or bike path.

Taurus: Meet them at a gourmet restaurant, auction house, farm or place where there are animals, flower show, garden shop, art classes, stores—especially food or jewelry stores.

Gemini: Meet them working for a newspaper or radio station, at parties or social events, writing courses, lectures, watering holes where there's good talk.

Cancer: Family dinners, boating or boat shows, cruises, on the beach, at seafood dinners, fishing, cooking schools, gourmet food stores, photography classes, art exhibits.

Leo: Big parties, country clubs, golfing, tanning salons, acting classes, theatrical events, movies, dancing, nightclubs, fine department stores, classy restaurants, VIP lounges at the airport, first-class hotels and travel.

Virgo: Craft stores, craft shows, flea markets, adult education courses, your local college, libraries, book stores, health food stores, doctors' offices, your local hospital or medical centers, health lectures, concerts, fine art events.

Libra: Art shows, fine restaurants, shopping centers, tennis matches, social events, parties and entertainment, the most fashionable stores, exhibits of beautiful objects, antique shows, decorating centers, ballet and the theater.

Scorpio: In banks, tax-preparation offices, police stations, sports events, motorcycle rallies, at the beach or swimming pool, doing water sports, at the gym, at action movies or mysteries, psychic fairs, ghostbusting.

Sagittarius: At a comedy club or laugh-a-minute film, at horse races or horse shows, pet stores or animal breeders, walking your dog, taking night courses at your local college, at a political debate, traveling to an exotic place, at a car show, mountain climbing, jogging, skiing, discussion group.

Capricorn: At a country music show, decorator show house, investment seminar, prestigious country club, exclusive resort, mountain climbing, party for a worthy cause, self-improvement course.

Aquarius: At a political rally, sci-fi convention, restaurant off the beaten path, union meeting, working for a worthy cause, campaigning for your candidate, fund-raising, flying lessons or airport.

Pisces: At any waterside place, at the theater or acting class, arts class, dancing, ballet, swimming pool, seafood restaurant, psychic event, church or other spiritual gathering, visiting at a hospital, at your local watering hole.

For your sun sign's compatibility with every other sign, see chapter 21.

How to Keep Your Relationship Sizzling

The Aries Lover

To keep your Aries mate red-hot, be sure to maintain your own energy level. This is one sign that shows little sympathy for aches, pains, and physical complaints. Curb any tendency toward self-pity—whining is one sure Aries turnoff (water signs take note). This is an open, direct sign. Don't expect your lover to probe your innermost needs. Intense psychological discussions that would thrill a Cancer or Scorpio only make Aries restless. Aries is not the stay-at-home type. This sign is sure to have plenty of activities going on at once. Share them (or they'll find someone else who will)!

Always be a bit of a challenge to your Aries mate—this sign loves the chase almost as much as the conquest. So don't be too easy or accommodating—let them feel a sense of accomplishment when they've won your heart.

Stay up-to-date in your interests and appearance. You

can wear the latest style off the fashion show runway with an Aries, especially if it's bright red. Aries is a pioneer, an adventurer, always ahead of the pack. Play up your frontier spirit. Present the image of the two of you as an unbeatable team that can conquer the world, and you'll keep this courageous sign at your side.

Since they tend to idealize their lovers, Aries partners are especially disillusioned when their mates flirt. So tone down your roving eye to make sure they always feel like number one in your life.

The Taurus Lover

Taurus is an extremely sensual, affectionate, nurturing lover, but can be quite possessive. Taurus likes to own you. Don't hold back with them or play power games. If you need more space in the relationship, be sure to set clear boundaries, letting them know exactly where they stand. When ambiguity in a relationship makes Taurus uneasy, they may go searching for someone more solid and substantial. A Taurus romance works best where the limits are clearly spelled out.

Taurus needs physical demonstrations of affection—don't hold back on hugs. Together you should create an atmosphere of comfort, good food, and beautiful surroundings. In fact, Taurus is often seduced by surface physical beauty alone. Their five senses are highly susceptible, so find ways to appeal to all of them! Your home should be a restful haven from the outside world. Get a great sound system and some comfortable furniture to sink into and keep the refrigerator stocked with treats. Most Taurus would rather entertain on their own turf than gad about town, so it helps if you're a good host or hostess.

Taurus likes a calm, contented, committed relationship. This is not a sign to trifle with. Don't flirt or tease if you want to please. Don't rock the boat or try to make this sign jealous. Instead, create a steady, secure environment with lots of shared pleasures.

The Gemini Lover

Keeping Gemini faithful is like walking a tightrope. This sign needs stability and a strong home base to accomplish their goals. But they also require a great deal of personal freedom.

A great role model is Barbara Bush, a Gemini married to another Gemini. This is a sign that loves to communicate. Sit down and talk things over. Don't interfere: Be interested in your partner's doings, but have a life of your own and ideas to contribute. Since this is a social sign, don't insist on quiet nights at home when your Gemini is in a party mood.

Gemini needs plenty of rope but a steady hand. Focus on common goals and abstract ideals. Gemini likes to share—be a twin soul and do things together. Keep up on their latest interests. Stay in touch mentally and physically. Use both your mind and your hands to communicate.

Variety is the spice of life to this flirtatious sign. Guard against jealousy—it is rarely justified. Provide a stimulating sex life—this is a very experimental sign—to keep them interested. Be a bit unpredictable. Don't let lovemaking become a routine. Most of all, sharing lots of laughs can make Gemini take your relationship very seriously.

The Cancer Lover

This is probably the water sign that requires the most TLC. Cancers tend to be very private people who may take time to open up. They are extremely self-protective and will rarely tell you what is truly bothering them. They operate indirectly, like the movements of the crab. You may have to divine problems by following subtle clues. Draw them out gently and try to voice any criticism in the most tactful, supportive way possible.

Family ties are especially strong for Cancer. They will rarely break a strong family bond. Create an intimate family atmosphere, with an emphasis on food and family get-togethers. You can get valuable clues to Cancer appeal from their mothers and their family situation. Whatever you do, don't compete with a mother! Get her to teach you the favorite family recipes; take her out to dinner. If your lover's early life was unhappy, it's important that Cancer feels there is a close family with you.

Encouraging creativity can counter Cancer's moodiness,

which is also a sure sign of emotional insecurity. Find ways to distract them from negative moods. Calm them with a good meal or a trip to the seashore. Cancers are usually quite nostalgic and attached to the past. So be careful not to throw out their old treasures or photos.

The Leo Lover

Whether the Leo is a sunny, upbeat partner or reveals cat-like claws could depend on how you handle the royal Leo pride. A relationship is for two people—a fact that ego-centered Leo can forget. You must gently remind them. Appearances are important to Leo, so try to always look your best.

Leo thinks big—so don't you be petty or miserly—and likes to live like a king. Remember special occasions with a beautifully wrapped gift or flowers. Make an extra effort to treat them royally. Keep a sense of fun and playfulness and loudly applaud Leo's creative efforts. React, respond, and be a good audience! If Leo's ignored, this sign will seek a more appreciative audience fast! Cheating Leos are almost always looking for an ego boost.

Be generous with compliments. You can't possibly overdo here. Always accentuate the positive. Make them feel important by asking for advice and consulting them often. Leo enjoys a charming sociable companion, but be sure to make them the center of attention in your life. If you have a demanding job or outside schedule, make a point to pull out all the stops once in a while, to create special events that keep romance alive.

The Virgo Lover

Virgo may seem cool and conservative on the surface, but underneath, you'll find a sensual romantic. Think of Raquel Welch, Sophia Loren, Jacqueline Bisset, and Garbo! It's amazing how seductive this practical sign can be!

They are idealists, however, looking for someone who meets their high standards. If you've measured up, they'll do anything to serve and please you. Virgos love to feel needed, so give them a job to do in your life. They are great fixer-uppers. Take their criticism as a form of love and caring, of noticing what you do. Bring them out socially—they're often very shy. Calm their nerves with good food, a healthy environment, and trips to the country.

Mental stimulation is a turn-on to this Mercury-ruled sign. An intellectual discussion could lead to romantic action, so stay on your toes and keep well-informed. This sign often mixes business with pleasure, so it helps if you share the same professional interests—you'll get to see more of your busy mate. With Virgo, the couple who works as well as plays together stays together.

The Libra Lover

Libra enjoys life with a mate and needs the harmony of a steady relationship. Outside affairs can throw them off balance. However, members of this sign are natural charmers who love to surround themselves with admirers, and this can cause a very possessive partner to feel insecure. Most of the time, Libras, who love to be the belles of the ball, are only testing their allure with harmless flirtations and will rarely follow through, unless they are not getting enough attention or there is an unattractive atmosphere at home.

Mental compatibility is what keeps Libra in tune. Unfortunately this sign, like Taurus, often falls for physical beauty or someone who provides an elegant lifestyle, rather than someone who shares their ideals and activities, which is the kind of sharing that will keep you together in the long run.

Do not underestimate Libra's need for beauty and harmony. To keep them happy, avoid scenes. Opt for calm, impersonal discussion of problems (or a well-reasoned debate) over an elegant dinner. Pay attention to the niceties of life. Send little gifts on Valentine's Day and don't forget birthdays and anniversaries. Play up the romance to the hilt—with all the lovely gestures and trimmings—but tone down intensity and emotional drama (Aries and Scorpio take note). Libra needs to be surrounded by a physically tasteful atmosphere—elegant, well-designed furnishings, calm colors, good manners, and good grooming at all times.

The Scorpio Lover

Scorpios are often deceptively cool and remote on the outside, but don't be fooled. This sign always has a hidden agenda and feels very intense about most things. The disguise is necessary because Scorpio does not trust easily; but when they do, they are devoted and loyal. You can lean on this very focused sign. The secret is in first establishing that basic trust through mutual honesty and respect.

Scorpio is fascinated by power and control in all its forms. They don't like to compromise—it's all or nothing. Therefore they don't trust or respect anything that comes too easily. Be a bit of a challenge and keep them guessing. Maintain your own personal identity, in spite of Scorpio's desire to probe your innermost secrets.

Sex is especially important to those under this sign. They will demand fidelity from you though they may not plan to deliver it themselves, so communication on this level is critical. Explore Scorpio's fantasies together. Scorpio is a detective—watch your own flirtations—don't play with fire. This is a jealous and vengeful sign, so you'll live to regret it. Scorpios rarely flirt for the fun of it themselves. There is usually a strong motive behind their actions.

Scorpio has a fascination with the dark, mysterious side of life. If unhappy, they are capable of carrying on a secret affair. So try to emphasize the positive, constructive side of life with them. Don't fret if they need time alone to sort out problems. They may also prefer time alone with you to socializing with others, so plan romantic getaways together to a private beach or a secluded wilderness spot.

The Sagittarius Lover

Be a mental and spiritual traveling companion. Sagittarius is a footloose adventurer whose ideas know no boundaries. So don't try to fence them in! Sagittarius resents restrictions of any kind. For a long relationship, be sure you are in harmony with their ideals and spiritual beliefs. They like to feel that their lives are constantly being elevated and taken to a higher level. Since down-to-earth matters often get put aside by Sagittarius schemes of things, get finances under control (money matters upset more relationships with Sagittarius than any other problems), but try to avoid becoming the stern disciplinarian in this relationship (find a good accountant to do this chore).

Sagittarius is not generally a homebody (unless there are several homes). Be ready and willing to take off on the spur of the moment, or they'll go without you. Sports, outdoor activities, and physical fitness are important. Stay in shape with some of Sagittarius Jane Fonda's tapes. Dress with flair and style. It helps if you look especially good in sportswear. Sagittarius men like beautiful legs, so play up yours. And this is one of the great animal lovers, so try to get along with the dog, cat, or horse.

The Capricorn Lover

These people are ambitious, even if they are the stay-at-home partner in your relationship. They will be extremely active, have a strong sense of responsibility to their partner, and take commitments seriously. However, they might look elsewhere if the relationship becomes too dutiful. They also need romance, fun, lightness, humor, and adventure!

Generation gaps are not unusual in Capricorn romances, where the older Capricorn partner works hard all through life and seeks pleasurable rewards with a young partner, or the young Capricorn gets a taste of luxury and instant status from an older lover. This is one sign that grows more interested in romance with age! Younger Capricorns often tend to put business way ahead of pleasure.

Capricorn is impressed by those who entertain well, have class, and can advance their status in life. Keep improving yourself and cultivate important people. Stay on the conservative side. Extravagant or frivolous loves don't last. Capricorn keeps an eye on the bottom line. Even the wildest Capricorns, such as Elvis Presley, Rod Stewart, and David Bowie, show a conservative streak in their personal lives. It's also important to demonstrate a strong sense of loyalty to your family, especially to older members. This reassures Capricorn, who'll be happy to grow old along with you!

The Aquarius Lover

Aquarius is one of the most independent, least domestic signs. Finding time alone with this sign may be one of your greatest challenges. The are everybody's buddy, usually surrounded by people they collect, some of whom may be old lovers. However, it is unlikely that old passions will be rekindled if you become their best friend as well as lover, and if you get actively involved in other important aspects of their lives, such as the political or charitable causes they believe in.

Aquarius needs a supportive backup person who encourages them, but is not overpossessive when their natural charisma attracts admirers by the dozen. Take a leaf from Joanne Woodward, whose marriage to perennial Aquarius heartthrob Paul Newman has lasted more than thirty years. Encourage them to develop their original ideas. Don't rain on their parade if they decide suddenly to market their spaghetti sauce and donate the proceeds to their favorite charity, or drive racing cars. Share their goals and be their fan, or you'll never see them otherwise.

You may be called on to give them grounding where needed. Aquarius needs someone who can keep track of their projects. But always remember, it's basic friendship—with the tolerance and common ideals that implies—that will hold you together.

The Pisces Lover

To keep a Pisces hooked, don't hold the string too tight! This is a sensitive, creative sign that may appear to need someone to manage life or point the direction out of their Neptune fog; but if you fall into that role, expect your Pisces to rebel against any strong-arm tactics. Pisces is more susceptible to a play for sympathy than a play for power. They are suckers for a sob story, the most empathetic sign of the zodiac. More than one Pisces has been seduced and held by someone who plays the underdog role.

They are great fantasists and extremely creative lovers, so use your imagination to add drama and spice to your time together. You can let your fantasies run wild with this sign, and they'll go you one better! They enjoy variety in lovemaking, so try never to let it become routine.

Long-term relationships work best if you can bring Pisces down to earth and, at the same time, encourage their creative fantasies. Deter them from escapism into alcohol or substance abuse by helping them to get counseling, if needed. Pisces will stay with the lover who gives positive energy, self-confidence, and a safe harbor from the storms of life, as well as one who is a soul mate.

CHAPTER 15

Is There Prosperity in Your Future?

There are big changes in the stars ahead, so projecting astrologically a few years down the line could point your career and investments in the most profitable direction.

For long-term trends, look to the outer planets, which cause major changes as they move into a different sign. Soon there will be a shift in the atmosphere as Pluto, the planet of transformation, moves into Capricorn in 2008 until 2024. (You'll notice a different kind of energy starting a few months in advance.) What's more, Jupiter, the planet of luck and expansion, also moves through Capricorn during 2008, accelerating changes and bringing luck to Capricorn, so expect many of that sign to surge into prominence. Bet on the sea goat (Capricorn's symbol) and areas associated with it. Capricorns should prepare to move into the limelight. ("It's about time," you Capricorns may well say!)

If you're headed for the fast track, set your sights on Capricorn fields, which will be going through radical changes. This will affect Capricorn-associated corporations, big business, government, institutions of all kinds, mining, land speculation, property owners and dealers, builders and building trades, contractors and engineers, civil service, providers of status products. Capricorn-influenced fields are known for function, structure, discipline, and order, so consider careers that have these qualities or can provide them to others.

Everyone Old Is New

Want to cash in on a much-neglected market? Services and care for the aging should be booming with career opportunities, thanks to our elder population explosion. Remember that the generation now entering the aging population was born with Pluto in Leo; it's the rock-and-roll generation, who will resist the idea of aging and retirement as long as possible.

This particular elder population will be highly visible and financially viable. They are big spenders who will be remaining much longer in the workforce. Those who do retire may begin second careers, so the workplace will be rethinking its relationship to grandmas and grandpas and changing to accommodate them. Since America has been a youth-oriented culture, expect a major transformation in advertising, retailing, fashion, housing, and health care.

Since the Pluto in Leo generation is one of the most image-conscious ever, anything that keeps these folks looking and feeling great is sure to succeed. Don't expect your grandma and grandpa to hang around the house. This is a curious, adventurous generation that will welcome opportunities to explore the globe that are especially tailored to their age group and interests.

Cater to Horatio Alger

Capricorn is the Horatio Alger sign of rising through one's own volition and ambition. Self-improvement courses will be booming as we search for more fulfilling careers and try to keep up with new technology.

Do you enjoy helping others fulfill their potential? Career coaching—in fact, coaching in all aspects of life—is a hot field. In the corporate area, human resources is a much-touted area of job growth. You'll need skills in training and in helping other people find jobs. Get involved with helping people adapt to the times and retrain themselves for new careers. Leos, Sagittarius, Virgos, and Aquarius make excellent trainers and teachers. Aries are the supermotivators.

Education, especially high education, will be in for a whole new approach, as gray-haired students decide to complete their educations or simply enjoy expanding their knowledge. College towns will become hot retirement destinations, which provide intellectual stimulation plus an elder-compatible atmosphere.

The demand for teachers will increase and provide a steady stream of jobs. Look into special education, private education of all kinds, and unusual approaches to teaching. The natural teaching signs—Virgo, Leo, Sagittarius, and Aquarius—are winners here.

Since the world has become a smaller place and the trend toward international involvement escalates, demand for language skills also increases. Americans may need to speak several languages including some once considered exotic for the average American, such as Chinese or Arabic. Language teachers, translators, and linguists, especially those with a Gemini emphasis in their charts, should find many opportunities.

Waste Not, Want Not

Capricorn is an intensely practical sign that dislikes waste of any kind, so consider careers in recycling and waste management, antiques, renovation, preserving old buildings, land conservation, and teaching history.

Environment-related careers are hot options, since there will be so much cleaning up of toxic wastes, rebuilding after cataclysmic natural events, and redesigning of equipment. Engineers, attorneys, designers, bankers, and researchers should slant their career search in this direction. Taurus, Scorpio, Libra, Pisces, and Aquarius could make their fortune here.

Keep Treasured Traditions Alive

It looks like a conservative time, when people will be concerned with traditional values. Hospitality businesses can capitalize on this trend by promoting the beloved holidays of all cultures, reviving the old customs and memories. Holiday vacations for the whole family to share, reunions, and celebrations could revitalize the resort and cruise business. Tourism that caters to the needs of the aging, but still adventurous, traveler should thrive.

Head for the Hills

If you're thinking about a change of scene, consider relocating to a Capricorn-influenced place, which should have growth potential now. If you're adventurous, head for Central Europe, especially mountainous regions. The Balkans, Bosnia, Bulgaria, Lithuania, Macedonia, and Albania are Capricorn places. India, Belgium, Hesse and Constance in Germany, Mexico, and New Zealand are also on the Capricorn wavelength.

Health Care for the Antiaging Population

Have you considered the health-care field? Careers in medical services are among the hottest prospects as the nation begins to reform its health-care systems. Physical therapists, nurses, physicians' assistants, and pharmacists, as well as health services administrators, will all be in demand to service the aging population. If you have strong Virgo, Scorpio, or Capricorn placements, which give you a flair for the health field and excellent organizational skills, you should consider this area. Compassionate signs such as Pisces and Cancer make excellent health caregivers.

Consider the Capricorn fields of knee surgery and therapy, bone and joint diseases, chiropractic care, dermatology. New techniques in self-enhancement, such as plastic surgery, dental work, and hair replacement, should also do well for this aging generation who'd love to look and feel forever young.

Therapists specializing in treatment of disabling conditions, optometrists, nursing home operators and managers, and home care for the aged should be thriving.

The Talent Finder

Designers and manufacturers of clothing, furniture and equipment suited to the over-sixty consumer should also do well. Look into this area if you have planets in Capricorn (ruler of old age), Pisces (creativity, compassion), Taurus and Cancer (associated with the home environment and of nurturing), and Aries (pioneering ventures).

Do you thrive on life in the fast lane? Sports and special events are high-visibility careers where salesmanship and flair count, so they're especially suited to fire signs Aries, Leo, and Sagittarius. Good communicators like Gemini and Libra do well in public relations in this market.

Capricorn-favored sports require great discipline and endurance and are luckiest when they take place in the mountains. Rock and mountain climbing, hiking, and skiing are specially favored.

There will be a continuing boom in fitness careers, with the emphasis on well-run health clubs, personal attention, and social atmosphere. As the population ages, there will be more emphasis on weight training and rehabilitation aimed at elder bodies. Virgos, Sagittarius, Leos, and Aries are specially suited to the high-energy demands of this field, while Libras, Geminis, and Pisces provide good communication, diplomacy, and compassion.

We'll be eating more consciously as America slims down (Capricorn is the sign of discipline). Diet-specific restaurants, vegetarian restaurants, diet consultants, and organic food farmers and gardeners should be expanding. We'll be especially concerned with the quality of our meat and seafood. This is a fertile area for Taurus, Virgo, Cancer, Pisces, and Leos with skills in working with agriculture, diet counseling, cooking, restaurant management, organizing farmers' markets, and managing health food stores.

High-Tech Options

Though computer fields should continue to grow, the outsourcing of high-tech service jobs is also likely to continue. The good news is that there will still be a need for software designers, trainers, salespersons, and local repair staff, as computers have become an integral part of our lives. Aquarians are natural in all areas of computer work. Sagittarius and Geminis do well in teaching and sales, while

Capricorns excel in organization, Pisces in creative software design, and Cancers in applying high tech to industry.

Video-related careers can only get bigger in 2010 as Neptune, ruler of film, moves into Pisces, its strongest position. Video stores, cameras, and viewing equipment, new uses of video for education and entertainment, technical experts in production and performing—all should be booming. Pisces, Leo, Sagittarius, and Gemini should find plenty of opportunities in performance, sales, and marketing.

Take these tips from the stars and do your career planning with the planets!

CHAPTER 16

Heath and Diet Makeovers from the Stars

Health spas, fitness resorts, gyms, yoga studios, and sports complexes are multiplying around the country. Vitamin stores and juice bars are opening up in malls. We're buying shelves of diet books. Yet we're still one of the fattest nations on the planet! This year, the stars say we'll have more discipline to make over our bad eating habits and resolve to become as healthy as possible. Astrology can clue you in to the tendencies that contribute to good or ill health (especially when it comes to controlling your appetite). Finding the right diet and health program and having the patience to stick with them over time could be your big challenge this year. So follow these sun-sign tips on how best to lose those extra pounds and make this your healthiest year ever.

Aries Tips: Avoid the Quick Fix

Thanks to your hyperactive Mars-ruled lifestyle, you're sometimes too busy to bother with healthy meals in a calm atmosphere. You're more likely to grab carbohydrate-laden, calorie-packed fast foods for instant energy on the run. You need a regimen that gives you sustained energy, rather than a quick fix or a caffeine-fueled jump start. Aim for frequent small meals and carry healthy snacks with you to recharge your batteries. Protein and fruit smoothies in the morning might provide you with a quick, healthy head start to the day.

Aries is associated with the head, your most vulnerable area, which you should be especially careful to protect by wearing the appropriate headgear during risky activities and sports. Headaches warn you to slow down and take it easy for a while. If you've been stocking up on headache remedies, it might be time to consult a nutritionist for expert dietary advice.

Superbusy, impatient Aries tends to overschedule and stress out when others don't, won't, or can't keep up to your pace. Sports to the rescue! Swatting a ball, cheering on your favorite team, training for a marathon, or just running around the block can be the best remedies for whatever ails an Aries. Sports allow you to let off steam in an atmosphere of excitement and competition where you can feel the joy of winning. Your daring moves and Mars-powered energy should earn you a stellar spot on any team. If you're older, volunteer to coach local youngsters.

Martial arts of any kind appeal to your love of action. The slower, more flowing forms, such as tai chi, can be done throughout life. You don't have to be Jackie Chan or Russell Crowe to show your Aries flair for action heroics. Try racket sports (any sport that involves hitting or working with a swordlike object), fencing, tap dancing, or aerobics if martial arts don't give you a kick. However, remember to take time to check your equipment, warm up, and wait until you're properly conditioned before you jump to expert-level challenges.

Once you've found a sport you love, try not to push yourself too hard. Listen to your body when it tells you it's time to quit (never easy for Aries). Finally, know the difference between well-exercised, fatigued muscles and the pain that signals trouble.

Taurus Tips: Downsize Portions

Taurus loves all kinds of food in large quantities—especially rich, creamy desserts and fried goodies. (Once you start eating rich food, you find it almost impossible to stop.) Deprivation in any form is not going to work for you, so find a diet that allows you healthy variations of the foods you love most. Aim for smaller portions and fill up on skinny foods like salads. First, raid your refrigerator and eliminate any foods that are not on your diet. If it's there, you'll find it and eat it. The techniques for weight loss in Cher's diet books might inspire you.

Pleasure is the key to your exercise routine. You need an attractive place to work out, not a sweaty gym. Why not plan your workout to take place in one of the scenic areas of your town? Jogging or biking along a river or through a park, exploring the woodlands and seashore in your area with long nature hikes, or horseback riding along a scenic trail can make you look forward to exercising. Or plant an extensive garden that requires lots of active maintenance. If you live in an appropriate setting, get a dog that requires lots of exercise. Working with animals can also be a joy for Taurus.

Pay special attention to the Taurus area of the body: the neck. Yoga exercises, head rolls, the proper pillow, and a good masseur can make a big difference here. Though Taurus is a hardy sign with great stamina and endurance, you can become sluggish if you're overweight or if you have a thyroid problem. So, if you can barely drag yourself off the couch, be sure to check your thyroid. If you're not getting enough sleep, it could be due to tension in your neck. Try changing your pillow to one specially designed to support your neck.

Massage is one way to soothe the raging bull in you, especially if tension is lodging in your neck. Try shiatsu massage targeted to the acupressure points in the neck area. Neck massages are a sybaritic way to release tension and promote restful sleep.

Gemini Tips: Make a Game of It

Gemini is an on-the-go sign that does not usually have a weight problem, as long as you keep moving. If life circumstances force you to be sedentary, however, you may eat out of boredom and watch the pounds pile on. Your active social life can also sabotage your weight with sumptuous party buffets and restaurant meals where you have to sample everything. Your challenge is to find a healthy eating system with enough variety so you won't get bored. Develop a strategy for eating out—at parties or restaurants—and fill up the buffet plates with salad or veggies before you sample the desserts. Sociable Geminis on a diet can benefit from group support in a system like Weight Watchers. Find a diet twin who'll support you and have fun losing weight together.

Gemini is associated with the nervous system, our body's lines of communications. If your nerves are on edge, you may be trying to do too many things at once, leaving no time for fun and laughter. When you overload your circuits, it's time to get together with friends and go out to parties. Investigate natural tension relievers, such as yoga or meditation. Doing things with your hands—playing the piano, typing, craftwork—is also helpful.

Gemini is also associated with the lungs, which are especially sensitive. If you smoke, consider quitting. Yoga, which incorporates deep breathing into physical exercise, brings oxygen into your lungs. Among its many benefits are the deep relaxation and tranquillity so needed by your sign.

Combine healthful activities with social get-togethers for fun and plenty of fringe benefits for everyone. Include friends in your exercise routines; join an exercise class or jogging club. Gemini excels at sports that require good timing and manual dexterity as well as communication with others, like tennis or golf. Those who jog may want to add hand weights or upper-body exercises, which will benefit the Gemini-ruled arms and hands. If you spend long hours at the computer, try an ergonomic keyboard for comfort and protection against carpal tunnel syndrome.

Cancer Tips: Get the Emotional Support You Need

Dieting can be difficult for Cancers, who love good cuisine, find emotional solace with goodies, and fill up with comfort foods in tough times. There are sure to be conflicts in the Cancer who wants to be fashionably thin, but also to please the family with Grandma's favorite dishes. Cancer food conflicts sometimes lead to eating disorders, as with Princess Diana. Remember that you must be nurtured emotionally as well as physically. A diet-therapy group might help you deal with issues surrounding food and give you the support you need to stick to a diet. Find nonfood ways to baby yourself, such as a visit to a spa, walks along the beach, or beauty treatments to help you feel good about yourself while you lose weight.

Get the family behind you when you diet. You'll never lose weight if they insist on eating caloric favorites in front of you. Challenge yourself to create diet-conscious variations of family recipes so the whole family can eat healthy.

Your natural water-sign element is also your best therapy. Sometimes just a walk by a pond or a brief stop by a fountain can do wonders to relieve emotional stress and tension. You will be more likely to stick to an exercise routine if it's in or near water. Pool aerobics, swimming, fishing, sailing, and all other all water sports provide ideal ways for you to stay fit.

Health-wise, Cancer is associated with the breasts. Have regular checkups, according to your age and family health history of breast-related illness, and be sure to wear the proper supportive bra. Cancer is also prone to digestive difficulties, especially gastric ulcers and eating disorders. When emotionally caused digestive problems from those stomach-knotting insecurities crop up, baby yourself with extra pampering. If you're feeling blue, a visit with loved ones, old friends, and family could provide the support you need. Plan special family activities that bring everyone close together.

Leo Tips: The Downside of the Good Life

Leo's diet downfall might be your preference for the finer things in life, like dining on gourmet food at the best restaurants. And a Leo that is not getting the love and attention you need can easily turn to food for consolation. Give yourself the royal treatment in nonfood ways and imagine how great you'll look in that sexy gold dress.

Like your lion namesake, Leos often tend to be carnivores, so a low-carbohydrate, high-protein diet might work best for you, such as the Perricone or Atkins diet. If you're having trouble getting started on your diet, give yourself a jump start with a spa vacation. Some extra pampering, plus expert advice, could see you through the first difficult week and get you on the road to healthy eating.

Leo is associated with the spine and heart, two important areas to guard throughout your life. Be sure you have a good mattress to support the vulnerable Leo spine. Learn some therapeutic exercises to strengthen and protect your back. Aerobic exercises that benefit the heart and lungs are also musts for Leo.

Ruled by the sun, you're one sign that usually loves to tan. However, considering the permanent damage sun exposure can cause, you may elect to remain porcelain pale like Madonna or to use a spray-on tanning product. Don't leave for the beach without a big hat, umbrella, and sunblock formulated for your skin type. Many makeup foundations now come with a sunblock added, a good idea for Leo ladies.

Leos are proud of your body and usually take excellent care of it. Like the archetypal Leo male, Arnold Schwarzenegger, you can summon up great discipline and determination to maintain your public image. To make your body worthy of the spotlight, consider a bodybuilding regimen in which you're supervised by a personal trainer. Be sure any exercise routine you choose emphasizes good posture. The way you carry yourself can make the most of your figure type and dramatically affect your energy level. Get that regal bearing!

Virgo Tips: Find a Diet Coach

Since Virgo is associated with the digestive system, you can make quite an issue of food quality, preparation, and diet. Many of you will select a very detailed special diet to promote health, such as a macrobiotic diet. Potassium-rich vegetables are especially important, as is your relationship to whole grains. The mind-body connection to overweight has been emphasized by Virgo diet coach, Dr. Phil MacGraw. If you become overweight, it usually comes from coping with emotional or work-related stress. To counteract this tendency, add activities to your life that promote peace of mind. Exercises that use mental as well as physical techniques could help you stay with your program.

As one of the most health-conscious signs in the zodiac, caring for the health of yourself and others is usually a high priority with Virgos. Many great doctors, nurses, and dieticians were born under Virgo, such as the noted heart surgeon Dr. Michael DeBakey.

You tend to troubleshoot your health, scheduling medical exams and appropriate diagnostic tests promptly. You have probably learned that running your life efficiently does much to eliminate health-robbing stress. It's a great comfort to know you've got a smooth health-maintenance routine in place to back you up.

Virgos benefit from exercises that stress the relationship of the mind and body, such as yoga or tai chi. Sports that require a certain technical skill to master can also challenge Virgo. The key factor in Virgo-appealing exercises is to offer self-improvement on several levels simultaneously, not just a boring or repetitive routine.

Libra Tips: Resist Sweet Temptations

One of the most famous diet doctors, Dr. Robert Atkins, was a Libra. A well-spoken gentleman with a liking for sweets, he fit your sign's profile. At first, the low-carbohydrate diet he advocated was vilified by nutritional experts. In recent years, however, he has been vindicated, and the effectiveness of the Atkins diet proven. It could be the perfect diet for Libras who often put on too much weight from indulging in sweets. Because your sign rules the kidneys, it's no surprise that this diet advocates drinking plenty of water to cleanse the system as you reduce. Since you are one of the most social signs, you may entertain or be entertained often. Plan your food choices before you go out, so you'll know exactly what to eat. Then you'll be more likely to resist sweet temptations. Dieting with your mate or a group of friends could provide the support you need and keep you on track when you go out to dinner.

Restoring and maintaining equilibrium is the Libra key to health. Balance in all things should be your mantra. If you have been working too hard or taking life too seriously, a dose of culture, art, or music or perhaps some social activity will balance your scales. Make time to entertain friends, be romantic with the one you love, and enjoy the artistic life of your city.

Since Libra is associated with the kidneys and lower back, watch these areas for misalignment or health problems. Consider yoga, spinal adjustments, or a detoxification program if your body is out of balance. Working out in a gym may be unappealing to aesthetic Libras. Since yours is the sign of relationships, you may enjoy exercising with a partner or with loved ones. Make morning walks or weekend hikes family affairs. Take a romantic bicycle tour, picnic in the autumn countryside. Libra is also the sign of grace, so any kind of dancing may appeal. Dancing combines art, music, romance, relaxation, graceful movement, social contact, and exercise.

Put more beauty in all areas of your life, and you'll be healthier and happier.

Scorpio Tips: Diet for Self-Transformation

Scorpios never do anything halfway, so they need to be fully committed to their diets. Some Scorpios will go to great lengths to transform themselves, even resorting to extreme means like stomach stapling or gastric bypass, as Roseanne Barr did. You are gifted with amazing focus and discipline and can stick with any diet, once you have made up your mind. The trick is to eliminate self-destructive food habits. Finding a diet plan you can live with for long periods, such as the South Beach Diet, which worked for Hillary Clinton, will help you avoid the yo-yo diet syndrome.

Though Scorpio usually has a strong constitution that can literally rise from the ashes of extreme illness or misfortune, resist the temptation to take this for granted or sabotage your health with self-destructive habits. Try to curb excessive tendencies in any area of your life. Know when to quit and when to seek help; don't hesitate to ask for help when you need it.

Your sign is associated with regenerative and eliminative organs. Therefore, it follows that sexual activity can be a source of good or ill health for Scorpio. It is important to examine your attitudes about sex, to follow safe-sex practices, and to seek balance in sex, as in all other areas of your life.

It's no accident that Scorpio's month coincides with football season, which reminds us that sports are a very healthy way to defuse emotions. If you enjoy winter sports, be sure to prepare ahead of time for the ski slopes or the ice rinks. Be sure to warm up your muscles before you go all out. Water sports are a terrific outlet for Scorpio, so sign up for pool aerobics or competitive swimming and be sure to treat yourself to a vacation at a spectacular tropical beach resort. Somehow, just being near a saltwater environment can restore your equilibrium.

Sagittarius Tips: Aim for Long-Range Benefits

Dieting is something Sagittarius does with great difficulty. There has to be more to it than just getting thin. Therefore, an eating plan that is part of a spiritually oriented lifestyle, such as vegetarianism, might have more appeal. Aim for long-range benefits by balancing a sane, practical eating plan with plenty of exercise. Beware of fad diets that promise instant results and come with a high-pressure sales pitch. Avoid gimmicks, pills, or anything instant; these solutions are especially tempting to impatient Sagittarius. Exercise is the greatest antidote to overeating for your sports-loving sign, so follow your guru (Jane Fonda), go for the burn, and work off those calories.

Good health for Sagittarius is often a matter of motivation. If you set a fitness goal, it will be much easier to stay motivated than if you exercise or diet haphazardly, so aim for the best you can be and then set a plan to achieve it. Once you've decided on a course of action, get going. Being on the move and physically active keeps you in the best of health, improves your circulation, and protects your arteries. Problems could come from injuries to the hip or thigh areas, as well as arterial problems, so protect yourself with the proper equipment for your sports activity and don't push yourself beyond your capacity.

Exercise is your greatest antidote to stress. Your sign loves working out in groups, so combine socializing with athletic activities and team sports. Touch football, biking, hikes, and long walks with your dog are fun as well as healthy. Let others know that you'd like a health-promoting birthday gift, such as sports equipment, a gym membership, or an exercise video. In your workouts, concentrate on Sagittarius-ruled areas—the hips, legs, and thighs.

If you're already in shape, try out Sagittarius sports such as downhill or cross-country skiing, Rollerblading, and basketball. Since you like to travel, plan an exercise routine that can be done anywhere. Isometric exercises, which use muscle resistance and can be done in a car or plane seat, are a good travel option. If you are always on the road, investigate equipment that fits easily in your suitcase, such as water-filled weights, home gym devices, elastic exercise bands. Locate hotels with well-equipped gyms or parks nearby where you can jog.

Capricorn Tips: Disciplined Dieting

It was a Capricorn hostess and decorator, Lady Elsie de Wolfe Mendl, who introduced dieting to America, via the 1920s health guru Gayelord Hauser. Lady Mendl served very small portions of exquisitely prepared health food at her elegant dinner parties, a good tip for you who may need to downsize portions. One of the skinny signs, Capricorn has amazing self-discipline, a big help in maintaining weight loss. Exercise or active sports should help you keep the pounds off without strenuous dieting. Food and mood are linked with Capricorn, so avoid eating to console or comfort yourself; instead, choose upbeat relaxed companions. Since you are likely to mix business with pleasure, plan your work-related lunches and dinners in advance so you won't be led astray by the dessert tray.

As a Capricorn, you naturally take good care of yourself, getting regular medical checkups and tending toward moderation in your lifestyle. You're one of the signs that ages well and remains physically active in your senior years. But Capricorn's fast-paced, action-packed life can be stressful, so here are some ways to unwind and put the spring back into your step.

Since Capricorn is associated with the bone structure, you need to watch for signs of osteoporosis and take preventive measures. Good posture and stretching exercises such as yoga are essential to remain flexible. You might practice yoga, as Christy Turlington does. Another way to counteract osteoporosis is by adding weight-bearing exercise to your routine. If your knees or joints are showing signs of arthritis, calcium supplements may be helpful. For those who enjoy strenuous sports, remember to protect your knees by doing special exercises to strengthen this area, and always warm up beforehand.

Capricorn's natural self-discipline is a big help in maintaining good health. Keep a steady, even pace for lasting results. Remember to balance workouts with pleasurable activities in your self-care program. Grim determination can be counterproductive, especially if one of your exercise goals is to relieve tension. Take up a sport for pure enjoyment, not necessarily to become a champion.

Since you probably spend much of your life in an office, check your working environment for hidden health saboteurs like poor air quality, bad lighting, and uncomfortable seating. Get an ergonomically designed chair to protect your back, or buy a specially designed back-support cushion if your chair is uncomfortable. If you work at a computer, adjust your keyboard and the height of the computer screen for ergonomic comfort.

Capricorn, the sign of Father Time, brings up the subject of aging. If sags and wrinkles are keeping you from looking as young as you feel, investigate plastic surgery to give you a younger look and psychological lift. Teeth are also associated with your sign, a reminder to have regular dental cleanings and checkups.

Aquarius Tips: The Diet Trendsetter

Aquarius is a sign of reaching out to others, a cue to make your diet program a social one. Sharing your diet with friends might keep you interested and prevent boredom. It worked for Oprah Winfrey, an Aquarius whose yo-yo weight gains and losses became media events. If you know you'll be going public for a party or wedding, you'll be motivated to look your best. The trick is to segue from dieting to an ongoing healthy lifestyle. Otherwise you'll be back up the scale again. Try to find a flexible plan that adapts to individual personalities rather than one that imposes a rigid diet structure. Keep a diet diary or online blog to help monitor yourself, a tip from Oprah.

Clean air is top priority for a health-wise air sign especially vulnerable to airborne allergies and viruses. The effects of air pollution might influence where you choose to live. If you life in a polluted environment, get an air purifier, ionizer, or humidifier. Aquarius tends to travel a lot (or may fly your own plane, as John Travolta and Lorenzo Lamas do). Protect yourself from infections that flourish in the enclosed environments of trains, buses, and planes.

Since Aquarius is associated with the circulatory system, you especially benefit from a therapeutic massage. Find your local day spa and schedule one of their relaxing hands-on treatments. New Age treatments are favored by experimental Aquarius, so consider alternative approaches to health and fitness. Perhaps the Ayurvedic approach from India or Chinese massage therapies might work for you. Calves and ankles are also Aquarius territory, which should be emphasized in your exercise program. Be sure your ankles are well supported. Be careful of sprains and strains, especially if you're a jogger.

You'll follow a fitness routine only if you can make your own rules and exercise at a convenient time, which could mean odd moments. If your schedule makes it difficult to get to the gym or if you dislike the routine of regular exercise classes, videos might solve your problem. There is a vast selection of exercise videos to choose from. Exercising with friends could make staying fit more fun. Try several different kinds of exercise so you can vary your routine from yoga to kick-boxing when you get bored. Or set up a gym at home with portable home exercise equipment. (You're the type who will combine your treadmill sessions with a telephone conversation or TV news show.)

Pisces Tips: The Addictive Eater

Pisces is a sign of no boundaries, one of the most difficult to discipline diet-wise. You can get hooked on a fattening food like French fries (or alcohol), a habit like coffee with lots of sugar and a roll, and easily gain weight. Your water-sign body may have a tendency to bloat, holding water weight at certain times, especially around the full moon. The key for you, as with so many others, is commitment and support. Don't try to go it alone. Get a partner, a doctor, a group, or one of the online diet-related sites to help. Since you're influenced by the atmosphere around you, choose to be with slim healthy friends and those who will support your efforts. Avoid those seemingly well-meaning diet saboteurs who say just one cookie won't do any harm. A seafood-based diet, like the Perricone diet, could be the right one for you. Your Pisces sisters—Queen Latifah, Liza Minnelli, Camryn Manheim, and Elizabeth Taylor—have slimmed down, and so can you!

Health-wise, supersensitive Pisces, associated with the lymphatic system, reacts strongly to environmental toxins and emotional stress. It's no accident that we often do spring cleaning during the Pisces months. Start your birthday off right by detoxing your system with a liquid diet or supervised fast. This may also help with water retention, a common Pisces problem. Lympathic drainage massage is especially relaxing and beneficial to Pisces.

The feet are Pisces territory. Consider how often you take your feet for granted and how miserable life can be when your feet hurt. Since our feet reflect and affect the health of the entire body, devote some time to pampering them. Check your walking shoes or buy ones designed for your kind of exercise. Investigate custom-molded orthotic inserts if your arches are high. They could make a big difference in your comfort and performance.

Just as the sign of Pisces contains traces of all the previous signs, the soles of our feet contain nerve endings that connect with all other parts of our body. This is the theory behind reflexology, a therapeutic foot massage that treats all areas of the body by massaging the soles of the feet. For the sake of your feet, as well as your entire body, consider treating yourself to a session with a local practitioner of this technique.

Exercise is not a favorite Pisces activity, unless it is a creative activity like dance or ice-skating, or is related to your water element, such as water aerobics or swimming. A caring exercise instructor who gives you personal attention can also make a difference in your motivation. Walking regularly releases tension, gets you outdoors, and can be a way to socialize with friends away from the temptation of food and drink. Try doing local errands on foot, if you live in a city, or find a local park where you can take a daily hike. Invite someone you love or would like to get to know better to share this time with you, or get an adorable dog to accompany you.

CHAPTER 17

Discover Your Virgo Personality

Did you know that your Virgo sun sign colors all areas of your life? What and whom you like, how you behave as a parent, your attitude toward your career—all have a strong Virgo factor. The more you know about Virgo, the better you can use your personal solar power to help you make good decisions, from something as basic as what to wear today to deeper psychological issues, such as what compromises you might need to make in order to get along with a difficult boss or new lover. Your sun sign provides a time-honored guide to what's right for you, so why not turn to it when you're at a crossroads in your career, choosing a new hue for your walls, or deciding whether or not to pursue a romantic relationship? Let the following chapters empower you with the confidence that you're moving in harmony with your natural inclinations.

The basic characteristics of your sun sign are a blend of several ingredients. First there's your Virgo element: earth. Earth signs are practical, down-to-earth, realistic. Then there's the way Virgo operates: mutable, a sign of flexibility, change. Your sign's polarity adds yet another dimension: feminine, yin, negative, reactive. Let's not forget your planetary ruler: Mercury, the planet of learning, mental agility, communication. Add your sign's place in the zodiac: sixth, in the house of organization, maintenance, functionality, health. Finally, stir in your symbol: the virgin, a sign of purity, perfection.

This recipe influences everything we say about Virgo. For example, you could easily deduce that a practical earth sign with a Mercury ruling planet be well-organized, a good teacher. This sign would be concerned with details and the way things work. It would have high standards and be a bit of a perfectionist. But remember that your total astrological personality contains a blend of many other planets, colored by the signs they occupy, plus factors such as the sign coming over the horizon at the exact moment of your birth. The more Virgo planets in your horoscope, the more likely you'll follow your sun sign's prototype. However, if many planets are grouped together in a different sign, they will color your horoscope accordingly, sometimes making a low-key, mellow sun sign come on much stronger. So if the Virgo traits mentioned here don't describe you, there could be other factors flavoring your cosmic stew. (Look up your other planets in the tables in this book to find out what they might be!)

The Virgo Man: High Standards

Contradicting the virgin symbol of your sign is one of the pleasures of being a Virgo man, some of whom have been dubbed the "sexiest man in the world." You are the type who becomes even more attractive with age, like Sean Connery, Richard Gere, and Jeremy Irons. Maturity looks wonderful on you.

Part of the Virgo man's appeal is his subtlety. You never come on too strong. You are more likely to have a modest facade and to be as interested in a woman's mind as in her body. You usually let the opposite sex do the chasing. Though you may be sexually skilled, you prefer to keep your feelings under wraps, leave grand passion to others, and remain tantalizingly out of reach.

The Virgo man is not always as practical, health-conscious, aloof, and appraising as he appears. Underneath, you have a vivid fantasy life, full of adventure, like the world of James Bond, populated by perfect love partners (although the dream may get blurry at this point). You are never quite sure what the perfect partner is, but you know what she is *not*.

Virgo has extremely high standards in life and love. You reach your potential by seeing that everything is well run. Virgo usually chooses the functional over the flamboyant, mistrusting anything or anyone that seems uncontrollable. Your negative side is simply your good side carried to extremes. That happens when too-high standards make you overly critical of others, when concern for health becomes hypochondria, when extreme neatness and organization make you difficult to live with, and when careful budgeting turns into penny-pinching.

Virgo feels impelled to right whatever is not functioning or at least to point it out. Some Virgos, like Michael Jackson, actually create their own isolated perfect worlds, where the real world is excluded. This is one reason why the Virgo male is often called the bachelor of the zodiac. No one quite lives up to that fantasy image.

When forced to deal with the real world, Virgo becomes the efficiency expert, the demanding perfectionist, or the teacher in some way. You are best when you are improving someone in body or in mind—being the doctor or the teacher, and sometimes both at the same time.

In a Relationship

The Virgo man can be a devoted partner when you find a mate who meets your high standards. Like everything else, you work hard at your relationships, though you may not express your tender romantic side easily. You like to have your house in order, and will expect your partner to stick to your agenda. You will tolerate her having a career, as long as she also maintains the home as a well-ordered refuge from the outside world. However, a Virgo's woman is well advised to look beneath the surface of her man and encourages him to express his erotic sensual side, those hidden "Agent 007" fantasies. Otherwise, as the Virgo man ages, he may decide to take a risk and live out some of his fantasies with a younger playmate. Some Virgos leave their sensible mates for a glamorous, far riskier partner who provides them with the taste or adventure they've been missing. As one aging Virgo entrepreneur described his glamorous second wife, "She spends all my money, but she's worth it!"

The Virgo Woman: The Passionate Perfectionist

Like your male counterpart, the Virgo woman is a paradox. You're renowned for being a schoolmarm type, obsessed with neatness and tidiness. However, some of the world's most seductive women were born under the sign of the virgin—Raquel Welch, Sophia Loren, Cameron Diaz, and Salma Hayek, for example. Looking more deeply into the lives of these beauties, we find women who are extremely health-conscious, devoted to their families, and discriminating about relationships. They have cool business heads and often run multiple business ventures. These are not party girls by any means! Virgo is oriented toward work, not play (the personal digital assistant must have been invented by a Virgo). You are the type who will turn down a glamorous spontaneous invitation, or an exciting man, if you have scheduled that time to do your laundry. And this will make you all the more desirable to your pursuer! Remember the legendary Virgo beauty Greta Garbo, who wanted to be left alone yet always had a pack of admirers in pursuit.

When you set a goal, you proceed in a very methodical and efficient way to attain it. Your analytical mind will take it apart, piece by piece, to discover where you can make improvements. You do this to people, too. (Caution: With your critical Virgo nature, you can win points but lose your friends.)

Beneath the cool Virgo surface, there's a romantic in hiding, one who'll risk all for love, as did Ingrid Bergman, who scandalized the nation by leaving her family to run off with an Italian film director. Greta Garbo specialized in portraying the women who lived life romantically, like Mata Hari and Anna Karenina, the direct opposite of the Virgo image, and had a controversial ménage à trois in her personal life. Virgo Lauren Bacall blazed with Humphrey

Bogart on and off screen, in spite of their considerable age difference. Many Virgos choose men who are contrary to the expectations of others. Someone from an entirely different race, age group, or culture may tempt you to drop your careful plans and take a chance on love!

In a Relationship

The Virgo woman appeals to both mind and body, but even though you may appear supersensual, you are rarely promiscuous. You are more interested in commitment, in finding the perfect mate.

Virgo often has a high-strung temperament that zeroes in on your partner's weak points and doesn't rest until they are corrected. This constant nagging and faultfinding can make you difficult to live with. A better approach is to use your talent and charm to provoke others to take action or to set a good example for others to follow.

Once committed, you're an excellent companion and one of the most helpful mates in the zodiac. Since you have been very careful about giving away your heart, you'll be an adoring wife. You are the perfect partner for a man who needs a helping hand and someone to take care of details. Many Virgos are in business with their husbands, blending work and home life perfectly. You will pull your weight in the relationship, stick by him in difficult times, and even support him financially if necessary. Needless to say, his life will get organized and his diet improved. Virgo is not sparing of a man's ego, however, and must be careful not to let criticism degenerate into nagging. When you let go and allow laughter and fun to enter your relationship, you may indeed achieve the perfect marriage.

Virgo in the Family

The Virgo Parent

Virgo, who enjoys providing useful service, makes a very effective parent, expressing love through devotion and caring attention. Your special strength is in practical matters that prepare your child for survival on his or her own, such as teaching useful skills and providing health care and the best education possible. You'll also develop your child's basic common sense and organizational skills.

Virgo's tendency to worry and be overly critical is better soft-pedaled with sensitive children, who need to develop inner confidence. You'll be more comfortable with the mental side of parenting than with the emotional demands of a needy child. You may have to compromise your overly high standards to give affection and praise, as well as criticism. Though you naturally focus on perfecting details, be sure to give your child room to grow. Realize that making mistakes and taking risks are an important part of education that will help prepare your child for solo flights.

The Virgo Stepparent

Your Virgo objectivity and teaching skill will come in handy as a new stepparent. You'll keep the home running smoothly and deal with your extended family with intelligence and objectivity. You'll allow time for the children to adjust before you make friendly moves, never forcing the relationship. But you may have to tone down your tendency to give advice for their own good. Build up their confidence first by showing warmth, caring, and encouragement. In time, the children will respect your well-considered advice and come to you for constructive, analytical opinions.

The Virgo Grandparent

The perennial Virgo curiosity and interest in all things will serve you well in your senior years. You're likely to remain mentally sharp and as alert as ever! You'll know what's going on and have a well-considered opinion to offer. And, surprise, more people are paying attention now! Maybe that's because you are more relaxed, open, and warmer than ever, and your self-confidence is justified by years of experience. You're especially attractive to youngsters. They come to you for advice because you're the one who knows what works and what doesn't. And you won't hesitate to tell it like it is. They'll consult with you about all manner of problems or hash over the world situation—you're right up with the latest news. Though you're still a worrier, you realize now how many imaginary problems never came to pass, and you've become more philosophical with age. You'll happily offer advice and zero in with sharp criticism when necessary, but now it's tempered with psychological wisdom that truly reflects your deep concern for the welfare of others.

CHAPTER 18

Virgo Stellar Style: The Fashion Trends, Home Decor, Colors, and Getaways That Suit Virgo Best

Whether you're ready for an extreme makeover or simply want to update your wardrobe, look to your sun sign for the trends and colors that will harmonize with your Virgo personality.

Virgo Chic

"Less is more" should be your motto. Simple, comfortable, elegant clothes suit Virgo best. Be inspired by Virgo screen goddesses Ingrid Bergman or Lauren Bacall (or Greta Garbo in private life). Most Virgos look best in beautifully cut, uncluttered, classic clothes. Even the most curvaceous Virgos, like Salma Hayek, Sophie Dahl, Jacqueline Bisset, Raquel Welch, and Sophia Loren, keep their clothing styles simple, avoiding ruffles and flourishes. Nor will they clutter themselves with too many accessories or too much jewelry. Cameron Diaz looks best in clean-cut simple styles that let her beautiful eyes and smile take the spotlight. Beyoncé Knowles is a critical fashion perfectionist concerned with every detail of her appearance. Her look can be dramatic, but it is always carefully put together.

Elegant white and earth tones belong to Virgo. These are versatile colors that are always appropriate, in any season. You also look chic in navy and white or in gray tones.

Virgo style is sensual, but never obvious. (You look especially sexy in a tailored suit!) All-white linen is another Virgo look—remember Ingrid Bergman's grand entrance in the film classic *Casablanca*. Bright colors are tricky with Virgo, because the wrong shade or color combination might jar your nerves. Use bright colors as accents to your basic neutral palette.

Your makeup should be subtle and carefully applied using mostly earth tones. Again, "less is more." Virgo's hair should be perfectly cut and groomed in a classic style. You'll probably find the ideal hairstyle and stick to it for life, like Claudette Colbert, who was known for her bangs, or Greta Garbo for her famous pageboy.

As Paris is a city influenced by Virgo, it should come as no surprise that there are many fashion designers born under your sign. Current designers Stella McCartney and Karl Lagerfeld are perfectionists with an eye for detail. Lagerfeld, especially, takes an intellectual approach to fashion. In the past, designers James Galanos, Geoffrey Beene, Tom Ford, and Elsa Schiaparelli set high standards. Models Sophie Dahl, Claudia Schiffer, and Kirsty Hume strut the Virgo style in fashion magazines.

Time for a Home Makeover? Bring Virgo into Every Room!

Earth-bound Virgos should have an environment that speaks of calm and order. You make an art of creating a healthy home that is elegantly uncluttered. For that reason, many Virgos prefer modern architecture or Japanese-influenced rooms. Whatever your style preference, aim for clean lines and provide efficient storage space.

Use a subdued palette with lots of white, your special color, to reflect light and to set off the various shapes of your furniture. The elegant white and earth tones that work best in your wardrobe also look terrific on your walls. These versatile colors give you endless possibilities for change and can be easily adapted to the seasons. Navy and white is another classic Virgo look, especially if you collect blue and white china. Use brights as accents to your basic neutral color scheme.

Virgos have a special genius for organization and can make even the tiniest space functional and efficient. Antique secretaries, oak file cabinets, printer's trays, and closet organizers get pressed into service. Because you're a reader, there should be plenty of bookshelves and safe storage for your prized record collection. Beautiful compositions of objects you love, natural fibers, and a special air filtering system to provide you with the cleanest air possible would satisfy your Virgo instincts.

With the Virgo eye for detail, nothing shares your environment unless it passes muster. Like Greta Garbo, who even designed her own rugs, you may prefer to craft your own furniture or cabinets. Your kitchen should be especially well-planned, perhaps in germ-resistant stainless steel, equipped with blenders, juicers, sprouters, and shelves for vitamins. The Virgo bedroom should focus on a good night's sleep with an orthopedic mattress that is kind to the spine and a good reading light and bedside bookshelves for night readers. An all-white bedroom with natural fiber bed linens, perhaps embroidered or trimmed with lace, is an elegant Virgo look.

The Virgo Sound Track

Virgo musical artists, from Michael Jackson to Itzak Perlman, are known for their virtuoso style. Your discriminating taste in music makes you search out the definitive recordings of your favorites to be perfectly played on state-of-the-art sound equipment. In classical music, you might prefer string quartets, Puccini operas, or the Virgo composers Dvořák, Bruckner, and John Cage. Virgo conductor Leonard Bernstein had your passion for perfection. Some Virgo musicians and composers who might add variety to your collection are Michael Jackson, Elvis Costello, Maria Muldaur, Dinah Washington, Mel Tormé, Paul Winter, Itzak Perlman, Barry Gibb, Bobby Short, and Michael

Feinstein. Rock fans will go for Beyoncé Knowles, Pink, and Moby.

Virgo Away from Home

Planning a trip is part of the fun of travel for Virgo. You will stock up on guidebooks and research the Internet for the best values. You'll demand a beautiful setting that has some health or intellectual benefits.

As the great teacher (and student) of the zodiac, why not combine a vacation with a learning experience by taking a course at a local school? You could add a new language to your repertoire while you enjoy the pleasures of Mexico or Provence, improve your culinary skills at a gourmet cooking school in Paris, or join an archaeological dig in Turkey. Select a subject that is completely divorced from your business for a complete change of pace.

Health-minded Virgos should consider getting in top condition at a health spa, either in the mountains here or in a fascinating foreign country. Germany, Switzerland, and northern Italy have a wide variety of health resorts and hot springs to choose from. Select a spa with a medical emphasis, as well as beauty and fitness.

Indulging your interest in history with visits to the historical landmarks or houses of the period that interests you would make another stimulating and interesting vacation. Tours of antebellum mansions or English country houses can easily be arranged in advance. Many universities offer tours guided by an expert in antiquities and in local culture.

Other possibilities are rock climbing in Colorado, hiking through Wordsworth country (the Lake District of England), or exploring Amsterdam by bicycle. Special Virgo-blessed places are Boston, Paris, Greece, and Washington, D.C.—all places of learning with wonderful museums and a vibrant cultural life.

Your bags are probably well made and sturdy, as well as good-looking. Save yourself some time at the baggage claim by labeling your bags with brightly colored stickers. Save your meticulous and detailed packing lists from trip to trip.

Then, when you revisit the same destination or climate, you'll know just what to take. Be sure to take along a good book or some stationery to make use of the inevitable delays.

CHAPTER 19

Your Virgo Career Finder

What Does Virgo Bring to the Table?

What makes some Virgos more successful than others? Virgo has a special combination of talents and abilities that make you stand out. By discovering and developing your special sun-sign strengths, you'll not only be likely to find a career you truly enjoy, but you'll be able to channel your efforts to areas where you'll be most successful.

You are the efficiency expert who saves the company money and time, or who monitors quality control. Your meticulous neatness and concern for health make you a natural in the fitness, health, medical, and nutrition fields. This is not to say that Virgo is not glamorous or creative! Who could forget Bergman, Bacall, or Garbo? But even in the arts, you are a flawless performer who takes a craftsmanlike approach.

Your key word is service, so your career should be involved with helping others improve themselves or with providing a practical, useful product.

Where to Find Opportunity

Follow your natural Virgo tendencies. Glamour jobs that depend on a flashy presentation are not for you. Nor are you especially interested in public pizzazz. Mercury-ruled

Virgos have a talent for communicating knowledge. You are the zodiac's most natural teacher, in the educational system or in some facet of your job. The Virgo eye for detail is put to good use in editorial work, accounting, science, literary criticism (or any kind of critical problem solving), and law. Avoid jobs where too much diplomacy or flattery is required. Your critical mind has been known to deflate fragile egos. Political power plays also irritate your delicate nerves. You'll shine brightest in a position where others appreciate your dedication and attention to quality.

Though you can be a big money earner, thanks to your work ethic, financial rewards alone are not enough to satisfy your Virgo need to be of service to others. You must believe in what you're doing and be able to move ahead at your own pace.

The Virgo Leader

The Virgo boss is a passionate perfectionist who expects others to meet high standards. Your mind is systematic, always aware of how smoothly an organization is run. You do tend to micromanage. When you spot an error or something out of order, you are quick to report the misdeed or flaw, and may place a higher priority on efficiency than creativity. However, you are a wonderful coach, known for developing your team and eliciting peak performance. Though your underlings may find your attention to detail irritating at times, they will benefit by your caring attention, for you are always thinking of your subordinates' welfare. You will make sure they get requisite benefits, sick leave, vacation time.

For inspiration, you can't find a better Virgo mentor than billionaire sage Warren Buffet, one of the richest men in the world. Widely hailed as an investing genius, Buffett put his Virgo discrimination and critical qualities to work sizing up companies and amassing his fortune. Buffet's practical down-to-earth attitude, so typical of Virgo, extends to his understated lifestyle. He doesn't live in a huge house, collect cars, or take a limousine to work. Yet the witty and savvy pronouncements of the "Oracle of Omaha" are most eagerly followed in the financial world.

The Virgo Team Player

The Virgo worker is an employer's dream: punctual, efficient, detail-oriented, hardworking, willing to put in long hours. You are modest and quiet (except when something's wrong!) and do meticulously neat and thorough work. You are the perfect right-hand person who troubleshoots for the boss. You are best when you can organize your job yourself rather than cope with the inefficiency and slipups of others. On a team, your critical attitude may cause friction with less scrupulous types. You'll have to learn to phrase your criticisms diplomatically—usually you will not hesitate to deflate a fragile ego! You shine in a position where others appreciate your dedication and attention to quality.

Promote Yourself!

In doing your personal plan of action, think of how you can add value to an organization. Pick a job where your services are vitally needed, then show what you can do. Play up these Virgo talents:

- Analysis
- Your eye for significant detail
- Grace under pressure
- Constructive criticism
- Teaching ability
- Craftsmanship
- Organization
- Practicality

CHAPTER 20

Let Virgo Celebrities Teach You About Your Sun Sign

It's fun to find out who else was born under Virgo, especially if it's one of your favorite celebrities. Someone in the public eye who was born on or near your birthday is sure to have many of the traits you do. You may even have a Virgo twin born the same day and year. Notice how your famous sign mates used their Virgo qualities for better or for worse, how they rose from obscurity to fame (and vice versa), what helped or hindered their success, even how they dress to play up their Virgo star quality. Could this work for you as well?

You've got a host of fabulous Virgos to inspire you. Warren Buffet, Lance Armstrong, and Dr. Phil McGraw might motivate you to develop your confidence and leadership. The elegant classic Virgo style is displayed by Lauren Bacall and Queen Rania of Jordan. For Virgo's earthy sex appeal combined with uncommon business sense, there are Sophia Loren, Salma Hayek, and Beyoncé Knowles. If you're a tabloid fan, how do your sun-sign mates like Michael Jackson and Kobe Bryant show their Virgo traits as they cope with scandal and reinvent themselves?

If there are celebrities who intrigue you, go deeper into their lives by finding their other planets in the tables in this book. You'll learn more about them as you apply the effects of Venus, Mars, Saturn, and Jupiter to their sun sign traits. You'll be amazed at how the total planetary picture lights up when you have a living example to refer to.

If you've caught the astrology bug, you can move on to

analyze the charts of current newsmakers and match your astrology skills with the experts. Of the many celebrity sites on the Internet, the most accurate source of famous birthdays is www.astrodatabank.com, which has charts of world events and headline makers, plus the observations of amateur and professional astrologers. Try it!

Virgo Celebrities

Kobe Bryant (8/23/78)
Gene Kelly (8/23/30)
Patricia McBride (8/23/42)
Shelley Long (8/23/49)
Rick Springfield (8/23/49)
River Phoenix (8/23/70)
Cesaria Evora (8/24/41)
Steve Guttenberg (8/24/58)
Marlee Matlin (8/24/65)
Walt Kelly (8/25/13)
Van Johnson (8/25/16)
Mel Ferrer (8/25/17)
Leonard Bernstein (8/25/18)
Sean Connery (8/25/30)
Ann Archer (8/25/50)
Elvis Costello (8/25/54)
Claudia Schiffer (8/25/70)
Geraldine Ferraro (8/26/35)
Macaulay Culkin (8/26/80)
Lyndon Johnson (8/27/1908)
Martha Raye (8/27/16)
Yasser Arafat (8/27/29)
Tuesday Weld (8/27/43)
Barbara Bach (8/27/49)
Pee Wee Herman (8/27/52)
Charles Boyer (8/28/1899)
Donald O'Connor (8/28/25)
Ben Gazzara (8/28/30)
David Soul (8/28/43)
Scott Hamilton (8/28/58)

Emma Samms (8/28/61)
Shania Twain (8/28/65)
Ingrid Bergman (8/29/15)
Sir Richard Attenborough (8/29/23)
Dinah Washington (8/29/24)
John McCain (8/29/36)
Elliott Gould (8/29/38)
William Friedkin (8/29/39)
Robin Leach (8/29/41)
Michael Jackson (8/29/58)
Rebecca De Mornay (8/29/61)
Shirley Booth (8/30/1907)
Warren Buffet (8/30/30)
Jean-Claude Killy (8/30/43)
Peggy Lipton (8/30/47)
Cameron Diaz (8/30/72)
Lisa Ling (8/30/73)
Frederic March (8/31/1897)
James Coburn (8/31/28)
Paul Winter (8/31/39)
Van Morrison (8/31/45)
Itzak Perlman (8/31/45)
Richard Gere (8/31/49)
Queen Rania of Jordan (8/31/70)
Yvonne DeCarlo (9/1/22)
Vittorio Gassman (9/1/22)
George Maharis (9/1/33)
Lily Tomlin (9/1/39)
Barry Gibb (9/1/46)
Dr. Phil McGraw (9/1/50)
Gloria Estefan (9/1/57)
Christa McAuliffe (9/2/48)
Mark Harmon (9/2/51)
Jimmy Connors (9/2/52)
Keanu Reeves (9/2/64)
Salma Hayek (9/2/68)
Kitty Carlisle (9/3/15)
Irene Pappas (9/3/26)
Valerie Perrine (9/3/43)
Charlie Sheen (9/3/65)
Mitzi Gaynor (9/4/30)

Beyoncé Knowles (9/4/81)
Bob Newhart (9/5/29)
Werner Erhard (9/5/35)
William Devane (9/5/37)
Raquel Welch (9/5/40)
Swoosie Kurtz (9/6/44)
Jane Curtin (9/6/47)
Carly Fiorina (9/6/54)
Queen Elizabeth I (9/7/1533)
Grandma Moses (9/7/1860)
Elia Kazan (9/7/1909)
Peter Lawford (9/7/25)
Buddy Holly (9/7/36)
Susan Blakely (9/7/48)
Corbin Bernsen (9/7/54)
Michael Feinstein (9/7/56)
Sid Caesar (9/8/22)
Peter Sellers (9/8/25)
Cliff Robertson (9/9/25)
Otis Redding (9/9/41)
Billy Preston (9/9/46)
Michael Keaton (9/9/51)
Hugh Grant (9/9/60)
Kristy McNichol (9/9/62)
Rachel Hunter (9/9/69)
Charles Kuralt (9/10/34)
Jose Feliciano (9/10/45)
Margaret Trudeau (9/10/48)
Amy Irving (9/10/53)
Colin Firth (9/10/60)
Ryan Phillipe (9/10/74)
Earl Holliman (9/11/28)
Brian De Palma (9/11/40)
Harry Connick, Jr. (9/11/67)
Linda Gray (9/12/40)
Maria Muldaur (9/12/42)
Barry White (9/12/44)
Mel Tormé (9/13/25)
Jacqueline Bisset (9/13/44)
Nell Carter (9/13/48)
Stella McCartney (9/13/71)

Fiona Apple (9/13/77)
Zoe Caldwell (9/14/33)
Harve Presnell (9/14/33)
Nicol Williamson (9/14/38)
Joey Heatherton (9/14/44)
Mary Frances Crosby (9/14/59)
Agatha Christie (9/15/1890)
Claudette Colbert (9/15/1903)
Jackie Cooper (9/15/22)
Bobby Short (9/15/24)
Tommy Lee Jones (9/15/46)
Oliver Stone (9/15/46)
Greta Garbo (9/16/1905)
Lauren Bacall (9/16/24)
B. B. King (9/16/25)
Peter Falk (9/16/27)
Ed Begley, Jr. (9/16/49)
David Copperfield (9/16/56)
Marc Anthony (9/16/69)
Roddy McDowall (9/17/28)
Anne Bancroft (9/17/31)
Dorothy Loudon (9/17/33)
John Ritter (9/17/48)
Rossano Brazzi (9/18/16)
Jack Warden (9/18/20)
Frankie Avalon (9/18/40)
James Gandolfini (9/18/61)
Jada Pinkett Smith (9/18/71)
Lance Armstrong (9/18/71)
Frances Farmer (9/19/10)
Duke Snider (9/19/26)
David McCallum (9/19/33)
Jeremy Irons (9/19/48)
Twiggy (9/19/49)
Joan Lunden (9/19/51)
Sophia Loren (9/20/34)
Larry Hagman (9/21/31)
Leonard Cohen (9/21/34)
Stephen King (9/21/47)
Bill Murray (9/21/50)
Ricki Lake (9/21/68)

Nicole Richie (9/21/81)
Andrea Bocelli (9/22/58)
Paul Muni (9/22/1895)
Shari Belafonte Harper (9/22/54)

CHAPTER 21

The Virgo Power of Attraction: Your Chemistry with Every Other Sign

Understanding how your sun sign works as part of a couple can help you make wise decisions about your most important relationships: romantic, business, or friendship.

Traditional astrological wisdom holds that signs of the same element (for Virgo, that means other earth signs: Taurus and Capricorn) are naturally compatible. So are signs that are in complementary elements, such as earth signs with water signs. In these relationships, communications flow easily and you'll feel most comfortable with each other.

But do you want comfort at certain times of your life? What happens when you meet someone, sparks fly, and an irresistible magnetic pull draws you together, or when disagreements and challenges fuel intrigue, mystery, and passion? (Think of the sexy verbal sparring in Jane Austen's novel *Pride and Prejudice*.) Even though it may end sadly, you'll never forget or regret that passionate encounter. Indeed, many lasting marriages happen between incompatible sun signs, while some ideally matched couples fizzle after a few years.

Once you understand how your partner's sun sign is likely to view yours and what each of you wants from a relationship, you'll be in a much better position to judge whether this combination has happiness potential. Will there be chemistry or challenges where you'll both need to compromise . . . and are you willing to make them?

The celebrity couples can help you visualize each Virgo combination. Notice that some are legendary couples, others showed promise but broke up after a few years, and still others existed only in the fantasy world of film or television (but still captured our imagination).

Virgo/Aries

GOOD CHEMISTRY:

Aries sexual magnetism and positive energy warm you up. You both share high ideals in pursuit of love. Aries puts lovers on a pedestal; Virgo seeks the perfect lover. Aries' honesty and directness earn your trust. And Aries needs your meticulous follow-through.

COMPROMISES:

Aries can be recklessly impatient, which you will find a serious weakness. Virgo dedication to selfless service gets no credit from self-centered Aries, who wants recognition for services rendered. Virgo may get tired and feel abused or martyred by Aries' relentless demands. Unsympathetic Aries will see Virgo as a downer.

SIGN MATES:

Virgo Ryan Phillipe and Aries Reese Witherspoon

Virgo/Taurus

GOOD CHEMISTRY:

Taurus admires the Virgo analytical mind, while Virgo admires Taurus concentration and goal-orientation. Virgo feels secure with predicable Taurus. You enjoy taking care of each other. Relaxed, soothing Taurus brings out Virgo sensuality. Virgo brings the world of ideas home to Taurus.

COMPROMISES:

Virgo nagging can cause Taurus self-doubt, which can show up in bullheaded stubbornness. The Taurus slow pace and ideal of deep-rooted comfort could feel like constraint to Virgo, who needs the stimulation of diversity and lively communication.

SIGN MATES:

Virgo Mel Ferrer and Taurus Audrey Hepburn

Virgo/Gemini

GOOD CHEMISTRY:

Both Mercury-ruled, your deepest bond will be mental communication and appreciation of each other's intelligence. The Virgo Mercury is earthbound and analytical, while the Gemini Mercury is a jack-of-all-trades. Gemini shows Virgo the big picture; Virgo takes care of the details. Your combined talents make a stimulating partnership. Virgo becomes the administrator here, Gemini the idea person.

COMPROMISES:

Your different priorities can be irritating to each other. Virgo needs a sense of order. Gemini needs to experiment and is forever the gadabout. An older Gemini who has slowed down somewhat makes the best partner here.

SIGN MATES:

Virgo David Arquette and Gemini Courteney Cox

Virgo/Cancer

GOOD CHEMISTRY:

Your two vulnerable signs protect and nurture each other. Moody Cancer needs your cool analytical nature to refine and focus emotions creatively. You give Cancer protective care and valuable insight. The Cancer charming romantic tenderness nurtures your shy side. Here is the caring lover of your dreams. You'll have good communication on a practical level, respecting each other's shrewd financial acumen.

COMPROMISES:

Cancer extreme self-protection could arouse your suspicion. Why must Cancer be so secretive? Virgo protectiveness could become smothering, making Cancer overly dependent. You must learn to offer suggestions instead of criticism, to coddle Cancer feelings at all times. (This is a sign that doesn't take criticism well, even if given with the best intentions.)

SIGN MATES:

Sopranos costars Virgo James Gandolfini and Cancer Edie Falco

Virgo/Leo

GOOD CHEMISTRY:

Leo confidence, sales power, and optimism, as well as aristocratic presence, are big draws for Virgo. Virgo will have a ready-made job efficiently running the mechanical parts of the Leo lifestyle, which Leo is only too happy to delegate. And Leo social poise brings Virgo into the public eye, which helps your shy sign bloom! Both are faithful and loyal signs who find much to admire in each other.

COMPROMISES:

You may not appreciate each other's point of view. Virgo is more likely to dole out well-meaning criticism and vitamins than the admiration and applause Leo craves. Virgo will also protect leonine high-handedness with the budget. Virgo makes the house rules, but Leo is above them, a rule unto itself. Leo always looks at the big picture, Virgo at the nitty-gritty. You could dampen each other's spirits, unless you find a way to work this out early in the relationship.

SIGN MATES:

Virgo Marc Anthony and Leo Jennifer Lopez
Virgo Guy Ritchie and Leo Madonna

Virgo/Virgo

GOOD CHEMISTRY:

There's a strong mental turn-on, since you both approach love in an analytical and rather clinical way. Two Virgo sign mates have a mutual respect and an intuitive communication that are hard to beat. You'll evolve a carefully ordered way of being together, which works especially well if you share outside projects or similar careers.

COMPROMISES:

Be careful not to constantly test or criticize each other. You need to focus on positive values, and not forever try to meet each other's standards or get bogged down in details. Bring a variety of friends into your life to add balance.

SIGN MATES:

Virgos Sophia Loren and Sean Connery

Virgo/Libra

GOOD CHEMISTRY:

You are intelligent companions with refined tastes, both perfectionists in different ways. The Libra charm and elegant style work nicely with Virgo clearheaded decision making.

COMPROMISES:

Libra responds to admiration and can turn off to criticism or too much negativity. Virgo will need to use diplomacy to keep the Libra scales in balance. Virgo appreciates function as well as form, and sticks to a budget. Extravagant Libra spends for beauty alone, regardless of the price tag.

SIGN MATES:

Virgo Jada Pinkett Smith and Libra Will Smith

Virgo/Scorpio

GOOD CHEMISTRY:

With Scorpio, Virgo encounters intense feelings too powerful to intellectualize or analyze. This could be a grand passion, especially when Scorpio is challenged to uncover the Virgo earthy, sensual side. Your penetrating minds are simpatico, and so is your dedication to do meaningful work (here is a fellow healer). Virgo provides the stability and structure that keeps Scorpio on the right track.

COMPROMISES:

Virgo may cool off if Scorpio goes to extremes or plays manipulative games. Scorpio could find Virgo perfectionism irritating and the Virgo approach to sex too limited.

SIGN MATES:

Virgo Elvis Costello and Scorpio Diana Krall

Virgo/Sagittarius

GOOD CHEMISTRY:

Sagittarius inspires Virgo to take risks and win, brings fun, laughter, and mental stimulation to Virgo life. Virgo supplies a much needed support system, organizing and following through on Sagittarius ideas. These two signs fulfill important needs for each other.

COMPROMISES:

Virgo won't relate to the Sagittarius happy-go-lucky financial philosophy and reluctance to make firm commitments. Sagittarius would rather deal with the big picture, and may resent Virgo preoccupation with details. Sexual fidelity could be a key issue if the Sagittarius casual approach to sex conflicts with the Virgo desire to have everything perfect.

SIGN MATES:

Virgo Sophia Loren and Sagittarius Carlo Ponti
Virgo Beyoncé Knowles and Sagittarius Jay-Z

Virgo/Capricorn

GOOD CHEMISTRY:

This looks like a sure thing between two signs who have so much in common. You're good providers, and you both have a strong sense of duty and respect for order. You have similar conservative tastes and a basically traditional approach to relationships. You could accomplish much together.

COMPROMISES:

You may be too similar! The strong initial chemistry could give way to boredom. Romance needs challenges to keep the sparks flying.

SIGN MATES:

Virgo Lauren Bacall and Capricorn Humphrey Bogart

Virgo/Aquarius

GOOD CHEMISTRY:

Aquarius inspires Virgo to get involved in problem solving on a large scale. You are both analytical and inquisitive, and can both be detached emotionally. You'll appeal to each other's idealistic side, fueling interest with good mental communication.

COMPROMISES:

Virgo has a basically traditional, conservative outlook while Aquarius likes to stay open to all possibilities and can swing into spur-of-the-moment action. Virgo nerves could be jangled by Aquarius unpredictability and constant need for company. Aquarius could feel confined by the Virgo structured, ordered approach and focus on details.

SIGN MATES:

Virgo Lance Armstrong and Aquarius Sheryl Crow
Virgo Cameron Diaz and Aquarius Justin Timberlake

Virgo/Pisces

GOOD CHEMISTRY:

Virgo supplies what Pisces often needs most—clarity and order—while Pisces sensuality and creative imagination takes the Virgo lifestyle into fascinating new realms. If you can reconcile your opposing points of view, you'll have much to gain from this relationship.

COMPROMISES:

There are many adjustments for both signs here. Virgo could feel over your head with Pisces emotions and seeming lack of control and become frustrated when makeover attempts fail. Pisces could feel bogged down with Virgo worries and deflated by negative criticism. Try to support, not change, each other.

SIGN MATES:

Virgo Richard Gere and Pisces Cindy Crawford
Virgo Claudia Schiffer and Pisces Matthew Vaughn
Virgo Virginia Madsen and Pisces Antonio Sabato, Jr.

CHAPTER 22

Astrological Overview for Virgo in 2007

Welcome to 2007, Virgo! You're in for an intriguing year, with some excellent changes. Let's take a closer look.

The year begins with Mercury, your ruler, in Capricorn and your fifth house, so the first fifteen days of January really favor creative endeavors. It's a good time to plan and lay down your strategies concerning your creative projects. By January 15, Mercury moves into your sixth house, which indicates more communication with coworkers and employees.

The biggest change this year will happen in early September when Saturn, the planet that governs physical reality, moves into your sign. This two and a half year transit will test what you're made of. If your goals are solid and worthy of your talents, this transit will strengthen your resolve and provide a stronger structure through which to achieve your goals. If you've been floundering, Saturn will help you find your path. Relationships that have outlived their purposes may fall away from your life, but new, stronger relationships will enter. During this transit, Saturn will demand that you honor your responsibilities, obligations, and commitments.

Jupiter continues its transit through Sagittarius and your solar fourth house for most of the year. This transit should expand the foundation of your life in some way. You may move to a larger house with more property or your household could expand in some way.

Uranus, the planet of sudden, unexpected change, continues its transit through Pisces and your solar seventh house. Relationship begin and end abruptly, but the people who enter your life are unusual, perhaps even brilliant in some way. Embrace change. That's what Uranus expects of you.

The best times for romance this year occur when Venus is in your sign—between July 14 and November 7. However, from July 27 to September 7, Venus is moving retrograde, so its energies don't work as smoothly. It's best to get involved when Venus is moving direct. Another favorable time for romance is when Venus moves through your ninth house—March 17 to April 10. It's especially favorable for romance in a foreign country or with a foreign-born individual.

If you're planning a move, do it before September 2, when Saturn moves into your sign. One of the most opportune times to move is between August 6 and September 1.

From January 16 to February 24, your sex life should pick up in a major way! Mars will be transiting your fifth house of romance and pleasure during this time. As long as you aren't looking for commitment, this should be a terrific transit.

Another transit to watch for: Jupiter's transit into Capricorn and your solar fifth house on December 18. This transit will last for about a year and spells a period of expansion in your romantic opportunities, pleasurable activities, speculative ventures, and your creativity.

Your finances look especially good between November 8 and December 4, when Venus is transiting your second solar house of money.

Here are some dates to watch for this year:

March 18: Mercury and Venus travel at favorable angles to each other, through your solar seventh house. This combination favors romance, great communication, and intuitive connections in all partnerships.

April 12: Mercury and Venus are moving at favorable angles to each other again, stimulating activities in your career and in resources you share with others. You may have to make some adjustments in your love life or in your artistic endeavors, but Virgo excels at such details.

May 1: The sun and Mercury travel very close together through your solar fifth house. This combination favors your creative projects. You find your creative niche, and you are able to flow with your ideas. Your children and everything you do for enjoyment and pleasure also figure into the equation. Mars and Uranus are also traveling closely together though your solar seventh house. This combination adds excitement and visceral attraction to all your partnerships.

October 13–19: During this time, Venus and Saturn travel closely together through your sign. This combination can bring delays or restrictions in romance, or it can bring structure to your artistic endeavors. It's likely that responsibilities in some area of your life increase.

December 22: This day could be one of the best for you this year. The sun, Mercury, and Jupiter are traveling together through Capricorn and your fifth house. This trio favors speculation, gambling, your children, your pleasures, romance, and your creativity.

There are four eclipse dates to watch for this year. Two of them involve Virgo, two Pisces. Lunar eclipses tend to bring up emotional issues related to the sign and house in which they fall and solar eclipses tend to reveal something that has been hidden. On March 3, the lunar eclipse in your sign will bring up an emotional issue connected with how others perceive you. Two weeks later, on March 18, the solar eclipse in Pisces brings to light something that has been hidden from you in a partnership.

On August 28, there's a lunar eclipse in Pisces. This eclipse hits your seventh house of partnerships, so expect an emotional issue to surface in that area. On September 11, the solar eclipse is in Virgo. This eclipse reveals something to you concerning how others see you.

Every year, your ruler, Mercury, turns retrograde three times, and during these periods, it's easy to be misunderstood, travel plans often go awry, and computers and other appliances act up. It's a good idea not to negotiate or sign contracts. The times to watch for are:

February 13–March 7—Mercury retrograde in Pisces (your seventh house). This retrograde affects your partnerships, both romantic and professional.

June 15–July 9—Mercury retrograde in Cancer (your eleventh house). Friendships, your networks, and your ambitions and dreams are influenced.

October 11–November 1—Mercury retrograde in Scorpio (your third house). Be clear and concise in your communications with siblings, relatives, and neighbors.

CHAPTER 23

Eighteen Months of Day-by-Day Predictions—July 2006 to December 2007

Moon sign times are calculated for Eastern Standard Time and Eastern Daylight Time. Please adjust for your local time zone.

JULY 2006

Saturday, July 1 (Moon in Virgo) What better way to start the month than with the moon in your sign? You're in the right place at the right time today, and it pays off down the road. Contacts you make benefit you the rest of the year.

Sunday, July 2 (Moon in Virgo to Libra 1:07 p.m.) You're on top of things. You may be getting ready for visitors for the July Fourth holiday and want everything to be just so. Be careful that you don't overspend. A Gemini plays an important role.

Monday, July 3 (Moon in Libra) You're seeking balance in your affairs today, but balance may be the quality that eludes you. Don't fret. Things will unfold according to a plan you can sense, but can't see.

Tuesday, July 4 (Moon in Libra) Happy Fourth of July! Mercury turns retrograde in Leo. For the next few weeks, don't let unexpected changes unhinge you. This is actually an excellent time for revisions and rethinking current projects. It's especially good for writers who are reworking manuscripts.

Wednesday, July 5 (Moon in Libra to Scorpio 1:14 a.m.) Whenever the moon goes into Scorpio, you feel everything more intensely. Today you're researching something you need for a project. You're looking for the bottom line, and before the moon leaves Scorpio, you will find it.

Thursday, July 6 (Moon in Scorpio) Jupiter turns direct today in Scorpio in your third house. You're now able to integrate your worldview and spiritual beliefs into your communication projects. A Scorpio or another Virgo proves supportive.

Friday, July 7 (Moon in Scorpio to Sagittarius 9:14 a.m.) The moon joins Pluto in your fourth house. This combination can lead to power struggles with someone at home. But if you and other family members are clear on who is responsible for what, the risk of such power struggles is minimized.

Saturday, July 8 (Moon in Sagittarius) You're restless to travel. Either leave town for the weekend or start planning a trip overseas. Don't obsess about whether you can afford it. Just make your plans. That doesn't cost anything!

Sunday, July 9 (Moon in Sagittarius to Capricorn 3:25 p.m.) Did you read the Declaration of Independence on the Fourth of July? If not, do so immediately. Remind yourself about the founding tenets of the world's greatest experiment in democracy.

Monday, July 10 (Moon in Capricorn) Believe it or not, it's a day to play and have some fun, Virgo. Yes, fun is sometimes a foreign concept to you, but at least once a month, the stars support the pleasure principle!

Tuesday, July 11 (Moon in Capricorn to Aquarius 5:46 p.m.) It's time to tend to health concerns. Make appointments with your dentist and your eye doctor and anyone else you have put off seeing. You may be looking for a new health insurance policy too.

Wednesday, July 12 (Moon in Aquarius) Coworkers and you get together this evening for drinks and dinner. These contacts are important to you. Some of your coworkers are like family, and you can speak freely to them.

Thursday, July 13 (Moon in Aquarius to Pisces 7:00 p.m.) With the moon joining retrograde Uranus in your seventh house, your personal relationships may feel somewhat strained. Be honest about what you think and feel, and rest assured that the strain will vanish.

Friday, July 14 (Moon in Pisces) Your imagination and intuition are your strongest allies. Use them to negotiate the best terms on a contract. A Scorpio provides you with information that you need before making a decision about something near and dear to your heart.

Saturday, July 15 (Moon in Pisces to Aries 8:39 p.m.) Your focus is on resources you share with others—or which they share with you. Joint bank accounts and jointly held properties play an important role. Resist the urge to make a large expenditure.

Sunday, July 16 (Moon in Aries) This moon brings a certain restlessness to your daily life. You aren't sure what you want to do or achieve today. Best to begin with an agenda and then try to follow it so you'll feel you've accomplished something.

Monday, July 17 (Moon in Aries to Taurus 11:45 p.m.) Long-distance travel is a possibility. Or you may come home from work this evening and find your in-laws have dropped in for a surprise visit. Just roll with the punches, Virgo. Try not to have preconceived notions about anything.

Tuesday, July 18 (Moon in Taurus) Venus moves into Cancer today, favoring publicity, promotion, and advertising. Sometime between now and mid-August, romance is likely with a new acquaintance. Call it chemistry or fate, but the relationship proves beneficial for both of you.

Wednesday, July 19 (Moon in Taurus) You may be so stubborn about something today that you cut yourself off from other options. Remain open to other opinions and ideas, and realize that everyone wants to be heard.

Thursday, July 20 (Moon in Taurus to Gemini 4:39 a.m.) Your mind hums with ideas and plans related to your career. The challenge is to weed out the ones that don't seem to meet your discriminating standards. You may be left with a half dozen viable alternatives. Pick two, Virgo.

Friday, July 21 (Moon in Gemini) Your networking skills pay off today. You make contact with a Libra or an Aquarius who is excited by your talents and ideas. The partnership looks very promising.

Saturday, July 22 (Moon in Gemini to Cancer 11:29 a.m.) Mars moves into Virgo today. For the next six weeks, your energy is so powerful that you burn your candle at both ends. It's likely that you'll become involved in a highly charge sexual relationship that may challenge some of your deepest beliefs about what is possible between two people.

Sunday, July 23 (Moon in Cancer) With the moon in Cancer and Mars in your sign, you're a powerhouse of energy and activity today. Others recognize this and may depend on you to initiate action. But you have your own ideas about how to get things done. Don't let anyone push you around.

Monday, July 24 (Moon in Cancer to Leo 8:25 p.m.) This evening, you'll feel like being alone or with just one or two other people. Chill out. You need the relaxation. You excel at any work done behind the scenes.

Tuesday, July 25 (Moon in Leo) You're recognized privately by someone who appreciates your skills and abilities. You may confide in a close friend about certain issues related to your childhood that are surfacing now. Take heart, Virgo. You're preparing yourself for when the moon enters your sign the day after tomorrow.

Wednesday, July 26 (Moon in Leo) Your revisions are nearly done, and the new product really shines. You give the manuscript or product to someone whose opinion you trust, and that person loves the finished product as much as you do.

Thursday, July 27 (Moon in Leo to Virgo 7:37 a.m.) It's a good day. Your self-confidence is noticed by someone who has been watching you for quite some time; today that person musters the courage to strike up a conversation. A romance may be in the offing. Use your intuition to decide if this person is worth your time and effort.

Friday, July 28 (Moon in Virgo) Mercury finally turns direct again. Get out your maps, your e-tickets, and your travel plans. It's time to go see the world, Virgo. Yes, you can afford the time off work.

Saturday, July 29 (Moon in Virgo to Libra 8:28 p.m.) You feel the shift as the moon moves into Libra tonight. You're suddenly in the mood for romance, beauty, and soft music. Maybe it's the summer breeze or the scent of roses from your garden, but you're very optimistic about the future.

Sunday, July 30 (Moon in Libra) The arts, music, and your personal values come into play. If you have artistic aspirations, take a step toward achieving those dreams. Invest in your future.

Monday, July 31 (Moon in Libra) You have some extra money this week. Find a stock or investment that is in line with your deeper beliefs and put your money there.

AUGUST 2006

Tuesday, August 1 (Moon in Libra to Scorpio 9:08 a.m.) Your daily routine may be hectic today. You're running errands, carpooling, and generally doing cleanup duty for other people. It doesn't sound very appealing, but hey, Virgo, we all have days like this.

Wednesday, August 2 (Moon in Scorpio) You're recycling old memories of a former neighborhood and an earlier time in your life. This is fine as long as you don't get stuck in the past. You're much too future-oriented to let the old days influence your present course.

Thursday, August 3 (Moon in Scorpio to Sagittarius 7:14 p.m.) As the moon joins Pluto in your fourth house, you strive for a broader picture concerning your family and their goals and dreams.

Friday, August 4 (Moon in Sagittarius) You feel conflicted. A part of you wants to stay close to home, but another part of you wants to get out and about. A trip may be in order for your family and you. It doesn't have to be a long trip (although that would be okay)—just a change in perspective.

Saturday, August 5 (Moon in Sagittarius) Think big, Virgo. The world is your oyster—just make sure the oyster isn't rotten. Footloose and fancy free is the way to be!

Sunday, August 6 (Moon in Sagittarius to Capricorn 1:20 a.m.) It's a good day to build a foundation for your creative project. Whether you're writing a screenplay or putting together a portfolio of photos or art, build on what you've done so far. This is the kind of detail work at which you excel.

Monday, August 7 (Moon in Capricorn) If you've got a hunch on lucky numbers for today, then by all means play them. In fact, you're lucky in all speculative ventures today—including romance.

Tuesday, August 8 (Moon in Capricorn to Aquarius 3:48 a.m.) As the moon moves into your sixth house, be sure to watch your emotional barometer. There's a definite link between your emotions and your health. Stress often hits you in the stomach first. Try chewing a couple of papaya enzymes if your stomach is upset.

Wednesday, August 9 (Moon in Aquarius) Your ideas are cutting-edge, and you find support to implement them among coworkers. This evening, you get together with friends and have lively discussions about the latest books, movies, and political news.

Thursday, August 10 (Moon in Aquarius to Pisces 4:11 a.m.) The moon joins Uranus retrograde in your seventh house. You and your partner may disagree on the finer points today, but you agree on the larger picture. The Pisces moon stimulates your imagination. Even if, on a mundane level, something doesn't make sense to you, it certainly does on a larger scale.

Friday, August 11 (Moon in Pisces) Embrace the mysterious, Virgo. Toss your natural caution to the wind. It's time to spread your wings a bit and explore what's out there.

Saturday, August 12 (Moon in Pisces to Aries 4:23 a.m.) Venus moves into Leo, joining Saturn in your twelfth house. A love affair is possible during the next three weeks, and the significant other could be somewhat older than you. This relationship takes place hidden away from others.

Sunday, August 13 (Moon in Aries) You and your lover or significant other embark on a new venture together. It may involve a business or an adventure, but whatever it is, you're excited about it.

Monday, August 14 (Moon in Aries to Taurus 6:01 a.m.) You and a friend sign up for a course or workshop. It could be an adult education course or something more esoteric, like an alternative healing workshop. Whatever it is, you're excited about the options it will open up for you.

Tuesday, August 15 (Moon in Taurus) Your travel today may be related to your spiritual or political beliefs. A Leo or a Taurus tags along for the adventure. Your sensuality is heightened, and you revel in the scent of the air and the feel of the August sun.

Wednesday, August 16 (Moon in Taurus to Gemini 10:08 a.m.) You may feel like two people today. One side of you wants to kick back and take it easy; the other is raring to get moving. You solve your dilemma of course. Problem solving is one of your many gifts.

Thursday, August 17 (Moon in Gemini) Network, network. Your abundant energy serves you well today. You're able to tackle any number of things related to your career and smooth out glitches by the end of the day. A few months from now, this could pay off in a raise or promotion.

Friday, August 18 (Moon in Gemini to Cancer 5:04 p.m.) This moon is pretty comfortable for you. Its nurturing and intuitive aspects feed your need to be of service to others, and today you have an opportunity to do that. You do a favor for someone who shares your passions.

Saturday, August 19 (Moon in Cancer) You depend on friends today to support you through a tough time. It's not that the events are horrible, but you're frazzled. Take a deep breath. Then do the best that you can with what's available.

Sunday, August 20 (Moon in Cancer) You print up brochures today to advertise your business or product. A friend has good ideas about distribution and how to reach more people. You also find additional information on the Internet and in books. Get busy, Virgo!

Monday, August 21 (Moon in Cancer to Leo 2:34 a.m.) You wake this morning with a need for solitude. Even if you don't realize that you need it, you will before the day is out. It's as if there are too many people eating up your time. Today is for you.

Tuesday, August 22 (Moon in Leo) You may be on a gardening kick today. Just being outside in nature does wonders for your soul. As you weed and plant, you're also ridding yourself of the nonessentials from your life and seeding new ideas and energy.

Wednesday, August 23 (Moon in Leo to Virgo 2:08 p.m.) For the next couple days, you're flying high. These are your power days, with the moon in your sign and your inner and outer selves in sync. Schedule important meetings for today. Your energy is so abundant that if you do your part, the universe will do the rest.

Thursday, August 24 (Moon in Virgo) You have a chance to demonstrate your self-expression to people in authority or to someone you hope to impress. Just be yourself. Maintain your self-confidence. If you're interviewing for a job, you'll get it.

Friday, August 25 (Moon in Virgo) You land the project you've hoped for. All you have to do is make the deadline. But you're always efficient and conscientious, so that shouldn't be a problem. Just remember to enjoy yourself too!

Saturday, August 26 (Moon in Virgo to Libra 3:01 a.m.) You undertake some home beautification projects that begin small and end big. That's okay. It was time to tackle these projects; the end result will increase the value of your home.

Sunday, August 27 (Moon in Libra) Mercury moves into Virgo for a two-week stay that is beneficial for you. Your mind literally clicks along now, with barely a hiccup of hesitation. The transit favors writers or educators.

Monday, August 28 (Moon in Libra to Scorpio 3:56 p.m.) An intense day is before you, Virgo. Time to open up the heart and let powerful emotions out. Okay, so its overwhelming and scary. But it's also an experience, and if you can maintain that attitude, you'll make out remarkably well.

Tuesday, August 29 (Moon in Scorpio) You and a neighbor discover that you have more in common than you thought. The chemistry is there. Is this just a brief attraction or could it be the real thing?

Wednesday, August 30 (Moon in Scorpio) Your sister or brother needs some family support today. You give it gladly, yet wonder why this person has one drama after another.

Thursday, August 31 (Moon in Scorpio to Sagittarius 3:00 a.m.) Take off early today and head off for a long weekend with your family. You all need to reconnect. Whatever needs to be aired among you will certainly find its way into the open.

SEPTEMBER 2006

Friday, September 1 (Moon in Sagittarius)   A few tensions surface at home. It's nothing serious, but you need to clear the air of misunderstandings that may have developed over the past few months. A visitor from out of town is possible. Don't let the visit throw you off.

Saturday, September 2 (Moon in Sagittarius to Capricorn 10:35 a.m.)   You're a consummate planner today, and the plan is for a party this evening. Even if it's casual, you've got the details lined up so that the entire evening goes without a hitch. In some way, this evening's festivities feed into a creative project.

Sunday, September 3 (Moon in Capricorn)   Yesterday's party becomes today's creative project. Your creative adrenaline is racing and you're able to make significant strides on a project. A Virgo or a Pisces is helpful.

Monday, September 4 (Moon in Capricorn to Aquarius 2:15 p.m.)   Pluto turns direct in Sagittarius in your fourth house. This movement releases pent-up energy related to your home and personal environment. Life should go more smoothly now.

Tuesday, September 5 (Moon in Aquarius)   You're part of a team at work. Even if the idea initially turns you off, you realize by the day's end that a team effort was required for this particular project.

Wednesday, September 6 (Moon in Aquarius to Pisces 2:57 p.m.)   Venus moves into Virgo today. For the next three weeks, you attract opportunities related to the arts, money, and romance. If you're already in a committed relationship, you and your partner are in for a real treat!

Thursday, September 7 (Moon in Pisces) Mars moves into Libra and your second house today. This transit, which lasts about six weeks, signals a period of hard work. You may be putting in a lot of overtime to complete a particular project or simply to earn extra money.

Friday, September 8 (Moon in Pisces to Aries 2:24 p.m.) You may be fretting about your quarterly taxes. No point in worrying. Just pay the piper and move on. It may be time to consult an accountant, however, so you can get more write-offs.

Saturday, September 9 (Moon in Aries) You and your partner could be considering a join venture of some kind. Perhaps you're going to buy a house or property together. Whatever the venture, make sure you agree completely on the fine points.

Sunday, September 10 (Moon in Aries to Taurus 2:31 p.m.) You're feeling especially stubborn today. The issue could be related to a publishing venture or to some belief you hold. Be careful that you don't sabotage your own best interests.

Monday, September 11 (Moon in Taurus) This can be a sensuous placement for the moon, and if you're sensitive to it, you may be in the mood for romance and love. If you're not currently in a relationship, then the person on whom you turn your affections may be a foreign-born individual.

Tuesday, September 12 (Moon in Taurus to Gemini 5:00 p.m.) Mercury moves into your second house. For the next two weeks, your mind is focused on ways to earn more money for beautifying your surroundings. If you're in the market for a big-ticket item, look around, but don't make the purchase until Mercury has moved into Scorpio.

Wednesday, September 13 (Moon in Gemini) Your career is in the spotlight. Your boss sends you out of town to check on the competition. It's the kind of trip you enjoy. You manage to make some new professional contacts, as well.

Thursday, September 14 (Moon in Gemini to Cancer 10:54 p.m.) Late this evening, you feel a distinct shift in energy as the moon moves into a harmonious angle with your sun. Your intuition is now one of your strongest allies. You're gearing up for a very busy day tomorrow.

Friday, September 15 (Moon in Cancer) Your friends are your support group today; they help you publicize and advertise a product. You may be rethinking your goals and ambitions too.

Saturday, September 16 (Moon in Cancer) Your mother or some other nurturing female in your life presents you with ideas or a plan related to publicity. Listen with an open mind.

Sunday, September 17 (Moon in Cancer to Leo 8:15 a.m.) The moon joins Saturn in your twelfth house. Sometimes, this transit results in depression. The best way to use the lunar energy is to plan a project or activity that you can do in solitude ahead of time.

Monday, September 18 (Moon in Leo) You and a close friend kick back and take it easy today. Your withdrawal from activity and other people is actually good for you. You're preparing yourself for when the moon moves into your sign.

Tuesday, September 19 (Moon in Leo to Virgo 8:07 p.m.) By this evening, you're in top form. You're ready to take on anything or anyone. Your sex appeal is soaring. This energy shift is apparent to everyone who knows you, and it attracts the attention of someone special.

Wednesday, September 20 (Moon in Virgo) Yesterday's special someone makes a move today. Your romance begins to heat up. What are you really looking for, Virgo? Romance or fun? Long-term commitment or a short-term companion? You don't have to decide right away.

Thursday, September 21 (Moon in Virgo) Your ability to solve problems is noticed by your boss or someone else in authority. Down the road, this could pay off in a significant raise or a promotion. Just keep doing the work, Virgo. No one else excels at details like you do.

Friday, September 22 (Moon in Virgo to Libra 9:07 a.m.) Early this morning, the moon joins Mars in your second house. This transit brings an intuitive component to any investments that you make today. You may be somewhat short-tempered, though. Strive for patience.

Saturday, September 23 (Moon in Libra) You're especially artistic or musical today. This could mean that you satisfy the itch by buying stereo equipment or a new CD or that you stock up on art supplies. If you're really ambitious, you may decide to paint a couple rooms in your house.

Sunday, September 24 (Moon in Libra to Scorpio 9:55 p.m.) With the moon moving into intense Scorpio, you feel more deeply than usual. You may be researching or investigating trouble in your neighborhood. You won't rest until you get to the bottom of it.

Monday, September 25 (Moon in Scorpio) Is it possible that a neighbor or someone you know as a friend could become a romantic partner? Love happens in the strangest places, Virgo. Keep your options open.

Tuesday, September 26 (Moon in Scorpio) With the moon and Jupiter in your third house, your communication abilities and opportunities expand. You may be looking at other neighborhoods too, trying to decide if you want to move.

Wednesday, September 27 (Moon in Scorpio to Sagittarius 9:17 a.m.) Early this morning, you begin to grasp the larger picture of your family's goals. It may be time for a family meeting concerning where you all would like to be living in the future.

Thursday, September 28 (Moon in Sagittarius) You and your family leave town for a long weekend. It's a great opportunity to solidify family bonds and to get to know your kids as people.

Friday, September 29 (Moon in Sagittarius to Capricorn 6:02 p.m.) You and your kids are busy having fun today! What a concept, right, Virgo? Even though you may be champing at the bit to tackle work you've brought with you, resist the urge. Kick back and enjoy yourself.

Saturday, September 30 (Moon in Capricorn) Venus moves into Libra today, joining Mars in your second house. This transit is wonderful for financial opportunities and windfalls. It also brings pleasure to whatever you do to earn a living.

OCTOBER 2006

Sunday, October 1 (Moon in Capricorn to Aquarius 11:25 p.m.) Mercury moves into Scorpio, joining Jupiter in your third house. This transit expands your ideas and writing abilities. You may be doing more running around than usual during the next two weeks, but it all has a larger purpose.

Monday, October 2 (Moon in Aquarius) Coworkers are supportive and rally around an idea that you have for improving a work situation. You have more communication than usual with a group of friends. You volunteer for something the group has decided upon and the results are positive!

Tuesday, October 3 (Moon in Aquarius) It's time to seek out advice from an alternative medicine practitioner about a recurring health problem. It's nothing serious, and stress may be what's causing it. If you don't have a regular exercise routine, get started today.

Wednesday, October 4 (Moon in Aquarius to Pisces 1:34 a.m.) When the moon joins Uranus in your seventh house, your emotional responses are erratic and unusual. It may be that your responses are warning you about the potential pitfalls in a particular relationship. Listen to your intuition on this one.

Thursday, October 5 (Moon in Pisces) You may inadvertently uncover information about a particular past life you had. The issue in that life may have carried over into this one. Trust your intuitive information. You may want to find a past-life hypnotist who can help you delve even deeper.

Friday, October 6 (Moon in Pisces to Aries 1:33 a.m.) A possible mix-up occurs in an insurance payment. Call and get the matter cleared up. Your attorney contacts you with an idea about estate or tax planning.

Saturday, October 7 (Moon in Aries) You're feeling inordinately restless. It's time for you and your business partner to have a heart-to-heart talk about goals and plans for your venture. Stay on top of details.

Sunday, October 8 (Moon in Aries to Taurus 1:05 a.m.) You start planing an overseas trip. It's not strictly for pleasure; you can do business abroad. Or your trip is connected to your spiritual beliefs.

Monday, October 9 (Moon in Taurus) A Virgo or a Scorpio plays a vital role in your affairs. It's possible that you've hired another employee for your company or an assistant to help you with a publishing project. Your creative energy is powerful.

Tuesday, October 10 (Moon in Taurus to Gemini 2:06 a.m.) As the moon begins its transit through your tenth house, your energy turns toward your career. Books, communication, and travel figure prominently. If you're in sales, you do extremely well before the day's end.

Wednesday, October 11 (Moon in Gemini) You move ahead on your manuscript, portfolio, or some other creative project. If you're interviewing for a job, all goes very well. People are impressed with your abilities and your gift of gab.

Thursday, October 12 (Moon in Gemini to Cancer 6:21 a.m.) You get together this evening with your support group. These people share your interests and passions and form an important part of your life. In fact, tonight's meeting may take place in your home.

Friday, October 13 (Moon in Cancer) You may have to rearrange a few details concerning goals you've set for yourself. The timing may be off or perhaps you've overestimated what's involved.

Saturday, October 14 (Moon in Cancer to Leo 2:38 p.m.) As you move into autumn, you need days like today, when you spend time alone or with a partner or close friend. You shine at anything you do behind the scenes. You may visit a friend who is in the hospital or recuperating from an illness.

Sunday, October 15 (Moon in Leo)   Issues from your childhood or even a past life may be surfacing. Rather than ignoring the problem, dive in. Gain some insight before the moon goes into your sign the day after tomorrow.

Monday, October 16 (Moon in Leo)   Children figure into the day's events. They may not be your kids, but their energy boosts your spirits. One of these children says or does something that becomes fodder for a creative project you've been working on.

Tuesday, October 17 (Moon in Leo to Virgo 2:16 a.m.)   You never know where inspiration will come from, so be open to everything. People are attracted to you for a variety of reasons: help, friendship, romance. Life is a feast, Virgo. Enjoy it.

Wednesday, October 18 (Moon in Virgo)   Your writing skills are at their peak. You know exactly where you're going with a book you're working on, and your excitement spills over into other areas of your life. Look to a Capricorn for help in structuring your time so that you always make time for this project.

Thursday, October 19 (Moon in Virgo to Libra 3:20 p.m.)   An admirer brings you an expensive gift. You may be conflicted about accepting it because you're afraid strings are attached. Address the issue. Make your position understood.

Friday, October 20 (Moon in Libra)   Something you lost recently is found. The missing object may return to you in a strange way. Take note of any synchronicities involved.

Saturday, October 21 (Moon in Libra)   You get together with friends and visit an art gallery or take in a new film. Your artistic sensitivities are powerful, and you may dig out a canvas and paints that you haven't used in a while. Or maybe photography is your thing. It's a fine day to indulge yourself in the arts or music.

Sunday, October 22 (Moon in Libra to Scorpio 3:55 a.m.) An emotional confrontation is possible with a sibling or neighbor. It could be caused by feelings of possessiveness and a general misunderstanding of personal boundaries.

Monday, October 23 (Moon in Scorpio) As Mars joins the moon in your third house, yesterday's rift deepens. Mars always energizes whatever it touches, so be careful that you don't lose your temper or blow something small way out of proportion.

Tuesday, October 24 (Moon in Scorpio to Sagittarius 2:54 p.m.) Venus moves into Scorpio and joins Mercury, Mars, and Jupiter in your third house. It's getting crowded! Your passions are running deep, and you're in the mood for an affair, a romance, or a combination of the two. Any relationship that begins under these transits is sure to be sexually charged.

Wednesday, October 25 (Moon in Sagittarius) You're in love with love today, and this feeling affects everything you do and everyone with whom you come into contact. Spread the cheer, Virgo!

Thursday, October 26 (Moon in Sagittarius to Capricorn 11:48 p.m.) Any speculative ventures that you undertake today should be done by following your intuitive guidance. You can listen to the experts, but ultimately, your own wisdom is the best.

Friday, October 27 (Moon in Capricorn) Your ambitions include having fun, and this is a day to do exactly that. Pack the kids in the car, and head out to the country for some fresh air.

Saturday, October 28 (Moon in Capricorn) Mercury turns retrograde in Scorpio. Until mid-November, be clear about what you want, particularly when dealing with siblings, relatives, or neighbors. This is the final Mercury retrograde of the year, but it could be a humdinger! Neptune turns direct today in your sixth house. Expect a shift in energy at work.

Sunday, October 29—Daylight Saving Time Ends (Moon in Capricorn to Aquarius 5:17 a.m.) Any health reports that you get back may contain erroneous information. Seek a second opinion.

Monday, October 30 (Moon in Aquarius) With Mercury retrograde, your communication with coworkers and employees could be slightly off center. Take time to explain what you want and when you want it.

Tuesday, October 31 (Moon in Aquarius to Pisces 10:11 a.m.) Happy Halloween! You and your partner or spouse may get a bit nuts tonight. You don costumes and hit the streets with the other trick-or-treaters and have a barrel of fun!

NOVEMBER 2006

Wednesday, November 1 (Moon in Pisces) The month begins with your ruler, Mercury, retrograde in your third house. Until the middle of this month, it's a good idea not to sign contracts. Be as clear and concise as possible when you communicate with others. There's plenty of room for miscommunication.

Thursday, November 2 (Moon in Pisces to Aries 10:47 a.m.) With the moon moving from your seventh to the eighth house this morning, your focus shifts from relationships to resources you share with others. Is it possible that your partner or spouse is in the running for a promotion or raise? If so, this can free you to pursue investments in land or other property.

Friday, November 3 (Moon in Aries) With the moon in Aries and Mercury, Mars, Jupiter, and Venus all in Scorpio in your third house, you've got your hands full! Life may be a bit nuts today, with lots of running around that doesn't seem to have any point. Take heart. Things calm down tomorrow.

Saturday, November 4 (Moon in Aries to Taurus 11:05 a.m.) The moon in Taurus is more to your liking. You feel more grounded and are more conscious of security issues today—not security in terms of safety, but in what makes you feel emotionally secure. Make lists. Maybe you need a certain amount of money in the bank or certain types of perks at work. Whatever it is, write it down.

Sunday, November 5 (Moon in Taurus) Yesterday's list becomes today's issues. Once you know what you need, you'll be able to get it. An in-law or a visitor from out of town figures into events.

Monday, November 6 (Moon in Taurus to Gemini 11:47 a.m.) A short trip is in order. Since Mercury is still retrograde, expect unexpected changes in your itinerary. Remain flexible and try to go with the flow, even if that flow doesn't seen very smooth at times.

Tuesday, November 7 (Moon in Gemini) Remain upbeat today. There could be a glitch in something you've planned or an appointment you have. If you can look at the day's events as an adventure, you'll come out ahead of the game.

Wednesday, November 8 (Moon in Gemini to Cancer 2:46 p.m.) Your energy flows smoothly today. With the help of friends, you're able to achieve most of what you set out to do. A Scorpio provides information you need to make an informed decision about an advertising or publicity matter.

Thursday, November 9 (Moon in Cancer) Intuitively, you're on top of everything. But your left brain is champing at the bit today, demanding that you cull facts and figures that support your hunch. Do your homework and then act.

Friday, November 10 (Moon in Cancer to Leo 9:35 p.m.) Old issues could surface today in strange ways. These issues may be related to events and relationships from your early childhood. If you're not in therapy, you should consider signing up for a few sessions with a therapist you trust. Or just get together with a close friends whose advice you respect.

Saturday, November 11 (Moon in Leo) You move ahead on a creative project. Even if you're revising and reevaluating, you make significant strides and can see the proverbial light at the end of the tunnel.

Sunday, November 12 (Moon in Leo) Take one more day to rest and replenish your inner resources. Your mother or a sibling has an opinion or advice you should heed. Your dream recall should be strong tonight. Request advice from a dream. Then have your pad and pen handy.

Monday, November 13 (Moon in Leo to Virgo 8:20 a.m.) Your inner and outer selves work together seamlessly today. A Capricorn is attracted to you and admires your dedication and your work ethic, but may not be much fun. Think twice, Virgo.

Tuesday, November 14 (Moon in Virgo) Any relationship that begins today may have communication glitches, and any contract that is signed may have to be revisited later in the month. A Taurus asks you to ride along on an out-of-town trip. You're not sure you can afford to take time off from work or if you even want to go. Follow your heart, Virgo.

Wednesday, November 15 (Moon in Virgo to Libra 9:15 p.m.) You may want to take out additional insurance on your belongings. But before you send a check, consider your deeper beliefs and how fear motivates you.

Thursday, November 16 (Moon in Libra) You may decide to bank the money that would have gone to the additional insurance you were considering yesterday. It's probably a smart move at this time. But the shift in your beliefs may cause you some anxiety. Don't waste time fretting, Virgo.

Friday, November 17 (Moon in Libra) Mercury turns direct. Put on your traveling shoe and sign contracts! Also, Venus moves into Sagittarius and your fourth house. This transit certainly makes for a more harmonious home life. If you're not in a committed relationship, watch out! Romance is rushing toward you—in an unexpected and exciting way!

Saturday, November 18 (Moon in Libra to Scorpio 9:48 a.m.) The moon joins Jupiter in your third house. You have magnanimous feelings toward siblings and neighbors and are able to mend a rift in a significant relationship.

Sunday, November 19 (Moon in Scorpio) Uranus turns direct in your seventh house. You'll feel this shift in your relationship with your romantic and business partners. Smoother communication is indicated and also some pleasant surprises!

Monday, November 20 (Moon in Scorpio to Sagittarius 8:16 p.m.) The moon joins Pluto and Venus in your fourth house. This powerful lineup of planets could bring power issues to the surface this evening. It doesn't necessarily mean a big blowout, but be aware of alternate ways to channel the energy.

Tuesday, November 21 (Moon in Sagittarius) One of your parents could be in need of your caring and support today. Service and problem solving are areas where you excel, so get busy untangling a complicated situation.

Wednesday, November 22 (Moon in Sagittarius) Treat yourself to a mental trip. Buy a book that expands your spiritual concepts or go to a movie that you've been wanting to see. Whatever you do, be sure that it's good for you.

Thursday, November 23 (Moon in Sagittarius to Capricorn 4:26 a.m.) Jupiter moves into Sagittarius and your fourth house, where it will remain for about a year. If you're going to move, between now and next summer is the time to do it. If you've been considering an overseas trip, why not schedule it for the Christmas holidays?

Friday, November 24 (Moon in Capricorn) You may set up an office in your home today or, at least, take steps in that direction. You're building on past creative successes right now, and while that's certainly admirable, you may want to consider trying something new.

Saturday, November 25 (Moon in Capricorn to Aquarius 10:41 a.m.) You may feel confused or sort of dreamy for much of the day. In this creative state of mind, you can accomplish some amazing things—if you can force yourself off the couch long enough. Exercise would help.

Sunday, November 26 (Moon in Aquarius) You may take out a membership in a gym. Even if weight training isn't really what you're looking for, there are other classes that could interest you: yoga, Pilates, aerobics. Any of these pursuits will mitigate the confusion in your work.

Monday, November 27 (Moon in Aquarius to Pisces 3:21 p.m.) Your spouse or partner has a good surprise for you, possibly including a marriage proposal. Go with your heart, and don't allow your left brain to throw up a dozen barriers!

Tuesday, November 28 (Moon in Pisces) Your imagination and intuition move hand in hand today to help you negotiate beneficial terms on a contract. Even if other people disagree with what you're asking, follow your inner guidance.

Wednesday, November 29 (Moon in Pisces to Aries 6:30 p.m.) Remember that surprise from your spouse? Well, today is the first step you take together toward owning property jointly. Perhaps you put a down payment on a house or a piece of land. Perhaps you buy a new car. Whatever it is, you're excited. This is the beginning of a whole new journey.

Thursday, November 30 (Moon in Aries) You're restless and eager to do something new. You don't lack for ideas or energy, but you may be restricted by circumstances. Whenever you run up against an obstacle in your life, focus on breaking through it. You can do it!

DECEMBER 2006

Friday, December 1 (Moon in Aries to Taurus 8:27 p.m.) As you enter the final month of the year, you're in good shape, Virgo. This evening, you attend a seminar on the publishing industry or on some spiritual issue that fascinates you.

Saturday, December 2 (Moon in Taurus) News from abroad is likely. You may hear that your writing project is accepted for publication or you may find an agent who wants to represent you.

Sunday, December 3 (Moon in Taurus to Gemini 10:06 p.m.) You may feel torn between your devotion to your family and your dedication to your career. It's not an either-or issue. You can do both by balancing the demands in your life.

Monday, December 4 (Moon in Gemini) Your way with words doesn't escape the notice of a boss or an authority figure. Before the beginning of the year, you may land a significant promotion, if you haven't already.

Tuesday, December 5 (Moon in Gemini) Mars joins Venus, Jupiter, and Pluto in your fourth house. This could spell a love affair or an intensely sexual relationship that will prove to be very significant. Also, Saturn turns direct in Leo, so it's time for you to reclaim any power you have disowned.

Wednesday, December 6 (Moon in Gemini to Cancer 1:02 a.m.) Advertising, promotion, and publicity are highlighted today. If you've recently started your own business, you need to get the word out about your company and product and this is the best time of the month to do it.

Thursday, December 7 (Moon in Cancer) You enlist your mother or another nurturing female in your life to do some legwork. She's glad to help and even flattered that you asked!

Friday, December 8 (Moon in Cancer to Leo 6:53 a.m.) 2nd TRIAL
With Mercury moving into Sagittarius, five out of ten planets are in your fourth house. Talk about heat and activity! You may not know whether you're coming or going, Virgo, but try to relax into the energy. None of it's negative. It's just frenetic.

Saturday, December 9 (Moon in Leo) This lunar transit of your twelfth house should be a bit easier now that Saturn is moving direct. Even if you are still a bit blue, you have a good grasp on the issues that make you feel that way. You're in a more powerful position now to effect change in your own life.

Sunday, December 10 (Moon in Leo to Virgo 4:32 p.m.) The moon finally moves into your sign and it's like a breath of spring air. You're calling the shots today on many levels. You'll find that most people agree with you and support your ideas.

Monday, December 11 (Moon in Virgo) Venus moves into Capricorn, a sure sign of a romance full of fun and pleasure. This transit, which lasts into early next year, also favors your creativity. If you're making changes in how you approach your creativity, now is the time to try out what you've learned.

Tuesday, December 12 (Moon in Virgo) Your penchant for details is unparalleled today. You recognize a pattern in something you're working on and tackle it with typical Virgo vengeance, staying with it until you gain full understanding.

Wednesday, December 13 (Moon in Virgo to Libra 5:01 a.m.) The holiday season is starting to spill over into your mood. You shop today for some special gifts for loved ones. These gifts may be more expensive than you anticipated, but go ahead and splurge.

Thursday, December 14 (Moon in Libra) You update your personal appearance with a different haircut, different clothes, or even bolder colors in clothing and makeup. You're reinventing yourself.

Friday, December 15 (Moon in Libra to Scorpio 5:43 p.m.) An intense emotional experience is likely today. It's not necessarily bad, but it does purge you of negativity. Afterward you'll feel renewed, refreshed, and ready to move ahead.

Saturday, December 16 (Moon in Scorpio) Your mind is exceptionally intuitive. You notice connections between people and events or situations that would otherwise elude you. Somehow, these synchronicities play into the larger issues in your life.

Sunday, December 17 (Moon in Scorpio) A Cancer or a Pisces triggers an emotional response in you that shocks everyone. You need to ask yourself what the deeper issue is. Find the bottom-line and you'll have a clearer understanding of your own motives.

Monday, December 18 (Moon in Scorpio to Sagittarius 4:10 a.m.) A foreigner or someone in publishing or the law figures into the day's events. You could be called for jury duty or have to see an attorney about a legal matter. The events turn out in your favor.

Tuesday, December 19 (Moon in Sagittarius) You're feeling emotionally expansive. People remark on how good you look, how energetic you seem. Encouraged, you continue your workouts at the gym.

Wednesday, December 20 (Moon in Sagittarius to Capricorn 11:39 a.m.) Any inner work you do today feeds into your creative adrenaline. In fact, you've learned to create from the inside out rather than the other way around.

Thursday, December 21 (Moon in Capricorn) Frantic with last-minute shopping, you nonetheless find pleasure and immense enjoyment in buying for the people you love. There's a creative element to it that appeals to you.

Friday, December 22 (Moon in Capricorn to Aquarius 4:49 p.m.) Your focus isn't really on work, but on spending quality time with friends. You bring this energy and enthusiasm into the workplace, and the goodwill carries you through the new year.

Saturday, December 23 (Moon in Aquarius) You may need more rest now than usual. With all the activity of the holidays, your nerves are in need of repair! Take some vitamin B and ply yourself with antioxidants.

Sunday, December 24 (Moon in Aquarius to Pisces 8:44 p.m.) You and your partner trade gifts this evening or do something special together. You have your choice of holiday festivities to attend. If you're tempted to overindulge, think twice!

Monday, December 25 (Moon in Pisces) Merry Christmas! Good cheer is in the air. Whether you're spending the day with family or friends, your mood is high and your heart open.

Tuesday, December 26 (Moon in Pisces) You may volunteer for a charity organization today. Your time spent helping them is appreciated by others and makes you feel good about yourself.

Wednesday, December 27 (Moon in Pisces to Aries 12:05 a.m.) Mercury joins Venus in your fifth house. Your mind—and your heart—are focused on romance and pleasure. Anything speculative that you take on at this time should turn out in your favor.

Thursday, December 28 (Moon in Aries) Your accountant advises you on last-minute tax write-offs. You may even consult your attorney about a change in your will. Tend to the details today so that by New Year's Eve, you can cruise into the new year with an unfettered mind.

Friday, December 29 (Moon in Aries to Taurus 3:09 a.m.) You may have an opportunity to take a last-minute trip. Even if you didn't want to leave home during the holidays, this opportunity will be tempting!

Saturday, December 30 (Moon in Taurus) You're in need of some contact with the natural world. Perhaps you and a friend or partner go out for a hike. Make contact with the deeper parts of yourself.

Sunday, December 31 (Moon in Taurus to Gemini 6:17 a.m.) Your career is highlighted. Even though tonight is New Year's Eve, you can still hobnob and network. You never know which contact will prove valuable.

HAPPY NEW YEAR!

JANUARY 2007

Monday, January 1 (Moon in Gemini) Focus on your career. Make a symbolic gesture that underscores what you would like to achieve this year in your career. Books and information flow your way and clarify your resolutions for 2007.

Tuesday, January 2 (Moon in Gemini to Cancer 10:15 a.m.) The Cancer moon is comfortable for you. It forms a harmonious angle to your sun and softens your usual angst about perfection. With this moon, something surfaces concerning friendships.

Wednesday, January 3 (Moon in Cancer) Venus moves into Aquarius and your sixth house. This transit, which lasts through January 26, favors a romance at work or with someone you meet through work. If you are already involved, Venus in Aquarius makes your daily work routine more pleasurable.

Thursday, January 4 (Moon in Cancer to Leo 4:15 p.m.) As the moon moves into your twelfth house this afternoon, you feel the subtle nuances of the shift. You may want some time alone, or issues from earlier in your life may surface. Either way, you benefit from exercise, solitude, and inner searching.

Friday, January 5 (Moon in Leo) With Mars in Aquarius, your work day is hectic, and you could be working longer hours than usual. But you are so naturally diligent that hard work doesn't bother you—as long as you can see the results.

Saturday, January 6 (Moon in Leo) You've got the itch to shine in some way, but the opportunity to do so may not present itself. That's okay. You'll shine when the moon moves into your sign early tomorrow morning. In the meantime, kick back and take in a movie or read one of the novels stacked beside your bed.

Sunday, January 7 (Moon in Leo to Virgo 1:19 a.m.) Celebrate. The moon is in your sign, and that means you're feeling in control of yourself and your world. Your inner and outer selves are in complete agreement, Virgo, so go enjoy yourself!

Monday, January 8 (Moon in Virgo) Another terrific day with the moon in your sign. Be careful that you aren't self-critical. The day's accent is on health and fitness. If you've been thinking about starting an exercise routine, do it. The same goes with a diet or new nutritional program.

Tuesday, January 9 (Moon in Virgo to Libra 1:15 p.m.) You feel a bit more vulnerable in terms of your own beliefs and values. Someone may challenge you about a belief you hold. Rather than arguing or getting defensive, back off.

Wednesday, January 10 (Moon in Libra) You surround yourself with pretty things that comfort you. Soft silks, pastels, beautifully prepared foods, even gorgeous animals. You may tend to blow a lot of money on some pretty item you think you really want. Wait a few days and then decide if you can really afford it.

Thursday, January 11 (Moon in Libra) Relationships rise to the forefront. You need to be cooperative but not compliant, willing to bend but not to bend so much that you lose sight of your own needs. Find something that you love to do and then go do it!

Friday, January 12 (Moon in Libra to Scorpio 2:08 a.m.) Your emotions are more intense, your instincts more visceral. Your relationships with neighbors and siblings are accented. Your communications with people tend to be emotional.

Saturday, January 13 (Moon in Scorpio) The moon and Venus are companionable and feed your creative drive. Listen to your intuition, which is particularly strong. If you're conflicted about making a decision, wait until the moon is in your sign.

Sunday, January 14 (Moon in Scorpio to Sagittarius 1:12 p.m.) Both your home life and your career are accented. You may feel at odds about your obligations in these two areas. The secret to navigating the conflict lies in seeing the bigger picture.

Monday, January 15 (Moon in Sagittarius) Mercury moves into Aquarius, bringing a distinctive visionary flavor to your perceptions. Coworkers and your daily work routine figure prominently in the day's events. You have more contact than usual with coworkers and employees.

Tuesday, January 16 (Moon in Sagittarius to Capricorn 8:50 p.m.) Mars moves into Capricorn, forming a harmonious angle with your sun. Think of this transit as a booster rocket that gets you moving in a more creative direction. You're able to organize your creative activities. And as a great side benefit, you pursue pleasure and romance with terrific results!

Wednesday, January 17 (Moon in Capricorn) As the moon and Mars travel together through your solar fifth house, your creative energy is extraordinary. You're able to access the deeper portions of your psyche to find whatever you need to start or complete creative projects.

Thursday, January 18 (Moon in Capricorn) If you feel vulnerable and short tempered, take a few deep breaths and repeat, "I am safe." And you will be, Virgo. Belief is everything.

Friday, January 19 (Moon in Capricorn to Aquarius 1:16 a.m.) The moon joins Venus and Neptune in Aquarius in your solar sixth house. This combination certainly favors romance at work. Has a coworker attracted your attention? If so, observe that person from a distance. You may not have the full picture.

Saturday, January 20 (Moon in Aquarius) Kick back and relax. Get together with friends who share your interests and passions. You may feel intellectually daring, so run with whatever ideas you have. You won't regret it.

Sunday, January 21 (Moon in Aquarius to Pisces 3:49 a.m.) The moon moves into your seventh house. Since it's opposed to your sun, you may feel conflicted about a personal relationship. Try not to obsess about it. This conflict is just a phase.

Monday, January 22 (Moon in Pisces) You're attracted to pastel colors in your clothing, your decorations, even in your mood. Your intuition is heightened, and if you listen closely, it may lead you in some new and exciting direction!

Tuesday, January 23 (Moon in Pisces to Aries 5:53 a.m.) The Aries moon isn't very comfortable for you. You could feel irritable or impatient with the people around you. The best way to navigate this lunar energy is to focus yourself early in the morning through a few minutes of meditation and then, at some point during the day, engage in some sort of physical exercise.

Wednesday, January 24 (Moon in Aries) With Mars still in Capricorn, you should be reaping creative benefits. Your efforts are starting to pay off. Keep up the good work, Virgo!

Thursday, January 25 (Moon in Aries to Taurus 8:29 a.m.)
Breathe a sigh of relief. The moon is in a sign that's compatible with Virgo! You may be more stubborn than usual about a belief that you hold.

Friday, January 26 (Moon in Taurus) That overseas trip you've been considering becomes an itch that must be scratched! Be sure that you don't travel between February 13 and March 6, when Mercury will be retrograde. You may be on a quest of some sort.

Saturday, January 27 (Moon in Taurus to Gemini 12:10 p.m.) Venus moves into Pisces, a transit that should heat up your romantic life! All partnerships benefit from this transit.

Sunday, January 28 (Moon in Gemini) Focus on your career. Information and your network of friends and peers all play into the picture. Your emotions could feel somewhat torn by the duality of this moon, but as long as you are aware of it, you can deal with it.

Monday, January 29 (Moon in Gemini to Cancer 5:17 p.m.) Here's another moon that feels comfortable. Your intuition is quite strong again, especially where friendships are concerned. Trust whatever your intuitive guidance tells you.

Tuesday, January 30 (Moon in Cancer) Your mother figures into your activities. She may have advice or a bit of wisdom for you. You may resist what she says, but once you mull things over, you realize what she has told you is useful.

Wednesday, January 31 (Moon in Cancer) Your dreams may be undergoing a subtle but important shift as you alter your priorities. It's nothing major, so don't fret about it. A friend may need your compassion and clarity.

FEBRUARY 2007

Thursday, February 1 (Moon in Cancer to Leo 12:15 a.m.) The moon moves into your solar twelfth house. You shine behind the scenes. You may want to take a break from the rat race and get off for some quiet time. Solitude is a plus.

Friday, February 2 (Moon in Leo) Mercury moves into Pisces and your solar seventh house. This transit favors communication with partners. Mercury turns retrograde on February 13, so be sure to say everything you want to say to your partner by then.

Saturday, February 3 (Moon in Leo to Virgo 9:34 a.m.) The moon is finally in your sign again, and even better, it's the weekend. Get out there and enjoy yourself. People see you as a gregarious, outgoing person with wit, enthusiasm, and compassion.

Sunday, February 4 (Moon in Virgo) Another positive day, Virgo. Your sex appeal and charisma move your life in a new, unexpected direction, and you're pleased with the results. If you've been considering a move, sign the contract before Mercury turns retrograde on February 13.

Monday, February 5 (Moon in Virgo to Libra 9:15 p.m.) Emotional-security issues surface. What will it take to make you feel truly at home within yourself and your life? Define the qualities and then seek to bring them into your life.

Tuesday, February 6 (Moon in Libra) Balance is key to your success. You want to be fair with all parties involved in the issue, but to do that you'll have to detach emotionally from the situation. You can do it, Virgo!

Wednesday, February 7 (Moon in Libra) The arts feature into your activities. You have your eye on some expensive little item and aren't sure whether you can afford it.

Wait until the moon has moved into Capricorn before you decide.

Thursday, February 8 (Moon in Libra to Scorpio 10:10 a.m.) Despite the emotional intensity of this moon, its water element is compatible with Virgo's earth. Your emotions flow smoothly and facilitate your communications with everyone.

Friday, February 9 (Moon in Scorpio) Draw on the clarity and power of your emotions to change what you don't like in your life. Use visualization, affirmations, and all the tools at your disposal. The results will shock you!

Saturday, February 10 (Moon in Scorpio to Sagittarius 10:02 p.m.) The moon joins Jupiter in your solar fourth house. Your passions are on fire, and the issue concerns your home or family. Your feelings push you in a more positive direction.

Sunday, February 11 (Moon in Sagittarius) One of your parents or another family member needs your help and emotional support. You're a pro at helping others, Virgo. Just be careful that you don't become a victim of your own emotions.

Monday, February 12 (Moon in Sagittarius) You've got the big picture. You understand the conflict between your home and career obligations, and you are much closer to resolving it.

Tuesday, February 13 (Moon in Sagittarius to Capricorn 6:43 a.m.) You're able to draw on the Capricorn energy to build your creative projects and to get your kids in line. Mercury, your ruler, turns retrograde in Pisces, impacting your partnerships. Be as clear as possible in your communications.

Wednesday, February 14 (Moon in Capricorn) If your natal moon or rising is in Pisces, this Mercury retrograde will feel like a double whammy. Your emotions or the way others perceive you may seem to be muddled and confused. Happy Valentine's Day!

Thursday, February 15 (Moon in Capricorn to Aquarius 11:36 a.m.) It looks as if your coworkers or employees have things to say to you. Remove your emotions from the equation, and you'll come out way ahead of the game.

Friday, February 16 (Moon in Aquarius) You and coworkers get together after work. Someone is throwing a party, and it could be at your place! Don't worry about the state of your house. Just invite people in, have them bring something to eat and drink, and enjoy the evening.

Saturday, February 17 (Moon in Aquarius to Pisces 1:31 p.m.) The gentler nature of the Pisces moon infuses you with compassion and idealism. If your rising is Pisces, this transit certainly urges you to listen with an open heart to friends and family. Any strays that come to your door may end up as members of the family!

Sunday, February 18 (Moon in Pisces) You may be downright psychic. Test yourself with the tarot. See how proficient you really are at divining the future and the patterns in your own life. For a real challenge, sample the *I Ching*.

Monday, February 19 (Moon in Pisces to Aries 2:07 p.m.) Your patience may be tested. The issue could involve resources that you share with someone else or perhaps a mortgage or loan for which you've applied. Take a few deep breaths, Virgo, and know that this too shall pass!

Tuesday, February 20 (Moon in Aries) You're in a trailblazing mood! Your ideas come fast and furiously. Do you have time to act on all of them? If not, choose one to develop.

Wednesday, February 21 (Moon in Aries to Taurus 3:04 p.m.) Venus moves into Aries and your solar eighth house. This transit, which lasts until mid-March, favors romance that may have roots in past lives. Whoever you meet under this transit could trigger visceral feelings.

Thursday, February 22 (Moon in Taurus) This moon grounds you, keeps you rooted, and helps you to stabilize areas of your life where you may be too flexible. You may be more stubborn than usual, which surprises the people who know you best.

Friday, February 23 (Moon in Taurus to Gemini 5:42 p.m.) You have your finger on the pulse of a new project or professional endeavor. You know exactly how to achieve what you hope to do. All you have to do is to act.

Saturday, February 24 (Moon in Gemini) Books and bookstores, the Internet, networks—all are sources of information, and information is what you're after. Use all available resources to get what you need. Then piece the picture together in the way that only a Virgo can.

Sunday, February 25 (Moon in Gemini to Cancer 10:48 p.m.) Mars moves into Aquarius and your solar sixth house. This transit, which lasts until April 5, energizes your daily work routine. You have the energy to work longer hours, but could be prone to burnout unless you pace yourself. A sexual affair with a coworker is also possible.

Monday, February 26 (Moon in Cancer) This lunar transit brings friendships to the forefront of the activities. Even if you feel like staying close to home, you do so with friends and family around you. Your intuitive connections to the world around you are strong and vivid.

Tuesday, February 27 (Moon in Cancer) An emotional issue may surface involving a friend or family member. It's nothing major. Consider it a glitch in an otherwise pleasant day!

Wednesday, February 28 (Moon in Cancer to Leo 6:30 a.m.) The Leo moon can grate on you at times. But if you have a rising moon, or even a node in Leo, this transit triggers a need to be recognized for something you're doing or have done. You want to shine.

MARCH 2007

Thursday, March 1 (Moon in Leo) Your frustration may be that you aren't recognized for your talent or personality. The lesson for you, Virgo, is that self-worth should come from within, not from external validation. By tomorrow, you'll know exactly where you stand.

Friday, March 2 (Moon in Leo to Virgo 4:32 p.m.) With the moon moving into your sign late this afternoon, you enter an upbeat cycle. Your sex appeal and charisma are remarkable and attract attention from someone who interests you. Are you prepared for the art of seduction?

Saturday, March 3 (Moon in Virgo) Another good day for you. Anything and everything you hope to achieve is possible. Your energy remains high. Your magnetism allows you to charm everyone with whom you come into contact. The lunar eclipse in your sign brings up an emotional issue.

Sunday, March 4 (Moon in Virgo) Friends and acquaintances figure into your activities. You may have an early case of spring fever and want to get out and about to enjoy the weather. Head to a town where you've never been before and relish whatever experiences come your way.

Monday, March 5 (Moon in Virgo to Libra 4:26 a.m.) You're in a spending mood. Just be sure that you can afford your spree, because that's what it may turn into. If you're shopping with friends, avoid peer pressure to buy items you're not crazy about.

Tuesday, March 6 (Moon in Libra) Your need for balance is paramount. But balance may be what eludes you. Step back, take a deep breath, and spend a few moments in silence. If you meditate, you may need to extend your meditation period.

Wednesday, March 7 (Moon in Libra to Scorpio 5:18 p.m.) Mercury turns direct! Celebrate, pack your travel bags, and sign those contracts. Communications issues begin to straighten out.

Thursday, March 8 (Moon in Scorpio) You're looking for the bottom line, Virgo. You may be searching for information or trying to mend a relationship with a sibling or other relative. Try to keep your conscious thoughts to yourself.

Friday, March 9 (Moon in Scorpio) You're on a quest for emotional resolution to a relationship. You'll get it, but you may not like the end result. However, this moon is compatible with your sign and you have the inner reserves to navigate any landscape.

Saturday, March 10 (Moon in Scorpio to Sagittarius 5:38 a.m.) A home issue surfaces, and it's imperative that you deal with it. Don't procrastinate. It may involve your siblings, your children, or one of your parents. On other fronts, your love life should be humming right along!

Sunday, March 11—Daylight Saving Time Begins (Moon in Sagittarius) You're in a gregarious mood. Friends or neighbors join in your celebration, and they may help you out with some household chore. Perhaps a barbecue or party is what it's all about, Virgo.

Monday, March 12 (Moon in Sagittarius to Capricorn 4:35 p.m.) Even though it's a regular workday, your creative adrenaline is racing. Be sure to allot time for your novel, photography, art, acting, or other creative pursuit. Yes, your job is important. But your outside endeavors feed your soul.

Tuesday, March 13 (Moon in Capricorn) Plan your activities for the rest of the week. You're more organized, and a weekly plan will help you to make time for yourself and your creative work. If you have kids, they play a part.

Wednesday, March 14 (Moon in Capricorn to Aquarius 10:53 p.m.) A coworker has an unusual idea that could feed into something you're already working on. Listen to other people's ideas and concerns.

Thursday, March 15 (Moon in Aquarius) You can detach emotionally about a work or health issue. Maintain patience and listen closely to what others say. Within their thoughts and opinions lie nuggets of inspiration that you can use.

Friday, March 16 (Moon in Aquarius) Join a gym. Take yoga. Make regular walking a part of your day. In other words, start a regular exercise program that you know you can maintain. Not only will it benefit your body, but it provides another outlet for your abundant energy.

Saturday, March 17 (Moon in Aquarius to Pisces 1:31 a.m.) Venus moves into Taurus, a great transit for romance. In fact, think romance with a foreign-born individual. Even better, if you're traveling between now and April 10, romance in a foreign country is certainly a distinct possibility!

Sunday, March 18 (Moon in Pisces) You and your partner have a meeting of the hearts. Emotional issues may surface that should be dealt with quickly and honestly. The solar eclipse in Pisces helps you to see aspects of a relationship that have been hidden from you.

Monday, March 19 (Moon in Pisces to Aries 1:42 a.m.) Now that Mercury is moving direct again, you're in the mood for conversation, new information, and even travel. A loan or mortgage for which you've applied could be approved.

Tuesday, March 20 (Moon in Aries) You give aid to others who need help or emotional support. You may do this through an outreach program or even through volunteer work at a local animal shelter.

Wednesday, March 21 (Moon in Aries to Taurus 1:16 a.m.) You make a short trip. Whether it's for business or pleasure, it involves foreign countries or individuals and proves beneficial for you.

Thursday, March 22 (Moon in Taurus) With the moon in sensual Taurus, you're in the mood for romance. Someone who has piqued your interest takes an interest in you. Keep it lighthearted and fun, Virgo.

Friday, March 23 (Moon in Taurus to Gemini 2:07 a.m.) Regardless of what work you do, you need to come across as a professional. Your knowledge and expertise impress your bosses and peers. Your efficiency is extraordinary.

Saturday, March 24 (Moon in Gemini) Contact with friends and neighbors seem especially important. Information, knowledge, even gossip is exchanged about a work matter. This evening, you may party with friends or professional peers.

Sunday, March 25 (Moon in Gemini to Cancer 5:49 a.m.) You may stick close to home. Your mother or a nurturing female somehow plays into the day's events. Your priorities shift, but you hold tightly to your dreams.

Monday, March 26 (Moon in Cancer) Your intuition is clear and direct. Heed the guidance you receive. It may come to you through meditation, sudden hunches, or animal messengers. Look for the metaphor.

Tuesday, March 27 (Moon in Cancer to Leo 1:05 p.m.) You're a fireball of energy. The best outlet for all this energy is physical exercise, creative projects, and time spent alone. If you're a movie buff, rent a couple of DVDs that make you laugh.

Wednesday, March 28 (Moon in Leo) You excel in any work you do behind the scenes. Pace yourself. Leave time for play and enjoyment. Old issues may surface that are related to your childhood or to power you have disowned.

Thursday, March 29 (Moon in Leo to Virgo 11:28 p.m.) As the moon moves into your sign, the shift in energy is palpable. Smile, Virgo. It's a fine day for accomplishing whatever you have postponed and for romance.

Friday, March 30 (Moon in Virgo) Lucky you! Your charisma and magnetism attract everything you need and could possibly want. And better yet, you can really feel spring in the air!

Saturday, March 31 (Moon in Virgo) There's no better way to end a month than to have the moon in your sign. Tackle things that require attention to detail and figure out how to make a current project more efficient and comprehensible to others.

APRIL 2007

Sunday, April 1 (Moon in Virgo to Libra 11:45 a.m.) If you're in a spending mood, indulge yourself. You can afford it, even if your cautious nature screams that you can't. Whether it's a gym membership or a piece of art, both feed you in different ways.

Monday, April 2 (Moon in Libra) Your fairness may come into question. Rather than getting into an argument, simply defend your actions and then move on.

Tuesday, April 3 (Moon in Libra) The intensity of the Scorpio moon sometimes takes you by surprise. Your emotions run deeper, your intuition is stronger, and the synchronicities in your life happen more frequently. Be alert for signs.

Wednesday, April 4 (Moon in Libra to Scorpio 12:37 a.m.) If you heeded yesterday's signs, you know exactly how to handle a particular relationship or issue. A friend, neighbor, or relative may be involved. On other fronts, you may be doing more running around than usual.

Thursday, April 5 (Moon in Scorpio) Jupiter moves into Sagittarius and your solar fourth house. This transit, which lasts about a year, signals a new time of expansion. A move is possible. It's also possible that your family expands in some way.

Friday, April 6 (Moon in Scorpio to Sagittarius 12:57 p.m.) Mars moves into Pisces. Until mid-May your partnerships will be more energized. This can be positive or challenging, depending on how you and your partner react to each other when you're both stressed. Your sex life should improve tremendously!

Saturday, April 7 (Moon in Sagittarius) The moon is moving through your solar fourth house with Jupiter. One manifestation of this combination is an expansion in your emotions. You may blow things out of proportion, so watch yourself. No drama, Virgo!

Sunday, April 8 (Moon in Sagittarius to Capricorn 11:36 p.m.) With the moon forming a harmonious angle to your sun, you're in sync with your environment. It's a good day to prioritize for the week ahead and to get busy on your creative projects.

Monday, April 9 (Moon in Capricorn) With spring here, get out with the kids and do something fun! Romance is also accented. In fact, Venus continues to transit sensual Taurus, so your love life should be in a very nice shape!

Tuesday, April 10 (Moon in Capricorn) Mercury moves into Aries. For the next sixteen days, you focus on how to do things faster and with more originality. You may be somewhat impatient with people around you and think that you can get stuff done without help.

Wednesday, April 11 (Moon in Capricorn to Aquarius 7:23 a.m.) Venus moves into Gemini and your solar tenth house. This transit, which lasts until early May, indicates favorable events related to your career. It's also possible, Virgo, that a romance or affair with a peer or even a boss takes off.

Thursday, April 12 (Moon in Aquarius) As the moon joins Neptune in your solar sixth house, you may experience some confusion concerning a coworker or employee. It may be that you don't have the full story, so collect the facts before making a decision.

Friday, April 13 (Moon in Aquarius to Pisces 11:39 a.m.) Even though the Pisces moon is opposed to your sun, it's a more comfortable transit than air- or fire-sign moons. Your intuitive awareness increases, and your compassion deepens. Just be cautious that your compassion doesn't distract you from your own obligations.

Saturday, April 14 (Moon in Pisces) If your tax forms aren't ready to mail off yet, get busy. Your partner or even a friend may need your emotional support and wisdom. This evening, settle in with a good book. Try *Life of Pi* by Yann Martel.

Sunday, April 15 (Moon in Pisces to Aries 12:47 p.m.) Patterns and synchronicities leap out at you. What's the bottom line? If you can't quite grasp the message, shut your eyes, open a dictionary at random, and point to a word. That word should sum things up.

Monday, April 16 (Moon in Aries) If yesterday's patterns still have you puzzled, pose a question to the *I Ching* or even to the tarot. Any oracular device will provide insight. You may want to consult a professional astrologer to read your natal chart and determine what's going on for you.

Tuesday, April 17 (Moon in Aries to Taurus 12:12 p.m.) You may encounter a situation that requires you to be more stubborn or persistent. Try not to be contrary. Remember that courtesy and a quiet voice take you much farther than arguments or hostility.

Wednesday, April 18 (Moon in Taurus) The planning of a foreign trip looks likely. Just be sure that you travel before June 15 or after July 9, the period when Mercury is moving retrograde. If you've been called for jury duty, don't ask for a postponement.

Thursday, April 19 (Moon in Taurus to Gemini 11:52 a.m.) Saturn turns direct in Leo and your twelfth house. This movement should make it easier for you to access your unconscious. Meditation and dream recall prove beneficial. If you've considered therapy, this movement helps you find the therapist who is right for you.

Friday, April 20 (Moon in Gemini) The moon joins Venus in your solar tenth house. This combination places the focus squarely on your career and professional concerns. Women are helpful and it's possible that you get an artistic break of some kind.

Saturday, April 21 (Moon in Gemini to Cancer 1:51 p.m.) This afternoon, friends and your network of acquaintances take the spotlight. It's a great day for publicity and promotion. You've got your finger on the public pulse.

Sunday, April 22 (Moon in Cancer) You feel nostalgia for something or someone in the past. Old photo albums could hold the key to why you feel like you do. But your point of power lies in the present.

Monday, April 23 (Moon in Cancer to Leo 7:39 p.m.) If you're in a social mood, keep your contacts small and manageable. In other words, don't throw a party! Pets need your attention and love. In fact, maybe you should stick to animal companionship!

Tuesday, April 24 (Moon in Leo)   You seek recognition for something you've done or achieved. You deserve the recognition. But try not to boast.

Wednesday, April 25 (Moon in Leo)   With Jupiter still moving retrograde in your fourth house and the fiery Leo moon in your twelfth house, this could be one of those days when emotional situations are exaggerated. Postpone making any important decisions. Wait until tomorrow or Friday, when the moon is in your sign.

Thursday, April 26 (Moon in Leo to Virgo 5:25 a.m.)   You wake to a brand-new day, with a positive and upbeat attitude. Examine your sense of optimism and try to carry it forward through the end of the month and beyond.

Friday, April 27 (Moon in Virgo)   Mercury moves into Taurus and your solar ninth house. This should be a pleasant transit for you, and it lasts through May 10. Your daily activities are more grounded, your interests more mystically inclined.

Saturday, April 28 (Moon in Virgo to Libra 5:46 p.m.)   With the moon in Libra and Mercury in Taurus, you feel a need to be surrounded by beauty. This need may result in expenditures that strain your checkbook. Be sure you can afford whatever you buy.

Sunday, April 29 (Moon in Libra)   Balance and fairness should rule the day. Both may be difficult to achieve, but your ability to connect the dots helps tremendously. A friend or a group of friends helps you define your own beliefs.

Monday, April 30 (Moon in Libra)   How far can you take your ideas? As far as you want. A positive attitude and a deep belief in your own abilities help you to move in a new, beneficial, and productive direction.

MAY 2007

Tuesday, May 1 (Moon in Libra to Scorpio 6:42 a.m.) A brother or sister plays into the day's events and activities. Even if you don't usually see eye to eye on things, you agree wholeheartedly. Your intuition is right on target today, so listen to it.

Wednesday, May 2 (Moon in Scorpio) You find something that has been missing. It could be an object, but it could also be information or even an emotion that helps you clarify a situation. The situation or event that triggers your discovery comes through a sibling, a relative, or even a neighbor.

Thursday, May 3 (Moon in Scorpio to Sagittarius 6:48 p.m.) The moon joins Jupiter in your solar fourth house. Your emotions concerning your family or your home life may be overblown. Whatever you feel about the situation is valid, of course, but be aware that you may be overreacting.

Friday, May 4 (Moon in Sagittarius) With Jupiter still moving retrograde, its usually expansive energies aren't quite up to snuff. Just the same, you consider adding on to your home, or perhaps your family is about to expand. Is it because a relative is moving in or because someone is pregnant?

Saturday, May 5 (Moon in Sagittarius) You have the larger picture on a family issue. It won't necessarily change your bottom-line opinion or belief, but it does offer you a fresh perspective.

Sunday, May 6 (Moon in Sagittarius to Capricorn 5:21 a.m.) Romance and fun are at the top of your list. You have an opportunity to try something different that may be somewhat risky. You're after the experience, whatever it may be, and aren't worried about the risk. Go for it, Virgo.

Monday, May 7 (Moon in Capricorn)   Your creative endeavors focus on a long-standing project. You're able to recognize and correct flaws that weren't apparent to you before. You can move toward completion, secure in the knowledge that you're on the right track.

Tuesday, May 8 (Moon in Capricorn to Aquarius 1:48 p.m.)   Venus moves into Cancer and your solar eleventh house. Since this transit, which lasts until early June, forms a harmonious angle with your sun, romance is possible with someone you meet through friends.

Wednesday, May 9 (Moon in Aquarius)   You're able to detach emotionally from a situation or relationship on the job. This detachment is necessary to achieve the day's goals. Your visionary clarity brings insight to a work-related project.

Thursday, May 10 (Moon in Aquarius to Pisces 7:32 p.m.)   An issue with a partner surfaces. The two of you are able to talk things through and arrive at a much better place than if the issue had never come up. Be careful that your compassion doesn't suck you dry.

Friday, May 11 (Moon in Pisces)   Mercury, your ruling planet, moves into Gemini. This transit, which lasts until May 27, indicates travel and communication related to your career and professional life. You feel a greater need to define yourself in the public eye.

Saturday, May 12 (Moon in Virgo to Aries 10:20 p.m.)   You're in a fighting, defensive mode and forging ahead on your own. Slow down and take a second look at what's pushing you recklessly ahead. Is it something internal that you need to examine and understand? Is it peer pressure?

Sunday, May 13 (Moon in Aries)   Other people's resources are available to you. Use them judiciously, and be willing to share your resources with others as well. You may sign up for a workshop or seminar concerning an esoteric area that interests you.

Monday, May 14 (Moon in Aries to Taurus 10:50 p.m.) Your worldview, your spiritual beliefs, or even your political affiliations are impacted. It's not that you're challenged by someone else, but that an experience or relationship prompts you to delve more deeply into these areas. It's always about perfection of the self for you.

Tuesday, May 15 (Moon in Taurus) Mars moves into Aries and your solar eighth house. This transit lasts until June 24 and galvanizes all resources that you share with others and vice versa. Your partner may be confronting transformative events and need your support.

Wednesday, May 16 (Moon in Taurus to Gemini 10:35 p.m.) The day cruises along smoothly until this evening. Then you need to bite your tongue, nurture patience, and be more understanding with a peer or boss. The emphasis is on the right and wrong way to conduct business.

Thursday, May 17 (Moon in Gemini) Focus on career matters. Information is vital to the smooth functioning of a project, and your mission, should you choose to accept it, is to find the information you need. Peers or bosses may help in this regard.

Friday, May 18 (Moon in Gemini to Cancer 11:39 p.m.) Finally, late tonight, the moon moves into a sign more compatible with yours. Your mom or friends who have your best interests at heart provide information or emotional support.

Saturday, May 19 (Moon in Cancer) It's a good day for publicity and promotion. Regardless of what product you're pushing, the public is receptive. A friend needs your emotional support.

Sunday, May 20 (Moon in Cancer) How far can your intuition take you? It depends on how closely you listen and whether you take the advice or the path your intuition provides. Make time to nurture yourself, Virgo.

Monday, May 21 (Moon in Cancer to Leo 3:57 a.m.) You're in a flamboyant, demonstrative mood. Dress the part—bright colors, bold styles. Don't hesitate to speak your mind and to articulate what's in your heart.

Tuesday, May 22 (Moon in Leo) Even though you want to shine publicly, you're better off working behind the scenes, in solitude. You'll shine despite the solitude and come out way ahead when the moon moves into your sign tomorrow.

Wednesday, May 23 (Moon in Leo to Virgo 12:27 p.m.) The moon in your sign! Make decisions you have put off. Your intellect is clear, and your communication skills are strong. You're able to convince anyone of anything.

Thursday, May 24 (Moon in Virgo) Neptune turns retrograde in Aquarius and your solar sixth house. This movement has subtle effects. You may feel somewhat confused about a personal issue related to work. Or situations at work may be vague, ill-defined. But then, the Neptune transit has been going on for a long time now and you may not even feel it.

Friday, May 25 (Moon in Virgo) A recent raise or perhaps a tax refund sends you off in search of an item you've considered buying for some time. It could be frivolous, but if its beauty appeals to your artistic self, buy it.

Saturday, May 26 (Moon in Virgo to Libra 12:17 a.m.) Finances—either yours or your partner's or both—rule the day. This can be either positive or negative, depending on where your finances stand right now. Are you in debt? Or are your bank accounts nicely padded?

Sunday, May 27 (Moon in Libra) You are unbalanced. If the feeling is connected to a relationship, just ride the tide of events and be assured that things will look brighter tomorrow.

Monday, May 28 (Moon in Libra to Scorpio 1:12 p.m.) Mercury moves into Cancer and your solar eleventh house. This transit helps you tap your intuition and may even clarify feelings you have about your friends and family. It lasts until early August.

Tuesday, May 29 (Moon in Scorpio) This intense moon stirs up emotions that disturb you. Deal with the feelings and move on. Traveling is a given—nothing too distant, but far enough so that you need to keep an eye on your gas gauge.

Wednesday, May 30 (Moon in Scorpio) Your exercise routine revs up another notch. You add something to your program—weights, yoga, or aerobics. All are necessary to maintain your physical health.

Thursday, May 31 (Moon in Scorpio to Sagittarius 1:07 a.m.) As you head into June, keep your sights on your summer goals. Be flexible, but not ambivalent, firm but not rigid.

JUNE 2007

Friday, June 1 (Moon in Sagittarius) A situation at home or connected to your family or even your career calls for flexibility on your part. You rise to the occasion, and your position eases someone else's dilemma.

Saturday, June 2 (Moon in Sagittarius to Capricorn 11:10 a.m.) Today is your creative day. It's a weekend, so you can afford to carve out time for yourself! Your soul needs it.

Sunday, June 3 (Moon in Capricorn) Your creativity takes an unexpected turn. Instead of working on your novel or screenplay, you decided to redecorate one of the rooms in your house. Or perhaps you redo your child's room with new paint or wallpaper or new furniture.

Monday, June 4 (Moon in Capricorn to Aquarius 7:16 p.m.) If you have summer fever, you may want to knock off work early. Get out into the world and embrace the environment. Maybe you should consider volunteering for a environmental group.

Tuesday, June 5 (Moon in Aquarius) Venus moves into Leo and your solar twelfth house. If romance or an affair begins under this transit, be aware that it may occur in secret. You probably won't be able to maintain the secrecy once Venus moves into your sign.

Wednesday, June 6 (Moon in Aquarius) If your new romance is with a coworker or employee, you may need to be secretive about it until one or both of you make other work arrangements. Drama, Virgo. So much drama!

Thursday, June 7 (Moon in Aquarius to Pisces 1:25 a.m.) There's a softness about you, a gentler heart. The day looks good for contract negotiations, open and honest communication with your partner, and intuitive connection with friends and loved ones.

Friday, June 8 (Moon in Pisces) When the moon teams up with Uranus, which it does at least once a month, your emotional responses are unusual. You tend to attract people who are idiosyncratic or even brilliant.

Saturday, June 9 (Moon in Pisces to Aries 5:27 a.m.) Mortgages, insurance, and inheritances are accented. It may be that you have the funding you need to launch your business or idea. Other people's resources are available to you.

Sunday, June 10 (Moon in Aries) Your partner or spouse has news about earnings—perhaps a raise or some sort of benefit that neither of you had counted on. Whatever the news, you both stand to benefit.

Monday, June 11 (Moon in Aries to Taurus 7:30 a.m.) Focus on your philosophies and views about the world. Heady stuff, Virgo. But all of this plays into your higher education and your eventual path through life.

Tuesday, June 12 (Moon in Taurus) You're security conscious. What makes you feel emotionally secure? Once you identify those factors, you can work to bring them into your life.

Wednesday, June 13 (Moon in Taurus to Gemini 8:24 a.m.) If you're in a profession you enjoy, take steps to ensure your job security. If you're unemployed, get out there with your résumé and your people skills!

Thursday, June 14 (Moon in Gemini) You may come up against a boss or another authority figure. Speak your mind, be firm but courteous, and then go about your business. Gossip—listening to it or being a part of it—doesn't serve your purposes at all.

Friday, June 15 (Moon in Gemini to Cancer 9:46 a.m.) Mercury, your ruler, turns retrograde in Cancer and your solar eleventh house. It's important that you communicate clearly with friends because you might be misunderstood. Don't shift your priorities around until after Mercury turns direct again on July 9.

Saturday, June 16 (Moon in Cancer) The moon joins retrograde Mercury in your eleventh house. You could feel more vulnerable when it comes to friends and the groups to which you belong. Someone is critical of you or something you have done, and you take offense.

Sunday, June 17 (Moon in Cancer to Leo 1:25 p.m.) Your privacy is paramount. Perhaps you're working on something secret, or perhaps you simply have secrets. Either way, it's best to keep your contact with others at a minimum, if you can.

Monday, June 18 (Moon in Leo) You're laying the groundwork for when the moon moves into your sign tomorrow evening. Yes, you may be champing at the bit to get moving. Be patient and bide your time.

Tuesday, June 19 (Moon in Leo to Virgo 8:46 p.m.) The shift may not feel so subtle when the moon moves into your sign. A palpable sense of relief washes through you. Your self-confidence suddenly soars. You're back in the game, Virgo, and tomorrow and the next day, you're making up the rules.

Wednesday, June 20 (Moon in Virgo) With summer definitely here and the moon in your sign, you're in exceptional spirits. Romance may be in the air, and it's possible that it catches you by surprise. Someone you considered to be just a friend has designs on you.

Thursday, June 21 (Moon in Virgo) You're a paragon of efficiency and wit. You're free to express exactly who you are without any worries that others will judge you. People genuinely enjoy your company, so bask in that enjoyment. Your inner critic has gone to lunch for the day.

Friday, June 22 (Moon in Virgo to Libra 7:44 a.m.) If you feel caught between the proverbial rock and a hard place, postpone making a decision and gather your facts. New information will come to light in several days.

Saturday, June 23 (Moon in Libra) Uranus turns retrograde in Pisces and remains that way until late November. A planet's energy doesn't work as smoothly when it's retrograde, so expect to revisit relationship issues you thought had been resolved.

Sunday, June 24 (Moon in Libra to Scorpio 8:27 p.m.) Mars moves into Taurus, a sign that's compatible with your own. This transit, which lasts until early August, energizes your ninth house. Education, your belief system, the courts, and long-distance travel are featured in the ninth house.

Monday, June 25 (Moon in Scorpio) It's decision day. The situation that puzzled you last Friday snaps into clarity. You find the bottom line that dominates the issue, and you are able to decide accordingly. It may involve a sibling or other relative.

Tuesday, June 26 (Moon in Scorpio) Mars in Taurus and the moon in Scorpio are opposite to each other, but form nice angles to your sun. You feel very good about the course of your education or your relationship with a brother or sister. You may be doing more running around than usual.

Wednesday, June 27 (Moon in Scorpio to Sagittarius 8:25 a.m.) The moon joins Jupiter in Sagittarius and your fourth house. This combination may lead to exaggerated emotional reactions concerning your home and family. A lot of activity takes place at home, and you actually enjoy every minute of it!

Thursday, June 28 (Moon in Sagittarius) If you're trying to expand your home-based business, wait until Jupiter turns direct again on August 6 before making a big push. Tend to the details and lay the groundwork.

Friday, June 29 (Moon in Sagittarius to Capricorn 6:06 p.m.) Romance? Love? Sometimes, Virgo, you're the quintessential loner. You prefer your own company to that of others. But today isn't one of those times. Enjoy the attention that comes your way.

Saturday, June 30 (Moon in Capricorn) Your creativity is highlighted. You see progress in a creative project, and you are delighted with the twists and turns the project is taking. Be sure that the blueprint you're following is exactly the way you want it.

JULY 2007

Sunday, July 1 (Moon in Capricorn) Plan for a long weekend or even a vacation. Just don't travel before Mercury turns direct on July 9. On other fronts, it's a great day for romance and fun. You and your partner should get away together.

Monday, July 2 (Moon in Capricorn to Aquarius 1:25 a.m.) You and coworkers may get together to discuss current projects in a casual setting. There could be some confusion about who's in charge of a particular project. Go with the flow, Virgo.

Tuesday, July 3 (Moon in Aquarius) A charity drive is under way where you work. You may be asked to direct the activities. If so, you perform with admirable attention to details, and you are able to put a positive spin on the situation.

Wednesday, July 4 (Moon in Aquarius to Pisces 6:53 a.m.) If your rising sign or your natal moon is in Pisces, today should be quite pleasant. Your intuition runs quickly and clearly, encompassing many issues and relationships. It's as if you're tuned in to something much larger than yourself.

Thursday, July 5 (Moon in Pisces) Don't sign the contract yet. Wait until after July 9, when Mercury is moving direct again. If you're pressed to sign, do so with the understanding that the contract will be revisited. Get an expert's advice.

Friday, July 6 (Moon in Pisces to Aries 10:57 a.m.) You're fired up and ready for battle. Take a few deep breaths and try to see the situation without emotions involved. Once you do that, forge ahead on your ideas.

Saturday, July 7 (Moon in Aries) Time to check documents related to insurance, wills, and taxes. If you haven't paid your quarterly taxes yet, get your forms in order. A gift of opportunity comes your way. Make your decision about it tomorrow afternoon.

Sunday, July 8 (Moon in Aries to Taurus 1:54 p.m.) Relax. It's Sunday, and you've earned a respite. Plan for your overseas trip. Get on the Internet, become a virtual traveler, and decide where you would like to go.

Monday, July 9 (Moon in Taurus) Mercury turns direct. Friendships damaged during the retrograde period heal themselves. You're in good shape to pursue travel plans, to negotiate and sign contracts, and to do all the things you postponed during the retrograde period.

Tuesday, July 10 (Moon in Taurus to Gemini 4:10 p.m.) Some petty annoyance in your profession may cause you to overreact. It's really not worth the expenditure of energy. Deal with the situation and move on.

Wednesday, July 11 (Moon in Gemini) Books, information, freedom of thought—all these issues come to the forefront. You may get together with peers or bosses this evening for a social gathering. You, with your wit and optimism, are center stage.

Thursday, July 12 (Moon in Gemini to Cancer 6:40 p.m.) A friend you helped in the past returns that support. On other fronts, publicize your company's product. If you're having second thoughts about a dream, don't abandon it! Just revise it.

Friday, July 13 (Moon in Cancer) You've got your finger on the pulse of the public's heart. Use this knowledge to your advantage. It's easier than you think. Listen to your intuitive guidance and act accordingly.

Saturday, July 14 (Moon in Cancer to Leo 10:44 p.m.) Buckle up, Virgo. You're in for a wild and wonderful ride in the romance department. Venus has just moved into your sign! It's going to be there until early August, highlighting your attractiveness and charisma.

Sunday, July 15 (Moon in Leo) Despite the fact that the moon is in the house of solitude, Venus in your sign still manages to get you out and about. People love what they see. Is it possible this entails a modeling or acting gig?

Monday, July 16 (Moon in Leo) Mull things over and make your decision tomorrow. Stay focused on what matters most to you and don't feel guilty!

Tuesday, July 17 (Moon in Leo to Virgo 5:40 a.m.) Early today, the moon joins Venus in your sign, a great combination. Your inner beauty and presence surface for everyone to see. Whatever you take on works out in your favor. Romance, a raise, a contract negotiation—take your pick.

Wednesday, July 18 (Moon in Virgo) Another positive day! You and your partner do something you both enjoy this evening. It may be something as mundane as having your favorite brand of coffee at a bookstore or something as uplifting as a concert.

Thursday, July 19 (Moon in Virgo to Libra 3:54 p.m.) Friends feature in the day's events. You may be called upon to mediate a dispute or disagreement and discover that you have a bias that prevents you from being completely fair. Bow out.

Friday, July 20 (Moon in Libra) This moon often brings out your artistic side. The arts, music, photography, and dance may receive the energy of this lunar transit. You may even collect things from any of these areas. You want to surround yourself with beauty.

Saturday, July 21 (Moon in Libra) There's your viewpoint and there's the other guy's viewpoint. And then there are hundreds of viewpoints in between. In fact, it seems that you step into everyone's shoes, try their lives or thoughts on for size, and decide it's not so bad being the Virgo you are!

Sunday, July 22 (Moon in Libra to Scorpio 4:19 a.m.) If you're in the acting profession, the Scorpio moon should help you to draw on all your inner abilities and resources to portray a character. You may find that you're drawing on past-life experiences when playing a particular character.

Monday, July 23 (Moon in Scorpio) The same emotional intensity that works for an actor also works for a writer in creating characters or plots. Even the hard sciences rely on intuitive connections. Whatever your work or profession, you're in the flow.

Tuesday, July 24 (Moon in Scorpio to Sagittarius 4:31 p.m.) Sometimes the Sagittarius moon feels like an itch you can't scratch. You may feel torn between your obligations to your family and to your profession. Or you may sense that something is amiss somewhere in your personal universe.

Wednesday, July 25 (Moon in Sagittarius) Stay the course. The bigger picture is available to you now if you need or want it. Your home is a hub of activity, and your family seems to be running in a dozen different directions.

Thursday, July 26 (Moon in Sagittarius) You either hold down the fort, or you and your partner leave the fort behind and take off for parts unknown. Either way, you benefit.

Friday, July 27 (Moon in Sagittarius to Capricorn 2:23 a.m.) Venus turns retrograde in your sign. This movement may signal some bumps and bruises in a partnership or even with an artistic or creative project. However, a Venus retrograde isn't a Mercury retrograde, so don't spend time fretting about it.

Saturday, July 28 (Moon in Capricorn) You may feel a bit out of sorts concerning a creative project or due to an issue that concerns your children. The feeling passes, but not without a little soul searching on your part. The stars actually favor your creativity, but you need to adjust your thinking.

Sunday, July 29 (Moon in Capricorn to Aquarius 9:14 a.m.) You can take your ideas as far as you dare. You have quite a bit of courage, or perhaps it's just a devil-may-care attitude. Use it to your advantage.

Monday, July 30 (Moon in Aquarius) You and co-workers get together to brainstorm. You recall yesterday's devil-may-care attitude, and you are able to call upon it to get your message across. Keep up the repartee, Virgo. Your wit gets you through.

Tuesday, July 31 (Moon in Aquarius to Pisces 1:41 p.m.) With Venus retrograde in your sign, opposite this Pisces moon, you feel vulnerable and out of sorts about a friendship or partnership. Yes, it's a temporary emotion. But get to the root of the emotion and you'll understand why you feel as you do.

AUGUST 2007

Wednesday, August 1 (Moon in Pisces) If you have a natal moon or ascendant in Pisces or another water sign, this lunar transit is apt to be quite positive for you. Otherwise, you may feel vulnerable where partnerships are concerned, particularly since Venus is retrograde in your sign and opposed to the moon. Still, your compassion and intuition run deep.

Thursday, August 2 (Moon in Pisces to Aries 4:43 p.m.) With fire in your belly and stars in your eyes, you're a force to be reckoned with. This isn't your favorite moon by any means, but it urges you to forge ahead in some area of your life and to leave your mark on the world.

Friday, August 3 (Moon in Aries) Be sure that your insurance policies, will, and tax documents are up-to-date and that your premiums are paid. You may want to sign up for a workshop on life after death or past lives. The information you glean from such a workshop could illuminate a question or concern you have.

Saturday, August 4 (Moon in Aries to Taurus 7:16 p.m.) Mercury moves into Leo and your solar twelfth house. This transit lasts until August 19 and allows you the opportunity to delve consciously into your own unconscious. It's a good time to read Carl Jung's autobiography *Memories, Dreams, Reflections*.

Sunday, August 5 (Moon in Taurus) You're more grounded and able to work longer hours. Start an exercise routine if you don't have one. A yoga class may be in order to stretch out your muscles and test out your flexibility.

Monday, August 6 (Moon in Taurus to Gemini 10:02 p.m.) Jupiter turns direct in Sagittarius. You can put your house on the market or start a renovation or expansion project on your home. Between now and the end of the year, your family may expand in some way—a birth or a relative moves in.

Tuesday, August 7 (Moon in Gemini) Mars moves into Gemini and your solar tenth house. This transit lasts until late September and energizes the career sector of your chart. You may work longer and harder during this period, but the payoff at the other end is worth it.

Wednesday, August 8 (Moon in Gemini) With both the moon and Mars in your tenth house, you have the physical stamina and the emotional sensitivity to dive into career matters. Your best bet lies in communications, written or spoken.

Thursday, August 9 (Moon in Gemini to Cancer 1:37 a.m.) Friends are accented. You may be expanding your online network of acquaintances or your e-mail database. Be innovative and use your intuition to speed up the process.

Friday, August 10 (Moon in Cancer) In nine days, Mercury joins Venus in your sign. Get ready for the combination by doing the footwork with publicity and promotion. Make appointments. Touch base with people. Despite the prodding of Mercury in your twelfth house, don't be a hermit!

Saturday, August 11 (Moon in Cancer to Leo 6:42 a.m.) The moon joins Mercury in your twelfth house; it's probably a good idea to hang loose and solitary. Paint your bedroom. Buy furniture for your home office. Hit a bookstore and sit for hours, sipping coffee and reading. Stay away from people who make you feel less than you are.

Sunday, August 12 (Moon in Leo) Another day to lie low. You're reserving your resources for the next two and a half days, when the moon will be in Virgo. Choose a novel you've been saving for a rainy day, and even if it isn't raining, get busy!

Monday, August 13 (Moon in Leo to Virgo 2:04 p.m.) Time to rock and roll. You feel good enough to shrug off anyone who criticizes you and to keep your inner censor sealed up in a back room. That's an excellent start. Then let that special person who has been after you inside the door.

Tuesday, August 14 (Moon in Virgo) Romance and prosperity are yours! Keep your options open, embrace change, and don't allow that inner critic to whisper to you. Good news comes your way on a partnership or career issue.

Wednesday, August 15 (Moon in Virgo) Late tonight, you may experience a letdown in your emotional bubble or optimism. It's okay. It's just the moon moving into Libra. Use this energy tomorrow by socializing, connecting, and mediating disputes or disagreements.

Thursday, August 16 (Moon in Virgo to Libra 12:05 a.m.) More than anything, you want to be fair with other people, and you may end up being unfair to yourself. You're attracted to beauty of all kinds and could feel the urge to buy something you can't afford.

Friday, August 17 (Moon in Libra)   With Mars and the moon forming harmonious angles to each other but not to your sun, the emphasis is on gathering and disseminating information to your friends and acquaintances. You may donate money or time to a charitable organization and inadvertently make new professional contacts.

Saturday, August 18 (Moon in Libra to Scorpio 12:14 p.m.)   Your research pays off. You find precisely what you're looking for—the right piece of information, the right contact, the ideal expert—and you are able to complete a project or bring closure to a relationship.

Sunday, August 19 (Moon in Scorpio)   Mercury moves into your sign. This transit puts you at the top of your game, Virgo. Everything you communicate is done so with clarity and attention to detail. You don't censor what you say.

Monday, August 20 (Moon in Scorpio)   As the moon joins Jupiter in your solar fourth house, family and home issues top your list. You may blow something out of proportion or feel so expansive that you embrace dramatic change.

Tuesday, August 21 (Moon in Scorpio to Sagittarius 12:45 a.m.)   Publishing, your spiritual beliefs, and education figure into the day's events. It's also possible that you're considering an overseas trip and it may have a larger purpose. Are you embarking on a spiritual quest?

Wednesday, August 22 (Moon in Sagittarius)   A concern about your family or home surfaces, and you finally understand what to do. If you're contemplating a move or the purchase of real estate, start an earnest search.

Thursday, August 23 (Moon in Sagittarius to Capricorn 11:20 a.m.)   With Mercury, Venus, and now the moon in earth signs, you feel grounded, rested, and charged up. It's time to take on whatever you have avoided doing creatively. You can achieve your dream, Virgo, but you have to believe in yourself and your talents.

Friday, August 24 (Moon in Capricorn) Now that the transiting sun is also in Virgo, you've got four earth-sign planets in your court! You're able to work longer hours without tiring, to anchor your creative endeavors, and to turn abstract notions into concrete terms that others understand.

Saturday, August 25 (Moon in Capricorn to Aquarius 6:35 p.m.) You, friends, and coworkers get together this evening to brainstorm about something that is near and dear to all of you. It may be a community, charitable, or work-related project. Your vision leads the way.

Sunday, August 26 (Moon in Aquarius) Kick back. You've earned the time off. A romance is looking quite promising. Even though Venus is still retrograde in your sign, you've got other planets tipping events and opportunities in your favor.

Monday, August 27 (Moon in Aquarius to Pisces 10:35 p.m.) You and your partner should be doing well. Communication between you is highlighted. If you've had something on your mind, then express it. Be calm, but firm.

Tuesday, August 28 (Moon in Pisces) The lunar eclipse in Pisces brings up an emotional issue related to partnerships. Events four days to either side of the eclipse can be quite telling about the patterns of the eclipse for you.

Wednesday, August 29 (Moon in Pisces) The Aries moon isn't comfortable for you. But its energy often acts as a booster rocket, spurring you in some new and exciting direction. If you're really daring, you may want to try a past-life regression.

Thursday, August 30 (Moon in Pisces to Aries 12:25 a.m.)
Listen carefully to your hunches. Something new is in the wind. Can you tap into it?

Friday, August 31 (Moon in Aries) If your birthday is today, make a list of what you would like to have and achieve in the next year. Visualize. Pour emotion in these desires. Then make them happen. *You* write the script of your life.

SEPTEMBER 2007

Saturday, September 1 (Moon in Aries to Taurus 1:36 a.m.) Once again, there are a number of earth-sign planets in your court. This grounding energy allows you to explore your spiritual beliefs and worldview in a practical way. Once you understand your beliefs, you have a better grasp about who you are.

Sunday, September 2 (Moon in Taurus) Saturn moves into Virgo. This major transit happens only once every thirty years or so. It brings stability to what you do and to how others perceive you. If you're on a path or in a relationship that isn't in your best interest or which has outlived its purpose in your life, this transit helps to end it. Think of Saturn as the karmic taskmaster. Its energy may seem cruel at times, but it can also bring about a harvest.

Monday, September 3 (Moon in Taurus to Gemini 3:31 a.m.) The moon joins Mars in Gemini way up there in your tenth house. This combination drives energy into your career. All professional concerns seem entirely personal. Get over it and move on.

Tuesday, September 4 (Moon in Gemini) Think, just for a moment, back to yesterday or last week, and try to recall what was going on. In the fleeting quickness of time, the only thing we can be utterly sure of is this moment, this breath, this all-encompassing *now*. Your power lies in the present.

Wednesday, September 5 (Moon in Gemini to Cancer 7:09 a.m.) Mercury moves into Libra and your second house. If you're in the communications business, you should be able to make money during this transit through your gift of gab.

Thursday, September 6 (Moon in Cancer) With your ruler, Mercury, and the moon both in cardinal signs, you're leading the pack. You're the Pied Piper followed by friends and strangers alike. Your words have impact.

Friday, September 7 (Moon in Cancer to Leo 1:00 p.m.) Pluto turns direct in Sagittarius and your fourth house. The effects of this movement are subtle because Pluto moves so slowly. Expect something new in your home life or career that permanently changes your course of action.

Saturday, September 8 (Moon in Leo) Venus turns direct—great news for your love life. If you're not involved with anyone, that may change before Venus moves into Libra in November. Whatever you do, act with conviction.

Sunday, September 9 (Moon in Leo to Virgo 9:11 p.m.) By this evening, when the moon moves into your sign, you're on your way toward acceptance of yourself. Try not to analyze and pick apart your flaws and weaknesses, Virgo. Just sink into the moment.

Monday, September 10 (Moon in Virgo) You're in peak form. But to make the day even better, silence your inner critic when it's whispering in your ear. Refuse to listen to that relentless inner voice that wants you to worry and fret over things that haven't happened yet.

Tuesday, September 11 (Moon in Virgo) Everything you experience begins within and, like a magnet, attracts certain experiences, people, and situations into your life.

Change the root belief that causes you trouble and watch your life change accordingly! There's a solar eclipse in your sign. It should reveal something that was previously hidden or unclear.

Wednesday, September 12 (Moon in Virgo to Libra 7:32 a.m.) Today's lunar shift happens early, so you wake into a different energy. This energy galvanizes your friendship needs, especially if you have a lot of natal planets in Libra. If you feel vulnerable with a particular friend, explore the reasons why.

Thursday, September 13 (Moon in Libra) You're in a spending mood. Maybe you buy a new video game that has caught your eye, or perhaps you're in the market for new clothes. Use some restraint; check out the sales racks first!

Friday, September 14 (Moon in Libra to Scorpio 7:37 p.m.) Events four days to either side of an eclipse often provide a hint about what the eclipse means for you personally. With the moon in intense Scorpio this evening, your emotions may be an issue as they relate to siblings, other relatives, and neighbors.

Saturday, September 15 (Moon in Scorpio) If you're working on a novel or screenplay, move ahead on it. The moon's position favors all kinds of communications. You're able to get to the heart of what you're trying to say.

Sunday, September 16 (Moon in Scorpio) Your emotional support for a friend or sibling brings you cosmic kudos, Virgo! More important, you feel good when you're of service to others.

Monday, September 17 (Moon in Scorpio to Sagittarius 8:21 a.m.) The moon joins Jupiter in Sagittarius. This combined transit can be as pleasant or as miserable as you make it. It all depends on your emotional reactions or situations and relationships. It favors some sort of renovation or expansion to your home.

Tuesday, September 18 (Moon in Sagittarius) You can take an idea as far as you want or need to. The beauty of Jupiter is that it expands whatever it touches and brings a deeper sense of optimism to all your concerns. As a result of the solar eclipse, a romance could get off the ground with a coworker.

Wednesday, September 19 (Moon in Sagittarius to Capricorn 7:52 p.m.) Your creativity is moving swiftly and furiously. You're able to ground what you're doing, making it tangible and more believable to others. You find the proper structure or venue for a creative project.

Thursday, September 20 (Moon in Capricorn) As the taste of autumn enters the air, you may feel nostalgic for certain events in the past, perhaps involving a child who has grown up and left home. Dive into your creativity to take your mind off things and put you in a forward-looking frame of mind.

Friday, September 21 (Moon in Capricorn) With Mars still moving through your solar tenth house and the solar eclipse in your sign only ten days in the past, you may get a surprise career boost. It's also possible that something about your personal life or early childhood becomes clear to you.

Saturday, September 22 (Moon in Capricorn to Aquarius 4:18 a.m.) The Aquarius moon may not be comfortable for you, but it does bring opportunities to detach emotionally from work issues. You're able to lay your course, have the vision to see how you're going to get from A to B, and set sail!

Sunday, September 23 (Moon in Aquarius) Kick back and relax. You've earned the time off, Virgo. You and friends get together for brunch and an outing to enjoy the early fall. You actually seem to be learning to leave your inner critic sealed up in a closet.

Monday, September 24 (Moon in Aquarius to Pisces 8:56 a.m.) You're helpful to partners, both business and romantic, who may not have your clarity of vision and intuitive awareness about the issues. If friends make you feel emotionally vulnerable, examine the feeling to get to the root of it. Then blame the Pisces moon!

Tuesday, September 25 (Moon in Pisces) You feel a need to look especially attractive. This could mean a new hairstyle or outfit or perhaps even a new way of communicating. Just be careful that you don't lose yourself in someone else.

Wednesday, September 26 (Moon in Pisces to Aries 10:23 a.m.) Pretty soon, Mars will move into Cancer, a sign much more compatible with your own. That transit should stimulate friendships, and it may prompt you to rearrange your dreams in some way. Explore the possibilities of new dreams.

Thursday, September 27 (Moon in Aries) Mercury moves into Scorpio, a terrific transit for all sorts of communications. Get to work on your novel. Finish those memos and new product blueprints. Everything you say until October 11, when Mercury turns retrograde, will be understood by others.

Friday, September 28 (Moon in Aries to Taurus 10:18 a.m.) Mars moves into Cancer and your eleventh house. You have an intuitive certainty about something you're promoting. It's easier for you to work long and hard to accomplish whatever goals you have established.

Saturday, September 29 (Moon in Taurus) How you love the Taurus moon. Your thoughts turn to foreign locales, and you become the prototypical armchair traveler. Research countries on the Internet; look for good deals in airfare and hotels. Then choose a date after November 1, when Mercury will be moving direct again.

Sunday, September 30 (Moon in Taurus to Gemini 10:35 a.m.) A boss recognizes that you're a consummate communicator and you get the gig you want. Some things really do have a payoff, Virgo!

OCTOBER 2007

Monday, October 1 (Moon in Gemini) With Mars in the friendship sector of your chart and the moon in your house of careers, it's possible that a friend provides a lead to a different kind of job. Consider your options carefully and don't make a decision until the moon moves into your sign or on Wednesday, when it's in Cancer.

Tuesday, October 2 (Moon in Gemini to Cancer 12:58 p.m.) Before noon, you feel the subtle shift of lunar energies. Your intuition is suddenly stronger and it's to your advantage to listen to it. Live to the beat of your own drummer!

Wednesday, October 3 (Moon in Cancer) Your mom has some advice for you. Even if you dislike her giving you unsolicited advice, listen to what she says. Does it resonate for you?

Thursday, October 4 (Moon in Cancer to Leo 6:28 p.m.) Even though the Leo moon can make you feel restless and unsettled, it's a good transit for delving into who you are. This evening, you talk things over with a Virgo friend who helps you define your strong points.

Friday, October 5 (Moon in Leo) In a sense, the Leo moon is usually a preparatory period for when the moon moves into your sign. It's wise to resolve issues you don't want to deal with or which you've put off. Tie up loose ends.

Saturday, October 6 (Moon in Leo) A fire-sign friend or family member plays into the day's events. An Aries urges you to strike out on your own. A Leo encourages you to do what you love. A Sagittarius recommends a trip to some exotic locale; if you can't afford it, sign up for a workshop or seminar.

Sunday, October 7 (Moon in Leo to Virgo 3:04 a.m.) You're ready for the Virgo moon! And what a promising day it is. You respond to someone who has been dying to meet you, and the encounter proves intriguing. Could this be the beginning of a romance? Quite possibly. After all, Venus is moving direct, and it's sure to light up on your love life!

Monday, October 8 (Moon in Virgo) With both the moon and Venus in Virgo, your charisma is noticed by everyone around you. You receive kudos at work for a job well done. You're recognized for your creativity and individuality.

Tuesday, October 9 (Moon in Virgo to Libra 1:58 p.m.) As the moon moves into Libra early this afternoon, you're feeling the lingering aftermath of achievement and recognition. Not too much can burst your bubble.

Wednesday, October 10 (Moon in Libra) It's a social day. Enjoy an outing with friends, or spend time with your family and loved ones. Tomorrow Mercury turns retrograde; since Mercury rules your sign, that's always a bit disturbing.

Thursday, October 11 (Moon in Libra) Mercury turns retrograde in Scorpio and your third house. This transit may add some bumps and bruises to your relationships with siblings and neighbors. Things in your neighborhood could feel somewhat off. It may seem that until November 1, you're like a rat in the maze, running hither and yon and not getting to where you want to be.

Friday, October 12 (Moon in Libra to Scorpio 2:14 a.m.) The moon joins retrograde Mercury in your third house. Okay, you may feel emotionally vulnerable. But you can deal with it through your attention to detail and your need to get the absolute bottom line. In fact, once you have that bottom line, you'll stop beating yourself up!

Saturday, October 13 (Moon in Scorpio) You get together with relatives and neighbors, perhaps for a barbecue or block party. You feel a certain instinctive gravitation toward someone in particular. It turns out this person has some advice you should listen to.

Sunday, October 14 (Moon in Scorpio to Sagittarius 2:58 p.m.) Your family or home is featured in some way. It could be that your family needs your presence. This could create a conflict with your professional obligations.

Monday, October 15 (Moon in Sagittarius) If you feel the urge to redecorate or refurbish your home in some way, experiment with feng shui to enhance certain energies in your home. First, determine what energy you need most: prosperity, romance, or a stable family life?

Tuesday, October 16 (Moon in Sagittarius) You grasp the bigger picture concerning your home life. An excellent book for the day is Caroline Myss's *Invisible Acts of Power: Personal Choices That Create Miracles*. You'll come away from this book empowered.

Wednesday, October 17 (Moon in Sagittarius to Capricorn 3:04 a.m.) Dive into your creativity. The universe supports your creative actions and projects. Plan and lay down a blueprint for something you're trying to achieve.

Thursday, October 18 (Moon in Capricorn) Earth-sign individuals play roles in your life. A Taurus urges you to continue an exercise routine you've started. Another Virgo admonishes you for being so self-critical and boosts your ego and self-esteem.

Friday, October 19 (Moon in Capricorn to Aquarius 12:52 p.m.) Coworkers or employees bring their gripes to you. And you must turn the pettiness of these gripes into something substantive to present to the boss. People are depending on you to get the job done.

Saturday, October 20 (Moon in Aquarius) Your vision is extraordinary. You're able to inspire the troops—whether at work or at home—and delegate responsibilities. A good leader never asks people to do more than he would.

Sunday, October 21 (Moon in Aquarius to Pisces 7:03 p.m.) You and your significant other spend the evening together, deep in conversation. You are each other's support group, offering and providing guidance and spiritual sustenance. With Mercury still retrograde, miscommunication is possible, so be clear and concise about everything you say.

Monday, October 22 (Moon in Pisces) Think about the provision you want in a contract, but don't negotiate or sign the contract until after November 1, when Mercury turns direct again. Your compassion and intuitive attunement run deep.

Tuesday, October 23 (Moon in Pisces to Aries 9:25 p.m.) Frustration this evening is the direct result of the Aries moon. It can make you impatient, rash, even careless. Try to kick back and do something that relaxes you. Allow this lunar energy to work on your mind, firing you with new ideas.

Wednesday, October 24 (Moon in Aries) You see a homeless person who has a sign asking for food or money on the street. What do you do? Do you drive past this person? Do you stop and drop some money into the jar? The way you react tells you a great deal about how you share (or don't share) your resources.

Thursday, October 25 (Moon in Aries to Taurus 9:08 p.m.) With Mercury retrograde in intense Scorpio and the moon moving into its opposite sign of Taurus, you may feel mighty strange. But you have the inner resources to turn the feeling into something creative and useful.

Friday, October 26 (Moon in Taurus) Thinking of far-away places, the next election, or what you believe in your heart of hearts? All of these issues and more are part of the Taurus moon. You're grounded and able to resist peer pressure with complete grace.

Saturday, October 27 (Moon in Taurus to Gemini 8:12 p.m.) A friend or professional peer is helpful in terms of your career. Travel is indicated, but if you choose to go, remember Mercury is still moving retrograde. This movement brings unexpected changes and snafus in travel plans.

Sunday, October 28 (Moon in Gemini) If you're in the mood for a party, be sure to invite people with whom you work. It's a chance to get to know people better, and since the party is on your turf, you're more relaxed and outgoing.

Monday, October 29 (Moon in Gemini to Cancer 8:50 p.m.) This evening, the moon joins Mars in Cancer in your eleventh house. The combination feeds your intuitive wisdom and sensitivity toward friends. It will be easier for you to remember your dreams, so have your journal and a flashlight handy!

Tuesday, October 30 (Moon in Cancer) Last night's dreams ushered in ideas and idealism. Decipher and decode the most vivid dream and write down your interpretation.

Wednesday, October 31 (Moon in Cancer) Happy Halloween! Get ready for the Leo moon near midnight by dressing up for the occasion. Get out there with your kids or throw a Halloween party. Neptune turns direct—great news if you have a Pisces moon or rising sign. The effects are subtle, but should impact your relationships in a positive way.

NOVEMBER 2007

Thursday, November 1 (Moon in Cancer to Leo 12:48 a.m.) Mercury finally turns direct. This is always good news for you, Virgo, since Mercury rules your sign. Invitations pour in for the holidays. You aren't sure yet what you're going to do, but you still have plenty of time to make up your mind.

Friday, November 2 (Moon in Leo)   You take a day off and tend to things that need attention. If you're an aspiring actor, you may be practicing for auditions or working on your techniques and voice. Believe in yourself and your talent.

Saturday, November 3 (Moon in Leo to Virgo 8:45 a.m.)   This is a *very* positive day. Mercury is moving direct, the moon and Venus are in your sign, and Mars is in the compatible sign of Cancer. Romance, possibly with someone you've known first as a friend, is likely. You're at your most appealing. Use it to your advantage.

Sunday, November 4—Daylight Saving Time Ends (Moon in Virgo)   Venus will be in your sign only until November 8. So if you haven't drawn on the artistic side of this planet, do so. This may mean experimenting with your own artistic abilities, visiting museums, or collecting art.

Monday, November 5 (Moon in Virgo to Libra 6:47 p.m.)   By this evening, it seems that you're surrounded by air signs. Gemini rushes in with books, information, Web sites you need to take a look at. Libra wants to get together with the gang. Aquarius enlists your aid with a charity project. The air-sign people in your life certainly can wear you down!

Tuesday, November 6 (Moon in Libra)   Money—how do you earn and spend it? Is prosperity thinking a foreign concept to you? Focus on the *energy* of money and examine your beliefs related to money.

Wednesday, November 7 (Moon in Libra)   Your mediation skills are called into play when you intervene in a dispute. Be careful that you don't bend over backward to accommodate a mate or partner. It's always wisest to say what you think rather than what you think the other person wants you to say.

Thursday, November 8 (Moon in Libra to Scorpio 7:19 a.m.) Venus moves into Libra, indicating a very nice period of friendship and socializing. It could also signal romance if the other person shares your values. Don't fret about everything that's going on in your life. Cultivate conscious, purposeful living.

Friday, November 9 (Moon in Scorpio) Oh, such intensity! But this positive emotion gets you moving in a profound way toward something you genuinely want. You're trying to crack the code of just who you are, Virgo, and once you do, entire new worlds open up to you.

Saturday, November 10 (Moon in Scorpio to Sagittarius 7:59 p.m.) All day, you will feel an urge to do or achieve something. This evening, you figure out what that something is. It may involve an activity as simple as rearranging furniture in your home or something as complex as putting down new floors.

Sunday, November 11 (Moon in Sagittarius) With the Sagittarius moon forming a beautiful angle to Venus, your day should be surprisingly positive. You're able to grasp the larger picture about a relationship and feel more confident about resolving issues that have surfaced.

Monday, November 12 (Moon in Sagittarius) Your mother or another nurturing female in your life may need some advice or emotional support. This person needs your input on a move she may be considering.

Tuesday, November 13 (Moon in Sagittarius to Capricorn 8:01 a.m.) There are good ways and bad ways to approach your creativity. The universe is on your side in terms of organizing and brainstorming. Use the energy to your advantage and to make strides on your creative work.

Wednesday, November 14 (Moon in Capricorn) Your children may need more discipline or structure. Delineate chores and responsibilities so that you aren't shouldering the burden alone.

Thursday, November 15 (Moon in Capricorn to Aquarius 6:31 p.m.) Mars turns retrograde in Cancer and your eleventh house. This movement lasts through the end of the year and could make you disagree with friends.

Friday, November 16 (Moon in Aquarius) The lunar energy accentuates your work environment, your coworkers, and your daily health. If you don't have a regular exercise routine, start one. You may want to schedule dentist and doctor appointments.

Saturday, November 17 (Moon in Aquarius) You and friends who share a common passion or belief meet to brainstorm and for mutual support. It could be a drama group, a writers' group, or even a bridge club. You come away energized and in a more upbeat frame of mind.

Sunday, November 18 (Moon in Aquarius to Pisces 2:15 a.m.) As the moon joins Uranus in your seventh house, your emotional reactions to personal situations may be unusual. It's also possible that you attract highly individualistic and unusual people.

Monday, November 19 (Moon in Pisces) With Mars retrograde in Cancer, Mercury in Scorpio, and the moon in Pisces, you have a triple dose of water signs hitting you. Even though retrograde Mars may be problematic, this trio heightens your intuition and emotions. You will be dealing with friends, partners, and siblings or other relatives.

Tuesday, November 20 (Moon in Pisces to Aries 6:25 a.m.) Think of the Aries moon as your booster rocket. It propels you out of your usual state of mind or a rut and urges you to move in fresh directions. You could be short on patience, so be careful!

Wednesday, November 21 (Moon in Aries) Don't speed; exercise caution when driving. The Aries moon makes you impatient and restless; it's important that you don't allow yourself to take out your aggressions in your vehicle.

Thursday, November 22 (Moon in Aries to Taurus 7:19 a.m.) Grounded, stubborn, sensual, artistic, mystical—these attributes all describe the Taurus moon. This moon urges you to delve deep into cosmic questions. Your quest for answers may result in an overseas trip or adventure! But for today, it means enjoying family and friends.

Friday, November 23 (Moon in Taurus) You and your partner spend a sensual evening, and you may enjoy unusual foods, exotic wines, and all the romance of candlelight and ocean walks. Keep yourself grounded, Virgo.

Saturday, November 24 (Moon in Taurus to Gemini 6:29 a.m.) Uranus turns direct in Pisces. As with all outer planet transits, this one is subtle, with effects that take place over a long period of time. It impacts your partnerships. You and a business or romantic partner find new ways to deal with each other.

Sunday, November 25 (Moon in Gemini) The Internet, bookstores, information, and communication play into events. You may be on the phone more than usual, fielding invitations for the holidays or even planning a party at your place for some time in December. News related to your career is involved. An Aquarius proves helpful.

Monday, November 26 (Moon in Gemini to Cancer 6:07 a.m.) The moon joins retrograde Mars in Cancer. You have an intuitive certainty about a particular person; it's a good idea to heed your gut instinct. This individual may not have your best interests at heart.

Tuesday, November 27 (Moon in Cancer) If your goals and dreams seem to be shifting, don't worry too much. Mars isn't at its best because it's moving retrograde; things will settle down early next year, when Mars turns direct again.

Wednesday, November 28 (Moon in Cancer to Leo 8:23 a.m.) Take time for yourself. If you feel you've been running yourself ragged, turn off the phones, stay away from the Internet, and do something that's just for you.

Thursday, November 29 (Moon in Leo) If you're a college student, start studying for finals. Find a secluded spot and hit the books. If a friend or classmate needs tutoring, help out.

Friday, November 30 (Moon in Leo to Virgo 2:45 p.m.) By midafternoon, you're in your element again. The moon moves into Virgo, and you suddenly feel more confident, more in control. It's a good way to head into the last month of the year. Enjoy!

DECEMBER 2007

Saturday, December 1 (Moon in Virgo) With the moon in your sign and Mercury joining Jupiter in your fourth house, you'll have your hands full! You may be doing upgrades to your home, or your family could be expanding in some way.

Sunday, December 2 (Moon in Virgo) You and a friend or family member get a jump on holiday shopping. You're looking for a gift for a special someone. Try not to go overboard, but don't be stingy! When you feel this good, it's easy to hook right into prosperity thinking.

Monday, December 3 (Moon in Virgo to Libra 1:02 a.m.) The moon joins Venus in Libra in your seventh house, accentuating your partnerships and contracts. If you're about to negotiate a contract, do it before December 5, when Venus moves into Scorpio.

Tuesday, December 4 (Moon in Libra) You feel pretty laid back and may be indecisive, as well. Your indecision could concern your feelings about a relationship, finances, or even an artistic project. Postpone making a decision about anything until the moon and Venus are in Scorpio.

Wednesday, December 5 (Moon in Libra to Scorpio 1:32 p.m.) Both the moon and Venus move into Scorpio and your third house. Rather than making a decision, wait until tomorrow, when both planets are firmly in Scorpio. List what you would like to happen; then focus on making those goals come about.

Thursday, December 6 (Moon in Scorpio) Make your move, and trust the results will be what you hope. You're building foundations for the future. A Cancer or a Pisces plays into the process.

Friday, December 7 (Moon in Scorpio) There's no doubt that the Scorpio moon causes you to feel deep. At times, your emotions are so intense you may feel nearly overwhelmed. Take a couple of deep breaths when that happens, and understand that strong emotions help you to break through barriers and obstacles.

Saturday, December 8 (Moon in Scorpio to Sagittarius 2:12 a.m.) If you start criticizing yourself, stop immediately. Ask yourself why you have to denigrate yourself all the time!

Sunday, December 9 (Moon in Sagittarius) In about nine days, Jupiter moves into Capricorn, where it will transit for about a year. This transit marks a highlight in your life, Virgo. In the meantime, keep your cool if someone confronts you.

Monday, December 10 (Moon in Sagittarius to Capricorn 1:51 p.m.) This moon, like the Taurus and Virgo moons, is comfortable for you. Your romantic quotient soars and so does your capacity for fun and enjoyment. Get out this evening with friends or loved ones.

Tuesday, December 11 (Moon in Capricorn) Dive into artistic and creative projects. You may not have all the answers you need, but you're on your way toward a deeper grasp of what you're attempting to do.

Wednesday, December 12 (Moon in Capricorn) It's a reality-check day. Make sure you know what your kids are doing, what your partner is up to, and where you stand on your creative endeavors. If you still have time, do a bit of armchair traveling, scoping out possible foreign destinations for vacation.

Thursday, December 13 (Moon in Capricorn to Aquarius 12:02 a.m.) If you have a moon, natal nodes or an ascendant in Aquarius, you tend to feel this transit powerfully. You may be questioning what you're doing in your present job and what happened to your dreams. This lunar transit could help you get back on track.

Friday, December 14 (Moon in Aquarius) Your network of friends and peers figures into the day's equation. You may register for an online class in something that interests you, or you could meet with your writers' group, your theater group, your photography club, or your political cronies.

Saturday, December 15 (Moon in Aquarius to Pisces 8:15 a.m.) It's time to get serious about the holidays. You shop for something special for a romantic or business partner and may be planning a party. In fact, what are you doing New Year's Eve?

Sunday, December 16 (Moon in Pisces) What sort of changes would you like to make in your life? Get started on your resolutions for 2008. With Jupiter about to move into Capricorn, a sign that's harmonious with you, you'll be thinking a lot about ways to expand your options.

Monday, December 17 (Moon in Pisces to Aries 1:53 p.m.) This moon sometimes urges you to think about money. You could be mulling over investments, and trying to figure out where your money will make the best return.

Tuesday, December 18 (Moon in Aries)   Jupiter moves into Capricorn, marking the beginning of what will surely be an extraordinary year for you. Jupiter in your fifth house will strive to expand your creativity, you may start a family or meet your soul mate, and your capacity for pleasure and enjoyment will increase tenfold. This is certainly a transit to anticipate.

Wednesday, December 19 (Moon in Aries to Taurus 4:38 p.m.)   Saturn turns retrograde in your sign. Even though the effects can be subtle, Saturn is such a powerful planet in the astrological scheme of things that you undoubtedly will feel a burden in some area of your life. The best way to navigate this transit is to use Saturn's energies to create structure and stability in your life.

Thursday, December 20 (Moon in Taurus)   Mercury joins Jupiter in Capricorn in your fifth house. Your thoughts and everyday activities turn toward enjoyment, creativity, love, and your kids. The Mercury transit, which lasts through the early part of the new year, is just about perfect for the holiday season. It should help to counteract the Saturn transit in your sign.

Friday, December 21 (Moon in Taurus to Gemini 5:14 p.m.)   Work is probably the last thing you want to think about. But with the moon moving into Gemini and your tenth house, your career is accentuated. Yet Gemini is a social sign, so use this energy to enjoy your office party and the holidays!

Saturday, December 22 (Moon in Gemini)   If you're feeling a bit ragged around the edges, treat yourself to extra sleep. Then head to the gym or a yoga class. You'll need to keep yourself physically fit during this busy part of the season.

Sunday, December 23 (Moon in Gemini to Cancer 5:19 p.m.) As your family and friends begin to pour into your house, prepare to celebrate the holidays, but don't overdo it!

Monday, December 24 (Moon in Cancer) Your thoughts turn to home, family, friends, and gratitude for what you have. You touch base with your network of friends and acquaintances by phone and the Internet. Invitations come in for New Year's Eve.

Tuesday, December 25 (Moon in Cancer to Leo 6:53 p.m.) Merry Christmas! Your plate is exceptionally full, but you're up to the task. By this evening, you could be craving a bit of solitude and may steal some time just for yourself. A long walk alone might be the ticket.

Wednesday, December 26 (Moon in Leo) Tempers could flare. Too much proximity to family stresses you out, and you may have to let off steam somewhere, like the gym. Your dreams are particularly vivid and may provide answers or illumination about something that concerns you.

Thursday, December 27 (Moon in Leo to Virgo 11:45 p.m.) The moon joins retrograde Saturn in your sign. The lunar transit certainly brightens your mood and boosts your self-confidence. Even if you feel you're shouldering more than your share of responsibilities, you have Jupiter in your court, urging you toward optimism.

Friday, December 28 (Moon in Virgo) You are definitely in a party mood. Make plans for New Year's. Chances are, the party is going to be at your place. Tend to details about food, beverages, and invitations. Spend some time this evening getting your family to list resolutions for 2008.

Saturday, December 29 (Moon in Virgo) There could be a few changes in your plans. Mars is still retrograde in Cancer and Saturn is still retrograde in your sign, so you may feel pinched for time. But love, romance, and creativity are soaring.

Sunday, December 30 (Moon in Virgo to Libra 8:38 a.m.)
Venus moves into Sagittarius. This transit, which lasts into 2008, should spice up your love life at home and attract opportunities in the arts. If you've thought about setting up a home office, get to work.

Monday, December 31 (Moon in Libra) With your resolutions in hand, your optimism at a very nice level, and everything to anticipate, you leap into today with your arms wide-open. You've learned a great deal this year, Virgo, so you have a better handle on how to stop self-defeating thoughts before they take hold.

HAPPY NEW YEAR!

SYDNEY OMARR

Born on August 5, 1926, in Philadelphia, Pennsylvania, Sydney Omarr was the only person ever given full-time duty in the U.S. Army as an astrologer. He is regarded as the most erudite astrologer of our time and the best known, through his syndicated column and his radio and television programs (he was Merv Griffin's "resident astrologer"). Omarr has been called the most "knowledgeable astrologer since Evangeline Adams." His forecasts of Nixon's downfall, the end of World War II in mid-August of 1945, the assassination of John F. Kennedy, Roosevelt's election to a fourth term and his death in office . . . these and many others are on the record and quoted enough to be considered "legendary."

ABOUT THE SERIES

This is one of a series of twelve Sydney Omarr® Day-by-Day Astrological Guides for the signs of 2007. For questions and comments about the book, e-mail tjmacgregor@booktalk.com.

✪ SIGNET

SYDNEY OMARR'S® SUN, MOON, AND YOU:
An Astrological Guide to Your Personality

Discover the effects of the moon and sun on LOVE, ROMANCE & SUCCESS

Nationally syndicated columnist Sydney Omarr® shows readers how to turn the tides in their lives! Included are all the keys to finding the perfect balance between day and night, featuring:

- An introduction to the sun and moon signs
- Easy-to-read tables
- How sun/moon signs contribute to personality, likes and dislikes, finding ideal mates and the perfect jobs

Filled with colorful examples of historical figures under each sign, and requiring no familiarity with astrology, this is the must-have guide for all fans of astrology!

0-451-21454-4

Available wherever books are sold or at
penguin.com

NOW AVAILABLE

THE NEW AMERICAN
Dream Dictionary

The Complete Language of Dreams
in Easy-to-Understand Form

Wake up to your dream life.

JOAN SEAMAN AND TOM PHILBIN

NAL 0-451-21747-0

Penguin Group (USA) Online

What will you be reading tomorrow?

Tom Clancy, Patricia Cornwell, W.E.B. Griffin,
Nora Roberts, William Gibson, Robin Cook,
Brian Jacques, Catherine Coulter, Stephen King,
Dean Koontz, Ken Follett, Clive Cussler,
Eric Jerome Dickey, John Sandford,
Terry McMillan, Sue Monk Kidd, Amy Tan,
John Berendt…

You'll find them all at
penguin.com

*Read excerpts and newsletters,
find tour schedules and reading group guides,
and enter contests.*

Subscribe to Penguin Group (USA) newsletters
and get an exclusive inside look
at exciting new titles and the authors you love
long before everyone else does.

PENGUIN GROUP (USA)
us.penguingroup.com